Reactive Programming with Swift 4

Build asynchronous reactive applications with
easy-to-maintain and clean code using RxSwift
and Xcode 9

Navdeep Singh

BIRMINGHAM - MUMBAI

Reactive Programming with Swift 4

Commissioning Editor: Kunal Chaudhari
Acquisition Editor: Isha Raval
Content Development Editor: Flavian Vaz
Technical Editor: Akhil Nair
Copy Editor: Shaila Kusanale
Project Coordinator: Devanshi Doshi
Proofreader: Safis Editing
Indexer: Rekha Nair
Graphics: Jason Monteiro
Production Coordinator: Shraddha Falebhai

First published: February 2018

Production reference: 1210218

Published by Packt Publishing Ltd.
Livery Place
35 Livery Street
Birmingham
B3 2PB, UK.

ISBN 978-1-78712-021-1

www.packtpub.com

`mapt.io`

Mapt is an online digital library that gives you full access to over 5,000 books and videos, as well as industry leading tools to help you plan your personal development and advance your career. For more information, please visit our website.

Why subscribe?

- Spend less time learning and more time coding with practical eBooks and Videos from over 4,000 industry professionals

- Improve your learning with Skill Plans built especially for you

- Get a free eBook or video every month

- Mapt is fully searchable

- Copy and paste, print, and bookmark content

PacktPub.com

Did you know that Packt offers eBook versions of every book published, with PDF and ePub files available? You can upgrade to the eBook version at `www.PacktPub.com` and as a print book customer, you are entitled to a discount on the eBook copy. Get in touch with us at `service@packtpub.com` for more details.

At `www.PacktPub.com`, you can also read a collection of free technical articles, sign up for a range of free newsletters, and receive exclusive discounts and offers on Packt books and eBooks.

Contributors

About the author

Navdeep Singh is a result-oriented software developer and research professional with more than 7 years of experience in both development and research positions. He strives to create software with the user in mind, creating applications with a usable and intuitive user interface experience. Navdeep spends most of his time learning about the latest trends in technology, writing blogs, playing cricket, or practicing classical Hindustani music.

Firstly, I would like to thank the Almighty, who gave me insights to follow this path of sharing knowledge. Thanks to my beloved wife, who has been in my life for less than a year and has been an inspiration for pushing me to spend hours writing this book, my parents and my family who believed in me right from the start till this very moment.

About the reviewer

Kevin Munc (@muncman) is a 20-year programming veteran with wide experience, from mainframes to mobile. Along the way, he's reviewed books on Objective-C, watchOS, UIAutomation, Sprite Kit, JavaFX, and Vim.

> *I'd like to thank all my colleagues —past and present— who have helped me sharpen my reviewing skills. I'm also thankful for the ongoing support of my family as I continue chasing new tech.*

Packt is searching for authors like you

If you're interested in becoming an author for Packt, please visit authors.packtpub.com and apply today. We have worked with thousands of developers and tech professionals, just like you, to help them share their insight with the global tech community. You can make a general application, apply for a specific hot topic that we are recruiting an author for, or submit your own idea.

Table of Contents

Preface

As a platform, iOS offers numerous APIs to write asynchronous code and, many a times, this choice becomes hard to manage and a single code base ends up comprising multiple Asynchronous API usages, for example, closures for small Async tasks, delegation for background tasks, notification center for event-based tasks, and such. Managing and modifying such a code base might become a headache even if it is written in the best way possible, and the problem becomes more severe if a big team is involved with a single code base. `RxSwift` brings in uniformity so that different types of requirements (mentioned earlier) are handled with `RxSwift` code and hence you, as a developer, get more control over the processes and different module interactions within the app.

The main mission of this book is to give you a platform to catapult your skills to be on par with the best RxSwift developers out there. Follow the content in the book as per the schedule, and rest assured that you will achieve the mission.

Who this book is for

This book is for iOS developers who have intermediate knowledge of Swift development for IOS and want to take their skill set to the next level. `RxSwift` offers more control over asynchronous code in your iOS environment, and, as a seasoned developer, even a slight advantage to the way asynchronous code is written is always welcome. This book will challenge the way you have been thinking about your apps' logic and guide you along the way as you turn the tables and start thinking in a more declarative way as compared to the traditional imperative way. In short, you will learn how to think in "what to do" terminology as compared to "how to do."

For those who are eager to become a Swift Ninja, this book aims to work in a slightly unique manner—we will dive straight into the code, and as we build on the demo applications, we will explain the concepts "on the fly," as they say! Development is all about practice, and this book abides by that rule right from the word go.

What this book covers

Chapter 1, *Migrating from Swift 3 to Swift 4*, teaches what's new in Swift 4 and how you can transition your code from Swift 3 to Swift 4. Unlike the previous Swift releases, this time the conversion is more seamless, and you will see this in practice with the help of an example.

Chapter 2, *FRP Fundamentals, Terminology, and Basic Building Blocks*, takes you through FRP and its basic building blocks, marble diagrams, and sequence diagrams to understand more about sequences and events in brief. Finally, the chapter will unleash Railway-oriented programming and a brief introduction on error handling in FRP.
You will learn how you can handle errors in one single place without having to care about handling errors at every single event.

Chapter 3, *Set up RxSwift and Convert a Basic Login App to its RxSwift Counterpart*, explains that the best way to get the feel about any topic is practice. This chapter will take a nosedive into the RxSwift world by converting an existing Swift app into RxSwift. You will see the RxSwift syntax for the very first time in this chapter and get to work with a real-world application.

You will get a feel of how to convert an existing code base into a RxSwift code base and compare the benefits of the newly learned reactive concepts.

You will note the increased readability and concise but clear code that can be written using the RxSwift library when compared to normal Swift. The gist of this chapter is to provide you with a comparison to understand the benefits that RxSwift code brings into play.

Chapter 4, *When to become Reactive?*, helps you to use your armor judiciously, as it might lead to increased complexity if not used in a proper setting. When writing any code, keep in mind that the best code might not be the smartest code out there, rather, the best code is the one that is easier to maintain and understand. This chapter will brief you about when to use RxSwift in your application. You will also work with playgrounds to understand some more core concepts that enable you to simplify your complex code base.

Chapter 5, *Filter, Transform, and Simplify*, along with the next chapter, teaches you how to apply operators to filter out events and then proceed to handle them. You will play with major building blocks of RxSwift and note the clarity and control that you get as compared to normal Swift code while dealing with event-driven concepts. In this chapter, you will work with Playgrounds to transform sequences by filtering them using map, flatmap, and other such operators as they are generated so that you can take respective actions as per the type of the event that is generated.

Chapter 6, *Reduce by Combining and Filtering and Common Trade Offs,* might sound tedious to read at first, but the concepts will get more clear as we practice with real examples. In this chapter, you will work with some more transforming operators to reduce the observable data stream by making use of combining and filtering operators in conjunction and then gradually work your way to know other operators, such as mathematical and time based.

You will also read about the trade-offs while incorporating these operators in your code so that you can be careful while making the choice to go reactive.

Chapter 7, *React to UI Events – Start Subscribing,* introduces you to another framework, which is part of the original RxSwift repository—RxCocoa.

Convert your simple UI elements such as UIButtons and UITextFields to Reactive components. You will learn how to subscribe to events emitted by your newly created reactive UI components and perform respective actions depending on the type of the event. For instance, a UIButton might have a touchUpInside or long press event, and you might want to respond to both the events differently.

This chapter will also introduce you to some reactive networking code and how you can subscribe to events while your code is interacting with API calls.

Chapter 8, *RxTest and Custom Rx Extensions – Testing with Rx,* discusses RxTest, and later, RxBlocking, by writing tests against several RxSwift operations and also writing tests against production RxSwift code. Also, you will create an extension to NSURLSession to manage the communication with an endpoint.

Chapter 9, *Testing Your RxCode – Testing Asynchronous Code,* says that almost every IOS app needs some sort of API access to fetch or save data over cloud to complete its workflow and hence it becomes important to test code that interacts with APIs. Since response from APIs is uncertain and error prone, the code that interacts with APIs should be tested rigorously before shipping with production code. This chapter introduces you to concepts such as mocking, stubbing, dependency injections, and expectations and sheds some light on how you can substitute your live APIs with dummy data.

You will also know how to continue development even when your API is not ready and, as a result, fasten your sprints.

Chapter 10, *Schedule Your Tasks, Don't Queue!, informs that in traditional Swift,* there are different ways to handle concurrency—GCD, Operational Queues, and so on. This chapter introduces you to the concept of schedulers. RxSwift encourages a developer not to work directly with locks or queues, and 99% of the times, you will be encouraged to use platform-provided schedulers rather than creating custom schedulers.

Chapter 11, *Subscribe to Errors and Save Your App*, describes that it does not take long for negative inputs to pour in when an app with users in production shuts down abruptly. This chapter will cover the beauty behind error handling in RxSwift. You can subscribe to errors and react to different types of errors either in one way or follow a specific path for specific errors, for instance, retrying if a download failed abruptly, reauthenticating a user behind the scenes if the session has expired, and so on.

Chapter 12, *Functional and Reactive App-Architecture*, compares different design patterns that can be used while writing RxSwift apps from scratch or modifying current apps to incorporate Reactive and functional behavior. You will know about observation, iteration, delegation, MVC, and MVVM and try to figure out which design pattern fits the puzzle in the best way possible. This chapter will also introduce you to different open source APIs that can be incorporated to your ongoing projects.

Chapter 13, *Finish a Real-World Application*, concludes that you would have covered a lot so far and worked on a lot of code examples; now, you will put everything that you have learned so far to practice in one place and finish an app that we started earlier in Chapter 2, *FRP Fundamentals, Terminology, and Basic Building Blocks*. This chapter will cover the MVVM application architecture and show how a well-designed ViewModel can power an RxSwift app.

To get the most out of this book

We assume that you, the reader of this book, already have intermediate knowledge of Swift programming language and have worked on iOS applications before.

Download the example code files

You can download the example code files for this book from your account at www.packtpub.com. If you purchased this book elsewhere, you can visit www.packtpub.com/support and register to have the files emailed directly to you.

You can download the code files by following these steps:

1. Log in or register at www.packtpub.com.
2. Select the **SUPPORT** tab.
3. Click on **Code Downloads & Errata**.
4. Enter the name of the book in the **Search** box and follow the onscreen instructions.

Once the file is downloaded, please make sure that you unzip or extract the folder using the latest version of:

- WinRAR/7-Zip for Windows
- Zipeg/iZip/UnRarX for Mac
- 7-Zip/PeaZip for Linux

The code bundle for the book is also hosted on GitHub at `https://github.com/PacktPublishing/Reactive-Swift-4-Programming`. We also have other code bundles from our rich catalog of books and videos available at `https://github.com/PacktPublishing/`. Check them out!

Download the color images

We also provide a PDF file that has color images of the screenshots/diagrams used in this book. You can download it here: `https://www.packtpub.com/sites/default/files/downloads/ReactiveSwift4Programming_ColorImages.pdf`.

Conventions used

There are a number of text conventions used throughout this book.

`CodeInText`: Indicates code words in text, database table names, folder names, filenames, file extensions, pathnames, dummy URLs, user input, and Twitter handles. Here is an example: "Setting up an `RxSwift` environment"

A block of code is set as follows:

```
use_frameworks!
target 'YOUR_TARGET_NAME' do
pod 'RxSwift'
pod 'RxCocoa'
end
```

Any command-line input or output is written as follows:

```
sudo gem install cocoapods
```

Bold: Indicates a new term, an important word, or words that you see onscreen. For example, words in menus or dialog boxes appear in the text like this. Here is an example: "Now pick the recently installed **Swift 4.0 Snapshot** and restart **Xcode IDE**"

Warnings or important notes appear like this.

 Tips and tricks appear like this.

Get in touch

Feedback from our readers is always welcome.

General feedback: Email `feedback@packtpub.com` and mention the book title in the subject of your message. If you have questions about any aspect of this book, please email us at `questions@packtpub.com`.

Errata: Although we have taken every care to ensure the accuracy of our content, mistakes do happen. If you have found a mistake in this book, we would be grateful if you would report this to us. Please visit `www.packtpub.com/submit-errata`, selecting your book, clicking on the Errata Submission Form link, and entering the details.

Piracy: If you come across any illegal copies of our works in any form on the Internet, we would be grateful if you would provide us with the location address or website name. Please contact us at `copyright@packtpub.com` with a link to the material.

If you are interested in becoming an author: If there is a topic that you have expertise in and you are interested in either writing or contributing to a book, please visit `authors.packtpub.com`.

Reviews

Please leave a review. Once you have read and used this book, why not leave a review on the site that you purchased it from? Potential readers can then see and use your unbiased opinion to make purchase decisions, we at Packt can understand what you think about our products, and our authors can see your feedback on their book. Thank you!

For more information about Packt, please visit `packtpub.com`.

1

Migrating from Swift 3 to Swift 4

This book aims to build on your current iOS development knowledge in Swift and gradually increase your Swift skills to master Reactive programming concepts in Swift. This book will guide you through the concepts while working with real-world apps and projects to give you a better understanding of `RxSwift` and related APIs.

Swift, as a programming language, has evolved many times over the years since its launch in 2014, and like any software update, we developers have to keep ourselves updated as well. We will start this book by giving you a hands-on update about what's new in Swift and how you can seamlessly migrate from your Swift 3 code to the latest Swift 4 syntax. You will then learn about Swift 4's new features and enhancements—from improvements in language syntax to the new protocols and APIs.

We will start with compatible Xcode IDE and how you can set up the environment required to work with the latest Swift release, some prerequisites before starting to migrate to the latest version, premigration preparation, things to do once the migration is complete, special cases, and other related stuff as we go through this chapter.

Unlike previous Swift releases, this release provides source compatibility with Swift 3 while working toward ABI stability. The main topics that will be covered in this chapter are as listed:

- Setting up the Swift 4 environment
- Changes/improvements to Swift
- Additions to Swift
- Migrating to Swift 4

What's new in Swift 4?

Swift 4 includes many changes; 21 proposals have been implemented to be specific, but we will only cover a subset of those. Around 10 of these relate to the Swift package manager and of the remaining 11, some of the changes are minor improvements, so we will cover the ones that you will encounter in your day-to-day work.

 Application Binary Interface (ABI) is the specification to which independently compiled binary entities must conform to be linked together and executed.

Setting up the environment

There are a couple of ways to run Swift 4.

It's a prerequisite that you have a developer account and then you can use either of the mentioned methods:

- Install Xcode 9, search for Xcode 9, log in with your developer account, and download the current beta available for downloads.
- In case you prefer to use Xcode 8, you can use the latest development snapshot for Swift 4.0 available at `swift.org`. Once the download finishes, open the package `.pkg` file and install the snapshot. Open **Xcode** and go to **Xcode** | **Toolchains** | **Manage Toolchains**. Now pick the recently installed **Swift 4.0 Snapshot** and restart **Xcode IDE**:

Now your projects or playgrounds will use Swift 4 while compiling. We will use Xcode 9 for writing and executing all the code in this book. At the time of writing, the current Xcode 9 is in beta release version 6.

In the subsequent sections, you will read about the new features available in Swift 4, how you can transition to the latest Swift version, that is, Swift 4, and what should be the strategy for switching a massive code base written in Swift 3 to Swift 4; however, before that, a word of caution- the language is still in beta, and we should expect some changes and bug fixes along the lines until the official release is announced. With that being said, there is nothing to worry about; to keep an eye on the changes and stay up to date with the new implementations and bug fixes, follow the official release notes.

What's changed?

Before we go ahead and discuss the new additions, let's see what has changed or improved in the existing language.

Changes/improvements in Dictionary

Many proposals were made to enhance the Dictionaries and make them more powerful. In certain scenarios, Dictionaries might behave in an unexpected manner, and for this reason, many suggestions were made to change the way Dictionaries currently work in certain situations.

Let's take a look at an example. Filtering returns the same data type; in Swift 3, if you used a filter operation on a Dictionary, the return type of the result would be a tuple (with key/value labels) and not a Dictionary. Consider this example:

```
let people = ["Tom": 24, "Alex": 23, "Rex": 21, "Ravi": 43]
let middleAgePeople = people.filter { $0.value > 40 }
```

After the execution, you cannot use `middleAgePeople["Ravi"]` since the returned result is not a Dictionary. Instead, you have to follow the tuple syntax to access the desired value because the return type is tuple, `middleAgePeople[0].value`, which is not implicitly expected.

Thanks to the new release, the current scenario has now changed as the new return type is a Dictionary. This will break any existing implementation in which you had written your code based on the return type, expecting it to be a tuple.

Similarly, while working with Dictionaries, the `map()` operation never worked the way most developers expected, since the return type could be a single value while you passed in a key-value tuple. Let's look at the following example:

```
let ages = people.map { $0.value * 2 }
```

This remains the same in Swift 4, but there is the addition of a new method `mapValues()`, which will prove to be of more use as it allows values passed to the method to be transformed and spit out as a Dictionary with original keys.

For example, the following code will round off and convert all the given ages to Strings, place them into a new Dictionary with the exact same keys, that is, Tom, Alex, Rex, and Ravi:

```
let ageBrackets = people.mapValues { "\($0 / 10) 's age group" }
```

 Mapping Dictionary keys is not safe as we might end up creating duplicates.

Grouping initializer

Grouping initializer is the new addition to the Dictionary that converts a sequence into a Dictionary of sequences grouped as per your ambition. Continuing our **people** example, we can use `people.keys` to get back an array of people names and then group them by their first letter, like this:

```
let groupedPeople = Dictionary(grouping: people.keys) { $0.prefix(1) }
print(groupedPeople)
```

This will output the following:

```
["T": ["Tom"], "A": ["Alex"], "R": ["Rex", "Ravi"]]
```

Here, T, A, and R are initializers to the distinct names. For instance, consider that you had one more name in the Dictionary, say "Adam" aged 55:

```
["Tom": 24, "Alex": 23, "Rex": 21, "Ravi": 43, "Adam": 55]
```

In this case, the `groupedPeople` array might look something like this:

```
["T": ["Tom"], "A": ["Alex", "Adam"], "R": ["Rex", "Ravi"]]
```

Alternatively, we can group people based on the length of their names, as shown:

```
let groupedPeople = Dictionary(grouping: people.keys) { $0.count }
print(groupedPeople)
```

This will output the following:

```
[3: ["Tom","Rex"], 4: ["Alex", "Ravi","Adam"]]
```

Key-based subscript with default value

To understand this change, let's first try to cite why it was required in the first place; let's take a look at the following code example:

```
let peopleDictionary : [String: AnyObject] = ...
var name = "Unknown"
if let apiName = peopleDictionary["name"] as? String {
name = apiName
}
```

Basically, our goal is to get the name of the user from some Dictionary (probably coming from some API) and in case it doesn't exist, we just want to keep the default name.

There are two problems with that approach. The first is the fact that we've probably got more than just a name field, and we end up with repetitive "if let" statements that are basically just making our code less readable.

The second problem is that just for the sake of unwrapping a value, we need to come up with some artificial name for the temporary assignment (and hey, we are not good at naming stuff anyway).

So the question now is, can we do better?

The previous solution would be to use generics or extensions to modify the behavior of the existing libraries used to write some generic method to retrieve the desired value, but with Swift 4, it's now possible to access a Dictionary key and provide a default value to use if the key is missing:

```
let name = peopleDictionary["name", default: "Anonymous"]
```

We can write the same thing using nil coalescing; you can alternatively use Swift 3 to write this line:

```
let name = peopleDictionary["name"] ?? "Anonymous"
```

However, that does not work if you try to modify the value in the Dictionary rather than just reading it. Accessing the key in the Dictionary returns an optional rather than an exact value and for this reason, we can't modify a Dictionary value in place, but with Swift 4, you can write much more maintainable and succinct code, as follows:

```
var friends = ["Deapak", "Alex", "Ravi", "Deapak"]
var closeFriends = [String: Int]()
for friend in friends {
   closeFriends[friend, default: 0] += 1
}
```

The preceding loop in code loops over each entry in the `friends` array and populates the count of each entry in the `closeFriends` Dictionary. Since we know that the Dictionary will always have a value, we can modify it in one line of code.

Convert tuples to Dictionary

With Swift 4, you can now create a new unique Dictionary from an array of tuples consisting of duplicate keys. Let's take an example of an array of tuples with duplicate keys:

```
let tupleWithDuplicateKeys = [("one", 1), ("one", 2), ("two", 2), ("three",
3), ("four", 4), ("five", 5)]
```

Also, you want to convert this array into Dictionary, so you can do this:

```
let dictionaryWithNonDuplicateKeys = Dictionary(tupleWithDuplicateKeys,
uniquingKeysWith: { (first, _) in first })
```

Now if you try to print `dictionaryWithNonDuplicateKeys`;

`print(dictionaryWithNonDuplicateKeys)`, the output will be as illustrated:

```
["three": 3, "four": 4, "five": 5, "one": 1, "two": 2],
```

This is along with all the duplicate keys removed in the resulting Dictionary.

Convert arrays to Dictionary

You can create a new Dictionary by mapping two sequences one is to one or by mapping a sequence of keys and values according to a custom logic; let's take a look at both the methods:

- Mapping two sequences (arrays) one is to one: Consider that you have two sequences `personNames` and `ages` as shown here:

  ```
  let personNames = ["Alex", "Tom", "Ravi", "Raj", "Moin"]
  let ages = [23, 44, 53, 14, 34]
  ```

  You can create a Dictionary contacts by joining these two arrays, as follows:

  ```
  let contacts = Dictionary(uniqueKeysWithValues: zip(personNames,
  ages))
  ```

The output will be this:

```
["Tom": 44, "Raj": 14, "Moin": 34, "Ravi": 53, "Alex": 23]
```

- Create a new Dictionary by mapping an array of keys and values according to a custom logic. Suppose you have two arrays- one with Strings representing all the odd numbers in words and other one with integers from 1 to 10:

```
let oddKeys = ["one", "three", "five", "seven", "nine"]
var numbers = [1, 2, 3, 4, 5, 6, 7, 8, 9, 10]
```

- Now, consider that you want to create a Dictionary in which you want to map the String values to corresponding int values; you can do this as follows:

```
numbers = numbers.filter { $0 % 2 != 0 }
let oddDictionary = Dictionary(uniqueKeysWithValues: zip(oddKeys, numbers))
print(oddDictionary)
```

- The output will be this:

```
["six": 6, "four": 4, "eight": 8, "ten": 10, "two": 2]
```

Easy, isn't it!

Resolving duplicates

Swift 4 allows us to initialize a Dictionary from a sequence with duple existence of entries and manage the duplicates easily. Suppose you have an array of friends as follows:

```
var friends = ["Deapak", "Alex", "Ravi", "Deapak"]
```

Also suppose that you want to create a Dictionary with all the friends, remove duplicates, and just maintain the count of the number of occurrences that occurred in the initial friends array; you can do this by initiating a new Dictionary, as follows:

```
let friendsWithMultipleEntries = Dictionary(zip(friends, repeatElement(1,
count: friends.count)), uniquingKeysWith: +)
```

The output will be the following:

```
["Deapak": 2, "Ravi": 1, "Alex": 1],
```

This helps you avoid overwriting key-value pairs, without putting in a word. The preceding code besides the shorthand +, uses zip to fix duplicate keys by adding the two contrasting values.

 `zip(_:_:)` creates a sequence of pairs built out of two underlying sequences.

Reserving capacity

Dictionary and sequence now have the capacity to explicitly, unambiguously `reserve capacity`.

Suppose you have a sequence of friends with an initial capacity of 4:

```
friends.capacity  // 4
```

You can now reserve the capacity by doing this:

```
friends.reserveCapacity(20)
```

This reserves a minimum of 20 segments of capacity:

```
friends.capacity // 20
```

Reallocating memory to objects can be an expensive task, and if you have an idea about how much space it will require to store an object, then using `reserveCapacity(_:)` can be an easy and simple way to increase performance.

Swift 4 brings in a number of modifications to the Dictionary, 12 to be exact as per the official Apple developers guide, and a number of additions that we will discuss in subsequent sections:

Changes/improvements in Strings

Undoubtedly, the String is one of the majorly used data types in all the programming languages. Apparently, it is the data type that mankind understands better. Strings are important to the extent that they have the ability to significantly change our perception of how difficult or simple it is to learn a programming language. Hence, it becomes really important to follow any development to this data type. Strings received a major overhaul with Swift 4, making them collections of characters. In the earlier versions, several times, Swift, with its complicated way of handling subStrings and characters, went overboard in advocating accuracy over convenience.

Bid bye to string.characters

As part of the changes, this is one of the most welcomed changes. This change eliminates the necessity for a characters array on String, which means now you can reverse them, loop over them character-by-character, `map()` and `flatMap()` them, and more than anything, you can now iterate directly over a String object:

```
let vowels = "AEIOU"
for char in vowels {
    print(char)
}
```

This prints the following:

```
A , E , I , O, U
```

Here, you not only get logical iteration through String, but also specific understanding for collection and sequence:

```
vowels.count , result is 5, no need of vowels.characters.count
vowels.isEmpty , result is false
vowels.dropFirst() , result is "EIOU"
String(vowels.reversed()) , result is "UOIEA"
```

There is a small improvement to the way characters behave—now you can obtain the `UnicodeScalarView` straight from the character, whereas earlier, instantiation of a new `String` was needed.

String protocol

Back in the days of Swift 1, Strings were a collection. In Swift 2, collection conformance was dropped because some of the behavior was thought to differ strongly enough from other collection types. Swift 4 reverses this change, so Strings are collection types again. One of the examples was described in the previous section where you were able to traverse over String vowels just like a normal array. In Swift 3, despite not being a collection, you could perform slicing operations on a String. Slicing a String in Swift 3 returned a String as well. This String was a String's own `SubSequence`, which led to some memory issues and one of the bigger changes in Swift 4 is the introduction of the `subString` types to remove these issues. For example, consider that we do this:

```
let secondIndex = vowels.index(after: vowels.startindex)
let subString = vowels[secondIndex...]
```

On doing this, if you inspect the type of `subString`, you will notice that it is `String.SubSequence` and not a String. With the existence of two types of String and `SubSequence` for adding functionality to Strings in your code base, you have to extend both types individually, which is quite cumbersome. Let's take a look at the following example:

We will add an extension to the `Character` type to determine whether a character is in uppercase:

```
extension Character {
    var isUpperCase : Bool {
        return String(self) == String(self).uppercased()
    }
}
```

Using this, let's define a stripped uppercase method on String:

```
extension String {
    func strippedUppercase() -> String {
        return self.filter({ !$0.isUppercase})
    }
}
```

So now that we have this method, we can use it on a String. So we can say that `vowels.strippedUppercase()` will return an empty String since all the characters in the vowels String are already uppercase.

If we grab a slice of the String though, that is, `subString` that we got earlier in the execution and use `subString.strippedUppercase()`, we get an error as `subString` is not a String anymore.

Does this mean that we need to extend the `subString` type and add this `strippedUppercase()` method as well? Thankfully NO!

Swift 4 also introduces String protocol. Both String and `subString` affirms to this new String protocol type. So anywhere we use extend String in our code base, we should now extend String protocol instead to ensure that `subString` gets the same behavior. So let's move the `strippedUppercase()` method into an extension of String protocol:

```
extension StringProtocol {
    func strippedUppercase() -> String {
        return self.filter({ !$0.isUppercase})
    }
}
```

When we do this, we get an error because we need to be aware of what self means inside the method; self can now mean either a String or `subString`. To ensure that we always account for this, we will always convert self, make it a String instance, and then do the work we need. So if self is already a String, nothing happens and the function does not throw an error, but if it is a `subString`, we will make it a String and then call filter, and the preceding function works just fine:

```
extension StringProtocol {
    func strippedUppercase() -> String {
        return String(self).filter({ !$0.isUppercase })
    }
}
```

There are more changes in String, but this should be the most used part that we might use from day to day.

Changed interpretation of grapheme clusters

An additional big advancement is the way String interprets grapheme clusters. Conformity of Unicode 9 gives resolution to this.

The use of extended grapheme clusters for character values in Swift 4 means that concatenation and modification of Strings may cause no affect on a resulting String's character count.

For example, if you append a COMBINING ACUTE ACCENT (U+0301) to the end of the String initialized to "cafe", the resulting String will have a character count of 4, and the fourth character will be "e", not e':

```
var word = "cafe"
print("total chars in \(word) is \(word.count)")
```

It prints "total chars in cafe is 4":

```
word += "\u{301}"    // COMBINING ACUTE ACCENT, U+0301
print("totalchars in \(word) is \(word.count)")
```

It prints "total chars in café is 4", whereas the count would increase by 1 to reflect 5 as a result of print statement earlier.

 Sequence of one or more Unicode scalars that when combined generate a single human-readable character is known as an extended grapheme cluster.

Similar to Dictionaries, the total number of modifications made to String API can be summed up by the following image:

Access modifiers

The `fileprivate` access control modifier was used in Swift 3 to make important data visible outside the class in which it was declared but within the same file. This is how it all works in the case of extensions:

```
class Person {
    fileprivate let name: String
    fileprivate let age: Int
    fileprivate let address: String
    init(name: String, age: Int, address: String) {
        self.name = name
        self.age = age
        self.address = address
    }
}
```

```
extension Person {
    func info() -> String {
    return "\(self.name) \(self.age) \(self.address)"
    }
}

let bestFriend = Person(name: "Robert", age: 31)
bestFriend.info()
```

In the preceding code, we created an extension for the `Person` class and accessed its `private properties` in the `info()` method using String interpolation. Swift encourages the use of extensions to break code into logical groups. In Swift 4, you can now use the `private` access level instead of `fileprivate` in order to access class properties declared earlier, that is, in the extension:

```
class Person {
    private let name: String
    private let age: Int
    private let address: String
    init(name: String, age: Int, address: String) {
        self.name = name
        self.age = age
        self.address = address
    }
}
    extension Person {
    func info() -> String {
      return "\(self.name) \(self.age) \(self.address)"
    }
}
let bestFriend = Person(name: "Robert", age: 31)
bestFriend.info()
```

These were all the changes introduced in Swift 4. Now we will take a look at the new introductions to the language.

What's new

In the next section, we will discuss new additions to the existing libraries and functionalities available in Swift.

JSON encoding and decoding

Everyone's favorite change to Swift 4 is of course the latest way to parse JSON. If you have been part of the Swift community for a while now, you'll know that every month we have a new hot way to parse JSON or so it feels, and now finally, we have an official way, so let's take a look. Let's talk about the Why first; Swift didn't ship with any native archival or serialization APIs and instead benefited from the Objective-C implementations available to it. While this allowed us to achieve certain end goals, it was both restrictive in that only NSObject subclasses can benefit, and we had to implement solutions for value types and as always, the existing solutions, `NSJSONSerialization` and so on, are far from Swift like.

The goal, therefore, for this proposal was to allow native archival and serialization of Swift Enums and Structs and to do that in a type safe way. Let's introduce some sample JSON to our playground to see how it works in practice and as an added benefit, we get to work with Swift 4's multiline String literal syntax:

```
import Foundation
let exampleJson = """
{
    "name": "Photography as a Science",
    "release_date": "2017-11-12T14:00:00Z",
    "authors": [
    {
        "name": "Noor Jones"
    },
    {
        "name": "Larry Page"
    }
    ]
}
"""
```

We cannot convert this raw JSON in a datatype, so let's say as follows:

```
let json = exampleJson.data(using: .utf8)!
```

Now, let's define a type, and we will keep it simple so that we can see how the new API works:

```
struct Book {
    let name: String
}
```

We want to decode the JSON into an instance of this `struct Book` and doing that in Swift 4 is super easy. First, we will make our model conform to our new `Codable` protocol, after which all we need to do is the following:

```
struct Book: Codable{
    let name: String
}
let photographyBook = try! JSONDecoder().decode(Book.self, from: json)
```

If we match the values on the instance, we can see that they match the value in the JSON data and that's it, easy isn't it?

Multiline String literals

With earlier versions of Swift, you had to use \n in your Strings to add line breaks, which meant if the String was very long, then your code would start looking ugly with heaps of \n sprinkled across it. Proposal SEO163 introduces multiline literals to Swift with a very simple syntax. Long Strings or multiline Strings are Strings delimited by triple quotes, that is, """ so we can say as follows:

```
let paragraph = """
This is a paragraph to demonstrate an example of multi-line String literals
and the use in the latest Swift 4 syntax!
"""
```

So you have to end the multiline String literals with triple quotes as well, as shown in the preceding code. The nice part about these multiline String literals is that they can contain newlines, single quotes, nested, and unescaped double quotes without the need to escape them. As an example, you can include some sample JSON to test against without escaping every single quote.

Smart key paths

Another important change introduced by Swift 4 is that of smarter key paths. Swift key paths are strongly typed and enforce a compile time check and remove a common runtime error.

You write a key path by starting with a backslash: `\Book.title`. Every type automatically gets a `[keyPath: ...]` subscript to get or set the value at the specified key path:

```
struct Book {
    var title = ""
    let price : Float
```

```
}
let titleKeyPath = \Book.name
let mathsBook = Book(name: "Algebra", price: 10.50)
mathsBook[keyPath: titleKeyPath]
```

The value in the earlier mentioned `keyPath` is `"Algebra"`.

The `titleKeyPath` object defines a citation to the name property. Then, it can be used as a subscript on that object. You can store and manipulate key paths. For example, you can append additional segments to a key path to drill down further. Key paths are composed of a root, and then you can drill down by following a combination of properties and subscripts.

If you change the variable of `mathsBook` from let to var, a specific property can also be modified through the `keyPath` subscript syntax:

```
mathsBook[keyPath: titleKeyPath] = "Trigonometry"
let newTitle = mathsBook[keyPath: titleKeyPath]
```

The value in the mentioned `keyPath` is `"Trigonometry"`.

One sided ranges

Swift 4 makes it optional to provide a starting index or finishing index of ranges, as used with earlier versions of Swift.

With earlier versions of Swift, you had to do the following to use ranges:

```
let contactNames = ["Alex", "Ravi", "Moin", "Vlad", "Mark"]
let firstTwoContacts = contactNames[0..<2]
let lastThreeContacts = contactNames[2..<contactNames.count]
print(firstTwoContacts)
print(lastThreeContacts)
```

You will get the result as follows:

```
["Alex", "Ravi"] , for [0..<2]
["Moin", "Vlad", "Mark"], for [2..<contactNames.count]
```

However, with Swift 4, you no longer have to be constrained to lower bounds or upper bounds of the range mentioned in the `for` loop mentioned earlier in the code example. You can now use a one sided range where the missing side will automatically be treated as the start or end of a sequence:

```
let firstTwoContacts = contactNames[..<2]
let lastThreeContacts = contactNames[2...]
print(firstTwoContacts)
print(lastThreeContacts)
```

You will get the result as shown:

```
["Alex", "Ravi"] , for [..<2]
 ["Moin", "Vlad", "Mark"] for [2...]
```

Pattern matching with one sided ranges.

Pattern matching works really well with one sided ranges in switch statements, but you should be mindful of the one hitch that it has.

While writing a switch case, be careful to add a default case since you have to make your switch case exhaustive and since one sided ranges are infinite now, adding a default case becomes mandatory:

```
let selectedNumber = 7
switch selectedNumber {
    case ..<0 :
        print("You have selected a negative number.")
    case 0... :
        print("You have selected a positive number")
    default :
        break
}
```

Here, note that we have already covered all the scenarios in the first 2 cases:

- **Case 1**: All negative numbers up to -1
- **Case 2**: All positive numbers from 0 onward

Hence, we simply break out the switch statement in the default case.

swap versus swapAt

The `swap(_:_: )` method in Swift 3 works on "pass by reference principle" and swaps two elements of a given array on the spot. In pass by reference, actual memory addresses are used rather than values:

```
var integerArray = [1, 2, 4, 3, 5]
swap(integerArray [2], integerArray [3])
```

As you can see, the parameters are passed as in out parameters, which means the actual references or placeholder addresses are accessible directly inside the function. On the other hand, Swift 4's `swapAt (_:_:)` works on "pass by value" principle and only the corresponding indices are passed to the function to be swapped:

```
integerArray.swapAt(2, 3)
```

The `swap(_:_:)` function will not be seen in Swift 4, because it will be deprecated and removed, and you have a couple of approaches to replace it. The first approach uses a temporary constant as follows:

```
let temp = a
a = b
b = temp
```

The second takes advantage of Swift's built in tuples, as follows:

```
(b, a) = (a, b)
```

Improved NSNumber

With earlier versions of Swift, behavior of `NSNumber` might be unexpected and casting to Uint8 might result in absurd results:

```
let number1 = NSNumber(value: 1000)
let number1ConvertedToUInt = number1 as? UInt8
```

In this scenario, logically, the value inside `number1ConvertedToUInt` should be nil, but this was not the case and the value would be 1000% 255, that is, 232 instead. This is because the maximum value that a UInt can hold is 255. Fortunately, this behavior has been resolved in Swift 4 and now if you execute the same code in Swift 4, you should expect the value of `number1ConvertedToUInt` to be nil.

Directly access unicode scalars of characters

Swift 4 allows direct access to unicode scalars associated with characters:

```
let character: Character = "A"
let unicodeScalar = character.unicodeScalars
```

Done! Easy, isn't it? Before you would have to convert the character to a String first and then try to access unicode scalar.

Migrating to Swift 4

As opposed to the previous releases of Swift, transitioning from Swift 3 to Swift 4 is less cumbersome when compared to the earlier migrations. The Swift migration tool is now bundled right into Xcode and is capable of handling most of the changes autonomously. Let's cover the steps required to update the version of a code base to the latest Swift release.

Preparation before migration

Ensure that the project that you are migrating builds successfully in Swift 3.2 mode, and all its tests pass. Keep in mind that Swift 3.2 does have significant changes from 3.1 as well as the SDKs against which you built, so you may need to resolve errors initially.

It's highly recommended that you manage your project under source control. This enables you to easily review the applied changes via the migration assistant, get rid of them, and retry the migration if required.

Different from last year, the migrator is built directly into the compiler and not a separate tool, so it can work with both the versions of Swift, that is, 3.2, and 4.

Swift migration assistant

If you open your project with Xcode 9 for the first time, you will see a migration opportunity item in the **Issue Navigator**; click on it to activate a sheet asking you if you'd like to migrate. You can be reminded later or invoke the migrator manually from the menu—**Edit** | **Convert** | To **Current Swift Syntax...**

You will be given a list of targets to migrate. Only those targets that contain Swift code will be selected.

There is only one migration workflow this year, although there is a choice between two kinds of @objc inference:

- **Minimize inference**: Add an @objc attribute to your code only where it is needed based on static inference. After using this option, you need to follow the manual steps.
- **Match Swift 3 behavior**: Add an @objc attribute to your code anywhere it would be implicitly inferred by the compiler. This option does not change the size of your binary as it adds explicit @objc attributes everywhere.

Clicking on **Next** will bring up the **Generate Preview** sheet and a migration build will be initiated by the assistant to get source changes. Once this is completed, you will be shown all the changes that will be applied when you click on **Save**. This will also change the Swift language version build setting for the migrated targets to Swift 4.

You may find some issues while processing the targets during the migration process. You can check the log for these errors by switching to report navigator and converting the entry that was added.

Swift 4 migration changes overview

Extensive changes that the migrator suggests occur from data produced by a comparison of the previous SDK and the current SDK, which may drive renaming of identifiers and types, for example; and from normal compiler fix-its. There are some special arrangements where the migrator can safely perform simple mechanical changes.

SDK changes

Moving global constants into static type properties and converting String constants into Swift enumeration cases are the two most common SDK changes. Migrator handles these automatically. You'll also see various type signature changes.

Notable special cases

The new release has many changes and additions, but there are some special cases that are worth mentioning. In the upcoming sections, we will cover some of these special cases.

New String

New APIs are added to String in Swift 4; the return types will be String or subString in certain cases. To ease this transition, the migrator will assist by adding explicit initializers in places where the API expects special cases.

We have already discussed some important changes in the String API earlier in the chapter.

Differentiating between single-tuple and multiple-argument function types

```
f: (Void) -> ()
```

When using f: (Void) -> () for the type of a function argument, it is generally meant to be f: () -> (), so the migrator will suggest that you use this type instead. Otherwise, with the new rules in SE-0110 for Swift 4, you will need to call the f function as f(()).

 To read more about the Swift proposals, you can visit https://Apple. github.io/swift-evolution/.

Adding tuple destructuring

Consider code such as the following:

```
swift func foo(_: ((Int, Int) -> ()) {} foo { (x, y) in print(x + y) }
```

The migrator must add explicit tuple destructuring to continue building in Swift 4, such as shown here:

```
swift func foo(_: ((Int, Int) -> ()) {} foo { let (x, y) = $0; print(x + y)
}
```

Default parameter values must be public

The compiler now checks accessibility of referenced objects a bit more strictly; non-literal values that you want to use in public functions as arguments should also be public. Among other things, this exposes an opportunity for optimizing access to the value at the call site. As this may involve API design, the migrator does not suggest fixes, although there are some possibilities for you to consider as an API author:

- Making the referenced default values public
- Providing public functions that return a sensible default value

In both cases, consider the impact of exposing a new API, ensuring that you document your public symbols.

After migration

After applying the migrator changes, you might need to do some manual changes in order to build the project.

Some compiler errors might have some fixits; Xcode suggests these fixits and most of them are applied already by the migrator, but if the fixit does not fit almost 100% in the given scenario, then you might need to do it manually.

It is not necessary that the code that the migrator supplies is ideal, even if it compiles correctly. Use your best judgement and check that the changes are appropriate for your project.

Known migration issues

With any beta release of Xcode, numerous bugs get reported and with iterative releases of the beta versions for IDE, these bugs keep reducing. Similarly, there are some known issues with the current beta version of Xcode, and they will be fixed in the upcoming releases. At the time of writing this chapter, the Xcode IDE version is 9 beta 6, and mentioning all the known issues with the current version of IDE might change quite a lot in a few months, so it is better to follow the official release notes provided by Apple that are released with every IDE release in order to stay up to date with the latest known issues.

Using Carthage/CocoaPods projects

Here are some important points to consider when migrating a project with external dependencies using package managers such as Carthage, CocoaPods, or the Swift package manager:

- It is recommended to use source dependencies rather than binary Swift modules, because Swift 3.1 modules will not be compatible with Swift 3.2/4 modules unless you can get distributions that were built in Swift 3.2 or Swift 4 mode
- Ensure that your source dependencies work smoothly with Swift 3.2 as well as your own targets
- You need to remove Carthage file's search path or clean the build folder if you have used Carthage in your project
- It is not necessary to migrate your source dependencies as long as they can build in Swift 3.2 mode

Summary

Swift is a fairly new language, and the Apple developers keep updating the underlying APIs and language syntax while enhancing the language features by adding new APIs. In this chapter, we learned about the changes and additions to Swift with its latest release, that is, Swift 4. We covered how to migrate our current IDE to support the latest Swift release, and then we went ahead and covered major changes to the existing APIs, followed by the new additions to the language. We highlighted the major changes that you will encounter most in your day-to-day programming practices. Toward the end of the chapter, we also covered how to migrate an existing code base to Swift 4 and tackle some of the issues that you might come across while trying to update the code base. This book is more about Reactive programming, so we will start working with Reactive concepts from Chapter 2, *FRP Fundamentals, Terminology, and Basic Building Blocks*, onward, but since we will be working with Swift 4 throughout the book, it made sense to start by getting you up to date with the development language; next up will be the setup of the overall development environment.

2
FRP Fundamentals, Terminology, and Basic Building Blocks

This chapter will introduce you to the basic building blocks that form the foundation of `RxSwift` as a library. We will introduce two different types of programming styles, the imperative and declarative style of doing things in code, and then establish the sweet spot between the two styles where `RxSwift` sits to take advantage of both programming paradigms.

We will elaborate on what functional reactive programming is and how you can adapt your code for it. The main topics covered in this chapter are as listed:

- Functional reactive programming: Basic building blocks, concepts, and frequently used terms
- Marble diagrams
- Railway-oriented programming

Functional reactive programming

Every programming language or technical domain has some kind of pictorial representation to explain certain concepts and make things easier to translate in logical pictorial representations. Similarly, we can express certain reactive concepts in logical pictorial representations. In this book, you will see the use of diagrams to represent functional and reactive concepts and hence it becomes important to have a basic understanding of these diagrams and how you can read them to understand the programming concept they want to showcase. In subsequent sections, we will give a brief introduction to the different types of Logical diagrams. You will get to learn more about concepts like state, side effects, signals, events, and so on in the later half of the chapter. Understanding these concepts is very important because these concepts form smaller elements of the bigger puzzle.

Programming as a whole is event driven most of the time and often, even the best code produces unwanted sequences of events that are unaccounted for; however, a developer should handle them as gracefully as possible. These unwanted or unexpected events are called exceptions and as soon as an exception springs up, the flow of code should digress a little from the normal flow in order to handle the exception so that the state of the app is maintained. It is like a train journey—you board a train and the train starts running on the track and in case there is some kind of congestion on the track, the train switches track to smoothly complete the journey. In programming concepts, this method of programming is called Railway-oriented programming. At the end, we will discuss the concept of railway-oriented programming and how this concept segregates exception flows from normal execution.

What is functional reactive programming (FRP)?

FRP represents an intersection of two programming paradigms, but before we dig deeper into the concepts, we need to know a bit more about some basic terms.

Imperative programming

Traditionally, we write code that describes how it should solve a problem. Each line of code is sequentially executed to produce a desired outcome, which is known as imperative programming. The imperative paradigm forces programmers to write "how" a program will solve a certain task. Note that in the previous statement, the keyword is "how."

Here's an example:

```
let numbers = [1, 2, 3, 4, 5, 6, 7, 8, 9]
var numbersLessThanFive = [Int]()
for index in 0..<numbers.count
    {
    if numbers[index] > 5
        {
        numbersLessThanFive.append(numbers[index])
        }
    }
```

As you can see, we sequentially execute a series of instructions to produce a desired output.

Functional programming

Functional programming is a programming paradigm where you model everything as a result of a function that avoids changing state and mutating data. We will discuss concepts such as state and data mutability and their importance in subsequent sections, but for reference, consider state as one of the different permutations and combinations that your program can have at any given time during its execution, whereas data mutability is the concept where a given dataset might change over a given course of time during program execution.

The same example that was given using imperative programming can be used in the following way using the functional approach:

```
let numbers = [1, 2, 3, 4, 5, 6, 7, 8, 9]
let numbersLessThanFive = numbers.filter { $0 < 5 }
```

We feed the filter function with a closure containing a certain criterion that is then applied to each element in the numbers array, and the resulting array contains elements that satisfy our criteria.

Notice the declaration of the two arrays in both the examples.

In the first example, the `numbersLessThanFive` array was declared as a `var`, whereas in the second example, the same array was declared as a `let`. Does it ring some bells? Which approach is better, which array is safer to work with? What if more than one thread is trying to work with the same array and its elements? Isn't a constant array more reliable? Let's answer all those questions in the data immutability section later in this chapter.

Reactive programming

Reactive programming is the practice of programming with asynchronous data streams or event streams. An event stream can be anything like keyboard inputs, button taps, gestures, GPS location updates, accelerometer, iBeacon, and such. You can listen to a stream and react to it accordingly.

You might have heard about reactive but it might have sounded too intimidating, scary, or cryptic to even try this style of programming; you might have seen something like this:

```
var twoDimensionalArray = [ [1, 2], [3, 4], [5, 6] ]
let flatArray = twoDimensionalArray.flatMap { array in
    return array.map { integer in
        return integer * 2
    }
}

print(flatArray)

Output : [2, 4, 6, 8, 10, 12]
```

At first glance, the preceding code might feel a bit obscure, and this might be the reason you turn your back on this style of programming. This book will help you grasp the main idea of reactive programming and help you think in reactive programming in order to apply in a real code base. As we cover the concepts in detail, you will note how this programming paradigm will help solve some major concerns that might spring up while working with a fairly large application doing a number of asynchronous tasks simultaneously.

Reactive programming, as we mentioned earlier, is programming with event streams.

However, the bigger question still remains unanswered, *What is functional reactive programming?*

FRP is the combination of functional and reactive paradigms, or to be more concise, it is reacting to data streams using the functional paradigm. FRP is not a utility or a library; it changes the way you architect your applications and the way you think about your applications.

Basic building blocks

Every massive structure has basic units that come together and make sense to the whole structure. For example, bricks, cement, paint, concrete, and so on make up basic building blocks on a building. Similarly, before we go ahead and discuss the massive field of functional reactive programming, it would be great if we understood the basic building blocks that will come together so that the massive applications that we create make sense. In the next subsections, we will cover the basic building blocks of FRP, starting with event streams.

Event streams

An event stream can be defined as a sequence of events happening over time; you can think of it as an asynchronous array. A simple description of an event stream is shown in the following diagram:

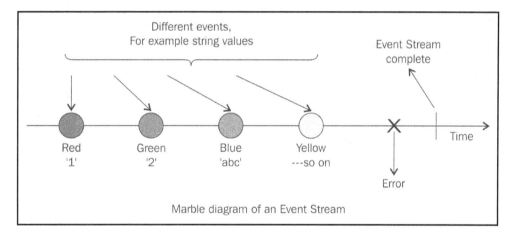

As you can see, we have expressed time on the arrow aligned from left to right, moving forward to the right, and events happen over time. *The colored bubbles (indicated by their names) drawn at intermittent intervals on the timeline represent the events*. We can add an event listener to the whole sequence and whenever an event happens, **WE CAN REACT TO IT** by doing something; that's the main idea!

We have numerous other types of sequence in Swift, for instance, arrays:

Suppose we have an eventStream array:

```
var eventStream = ["1", "2", "abc",  "3", "4", "cdf", "6"]
```

Let's try to compare eventStream to an array; arrays are sequences in space, which means all the items in the eventStream array now exist in memory; on the other hand, eventStreams don't have that property. Events might happen over time and you won't even know all the items that might happen and when will they happen. So if we have to relate between an array and event stream, then we can assert that if the ["1", "2", "abc", "3", "4", "cdf", "6"] values happen over a period of time and don't just exist in memory from scratch, the preceding array will act like an event stream where an event "1" might happen at 1st second, event "2" may happen at the 4th second, event "abc" might happen at the 10th second, and so forth. Here, note that neither the time at which the event is happening nor the type of event is known beforehand. The events are just addressed as they happen. The nice thing with event streams is that they have functions similar to arrays.

So let's say that our problem is to add all the numbers in the given array.

Solution to arrays: As you can see, the elements in the array are not numbers; they are strings, so we have to do some transformations here and go over a loop to filter out the strings that cannot be converted to a number and then add the rest if they are a valid number. We might loop over the array using a for loop, but while we traverse over the array inside a for loop, we will use the map and filter operations to provide a solution to the problem, which is the functional approach:

Step 1:

```
let result = eventStream.map{// inside map we will parse the array elements
to convert all the //integer compatible elements to integers
}
```

Step 2: Filter all the elements that are not numbers from the resulting array from step 1. So, the statement in step 1 can now be extended like this:

```
let result = eventStream.map({// inside map we will ... to integers
}).filter {
// filter all the non integers to form a pure integer array
}
```

Step 3: Add all the integer values to get the sum by extending step 2 with reduce. So, the same statement can be written as follows:

```
let result = eventStream.map({// inside map we will ... to integers
}).filter {
// filter all the non integers to form a pure integer array
}.reduce(0,+)
```

All those functions are called **Higher-order functions**, and the process of extending the functionality using dot notation in a single line is called **Chaining**.

We can do the same thing with event streams, the only difference being the availability of events at intermittent time intervals. As a result, processing of the event stream will take its own time and the result will not be populated instantaneously as it will be while working with an array.

State

To be precise, we need to understand more about the shared mutable state.

Before we can relate this term to programming concepts, let's try to come up with a definition in generic terms; consider an example. Suppose you bought a car and on the first day, you started the car and went for a drive. Everything just runs fine and smoothly. To start the car, you insert the key and rotate it clockwise; in the background, the spark plug ignites a controlled flow of fuel and your engine comes to life. This state of your car is the started state. You then switch the gear to drive mode and press the accelerator with your right foot. Voila! The car starts moving and now you can call this state of your car running and eventually you will stop your car at the destination, and then the state of the car will change accordingly.

So you noticed that your actions or inputs, engine ignition, pistons running, and so on—the sum of all the activities and processes either in foreground or background—comprise the state of the car and since, it can change with respect to several background processes and user actions, it is mutable:

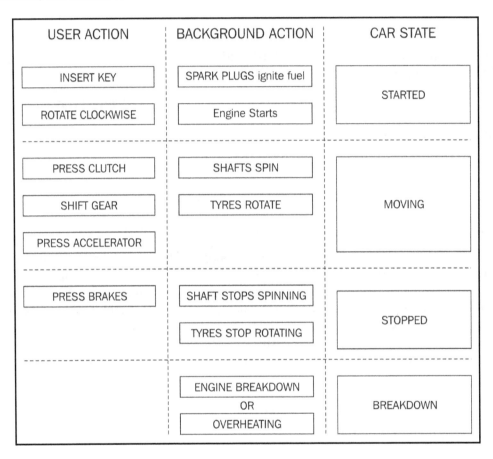

So many factors govern state of the car at a given point in time, and it is difficult to control the state of the car sometimes and then you have breakdowns! Well that's something for the car mechanic to worry about.

Mapping the same concept to the apps we build, each and every application has a state at any given instance of time. The application might be fetching data from a web service in the background, playing a song in the media player, responding to user inputs, and such—all these actions or processes (synchronous and asynchronous) at any given point in time are collectively termed the state of the application and unlike a car mechanic, it is our responsibility to manage the state of an app at any instance in time. This book will serve as a platform where you will manage the state of your app, especially dealing with multiple asynchronous tasks simultaneously.

Side effects

Since you are now aware of the shared mutable state in generic and programming worlds, you can pin down most issues with those two things to side effects.

Every function works in its scope to take an input, apply some logic, and generate an output; functions can have no inputs or outputs as well. For example, a function printing out the state of an object. Side effects occur when the state of the system changes because of the execution of a function. For example, suppose a function named `addAndStoreValue()` adds two integers and stores the result in the local database and raises a notification for the view to refresh in order to reflect the resulting value, then that change in the view will be the side effect that this function causes because of its execution. In other words, the state of the app changed once the function was executed. This change is called a **side effect**.

Any time you modify data stored on disk or update the text of a label on screen, you cause side effects.

You must be thinking that side effects are not bad at all; actually, that is the reason we code and execute our programs. We want the state of the system/apps to change once the program has executed.

You don't want your program to run and bring no change to the state of the mobile right? Who wants such an app? Imagine running an app for a while and causing no change in the state of the system at all, pretty useless, aye!

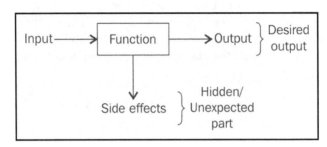

So from the discussion so far, we have understood that causing side-effects is desired, then what's the issue?

The issue with side-effects is that we want to control the side-effects and hence predict the state of the app once a function has finished execution. We want to control the execution to cause side-effects in a predictable manner and forecast the state of the device once our app starts running. We also need to segregate our app in modules to identify which pieces of code change the state of the app and which pieces process and output data.

RxSwift addresses the preceding issues by making use of declarative coding and creating reactive systems, both described earlier. We will delve deeper into these concepts in upcoming sections.

Functional programming mostly avoids side-effects; because of this the code becomes more testable and hence writing robust code becomes easier.

A well-written app differentiates code that causes side-effects from the rest of the program; as a result of this testing the app becomes easier, extending the functionality becomes clear, refactoring and debugging become a straightforward process, and maintaining such a code base is hassle-free. RxSwift serves a great deal in order to isolate side effects as expected.

Immutability

Before we discuss immutability, let's start by answering a question:

What datatype is more secure to work with in a multithreaded environment?

- Variable datatype, which can be changed over time, or
- Constant datatype, which cannot be changed once populated

Let me try to explain the question with the help of an example—suppose you had a variable dictionary of position coordinates:

```
var locationDictionary = ["latitude": 131.93839, "longitude": 32.83838]
```

locationDictionary is the location of the user that gets populated once every five minutes; this locationDictionary will, at some time in the near future, be converted to a locations JSON object and synced to the backend (an API pushing data to the server) from where the location will be picked and shown to some web view or it may be used for any other real-time location update purpose.

Imagine working with this location dictionary in a multithreaded environment; since it is a variable, locationDictionary can be updated anytime by any thread at any given moment in time, resulting in faulty location updates. You might end up sending unwanted or corrupt data to your API.

Simple fix: Make the variable a constant, and you can rest assured that once the value is populated in the dictionary, it will not be altered and hence you will have reliable results.

From the preceding discussion, we can now define an immutable object and what a mutable object is: an immutable object is an object that cannot be changed over the course of its existence or scope, whereas a mutable object can be changed within its scope.

Functional programming promotes the concept of immutability; remember the example:

```
let numbers = [1, 2, 3, 4, 5, 6, 7, 8, 9]
let numbersLessThanFive = numbers.filter { $0 < 5 }
```

Did you note how we can create a new numbersLessThanFive array as a constant rather then a variable? Try creating a similar array with imperative programming; can you have a constant array ? Let's try doing that:

```
var numbersLessThanFive = [Int]()
for index in 0..< numbers.count
    {
    if numbers[index] > 5
        {
        numbersLessThanFive.append(numbers[index])
        }
    }
```

The process is not only wordy but involves lossy data flow in the program, as any other thread executing in the memory can now change the values in this array since the array is now a variable. Working with immutable data streams is encouraged in any programming language, especially when you are trying to build complex applications that might spawn myriads of threads:

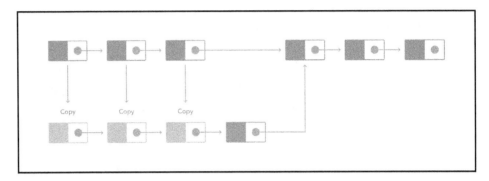

Since one aspect of functional reactive programming comprises a lot of functional programming, working with immutable data comes naturally while modeling logic in the FRP way and hence half the problems are addressed from the start. Well it is not as simple as it looks, but constant practice will make you perfect; this is the reason I encourage you not to miss any chapter or topic in this book, as each topic builds on top of another and strengthens your knowledge of FRP as a whole.

Since immutable objects cannot be changed over time during execution, it means they come at an cost and might not be reusable in certain scenarios. You have to dispose an immutable object or populate a new one if the current one does not fit the context. As you can see, there are certain drawbacks while working with immutable data types, but as intelligent programmers, we need to strike the right balance and make logical choices while modeling our data types:

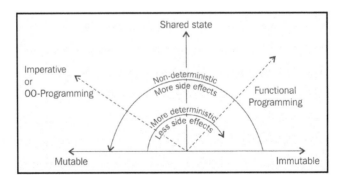

From the preceding diagram and our previous discussion, it is quite clear why working with mutable state can cause non-deterministic behavior in your program code. As mentioned earlier, we need to strike a balance between both to maintain a shared state to suit the problem at hand. More immutable data types mean more deterministic behavior.

RxSwift foundation

Reactive programming has been in the picture for more than 20 years now, but it did not really start to gain momentum until the introduction of reactive extensions in 2009. Reactive extensions or Rx are available for several languages, and they look and behave the same for the most part across all these languages. Development began on RxSwift in February 2015, and it became the official reactive extension for Swift in August the same year.

Reactive extensions

As mentioned earlier, all of the Rx extensions look and behave the same way, and that's because each language implements the same patterns and operators in a language-specific idiomatic way.

There are also platform-specific extensions such as `Cocoa` and `CocoaTouch`, which means that you can develop in the language and platform of your choice, which will be the native Swift platform in this case. The Rx skills that you learn in this book are universal and portable to other languages and platforms, which means that teams working with cross-platforms are able to better coordinate using reactive extensions.

To deliver a unique user experience, they are unique to each platform while ensuring that common behaviors and business rules are consistently implemented across all platforms.

Rx offers a common set of operators as mentioned earlier in this chapter: To perform various tasks based on events in an asynchronous fashion, Rx typically implements two common patterns:

- A subject maintains a list of dependents called **Observers**, and it notifies them of changes. Notification center and KVO are also implementations of this observer pattern.

- Rx also implements the iterator pattern, which is how sequences can be traversed. If you have spent time with Swift, then you will have definitely worked with the iterator pattern while trying to traverse over sequences and collections. We are talking about the same things here and in fact, in Rx, **Everything is a Sequence**:

do re mi ...
Everything is a Sequence

Pretty much everything is a sequence of data or events or something that operates on observable sequences. Note the term observable sequence; you will often read words like observable or sequence—these refer to the same thing. It's a sequence that's observable. We will refer to it as observable sequence throughout the book to help drive this point home.

Observable

An observable sequence is just a sequence. The key advantage of an observable sequence over Swift's standard sequence type is that it can also operate asynchronously. Before getting our hands dirty with the code where we will see the observable sequences in action, it is important to understand the lifecycle of an Observable sequence and what it does during that lifetime.

Lifecycle of an observable:

An observable sequence can emit things known as events. It can emit zero or more events; when a value or collection of values is added to or put onto a sequence, it will send a next event containing that value or collection to its observers. This is known as **emitting**, and the values are referred to as elements. This works the same way as observable sequences of events such as taps or other recognized gestures.

If an error is encountered, a sequence can emit an error event containing an error type; this will terminate the sequence.

A sequence can also terminate normally and in doing so it will emit a completed event.

If at any point you want to stop observing a sequence, you can cancel the subscription by calling `dispose()` on it; this is like removing an observer in KVO or the notification center API, or you can also just add subscriptions to an instance of `DisposeBag`, which will take care of properly canceling subscriptions on `deinit()` for you.

In `Chapter 3`, *Set Up RxSwift and Convert a Basic Login App to its RxSwift Counterpart*, we will see how we can create, subscribe, dispose, and terminate an observable.

Subject

Subject is a special type in RxSwift that can act as both of these:

- An **Observable sequence**, which means it can be subscribed to
- An **Observer** that enables adding new elements onto a subject that will then be emitted to the subject subscribers

There are four subject types in RxSwift, each with unique characteristics that you may find useful in different scenarios. They are as listed:

- `PublishSubject`
- `BehaviorSubject`
- `ReplaySubject`
- `Variable`

Let's discuss each one of these subjects in turn.

A `PublishSubject` emits only new next events to its subscribers; in other words, elements added to a `PublishSubject` before a subscriber subscribes will not be received by that subscriber. **This concept of emitting previous next events to new subscribers is called replaying, and publish subjects DO NOT replay.** If terminated, though, a publish subject will re-emit its stop event, that is, a completed or error event to its new subscribers; actually, all subjects will re-emit stop events to new subscribers. If you are creating a real-time indicator, you won't care what the last element was before a new subscription, you only want new elements coming in after the fact. `PublishSubject` will be useful in that scenario.

Sometimes you want new subscribers to always receive the most recent next event in the sequence even if they subscribed after that event was emitted; for this, you can use a `BehaviorSubject`. A `BehaviorSubject` is initialized with a starting value, and then it replays to the new subscribers a next event containing the most recent elements or the initial value if no new recent elements have been added to it beforehand. Remember that if any subject type is terminated, it will reemit its stop event, whether that is a completed or a new event to its subscribers. For example, in a chat app, you might use a `BehaviorSubject` to prefill a new posts tile text field beginning with the initial name untitled. As you will see later, you can then bind that text field to a submit button that is only enabled if the text field has text.

If you want to replay more than the most recent element on a sequence to new subscribers, you use a `ReplaySubject`. A `ReplaySubject` is initialized with a buffer size and that value cannot be changed after initialization. It will maintain a buffer up to the buffer size of the most recent next events, and it will replay the buffer to the new subscribers as if those events had happened immediately after each other, right after subscribing. It will also reemit its stop event to new subscribers. You can use replay subject to display as many as the five most recent search items whenever a search controller is presented.

A variable is essentially a wrapper around `BehaviorSubject`. It will replay a next event with the latest or initial value to new subscribers. A variable is guaranteed to never emit an error event and terminate. It also automatically completes when its about to be deallocated, which makes this subject unique. Unlike other subject types, a variable uses the dot `"."` syntax to get the latest value or to set a new value onto it. You can access a variable's `BehaviorSubject` by calling as `Observable()` on it.

We will cover all these subjects in code in the coming sections, so do not worry if your current understanding is not yet crystal clear. This section served to give you a brief introduction about what's to come in the next sections.

Marble diagrams

As discussed earlier, we know that Rx is all about working with Observable sequences; the way you work with them is by using one or more operators on them. Operators are methods of the various observable types as discussed earlier.

Marble diagrams are interactive diagrams that depict how Rx operators work with observable sequences. Consider this example:

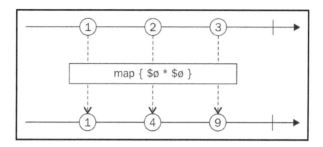

You can visit RxMarbles.com to view and play around with marble diagrams for most Rx operators that you will find in RxSwift. For instance, from the preceding marble diagram, you can see how a map operator works.

The elements in the top line represent elements emitted from an observable sequence and the elements in the bottom line represent the outcome sequence, that is, after invoking the operator with whatever parameters are specified on the original sequence or multiple sequences in some cases.

Here in map operator in the marble diagram, there are three elements emitted from the observable sequence. The map operator is used to map the operation specified inside the map operation and apply it to each element of the observable sequence as shown by the top line. So, in this case, the map operator will take each element from the observable sequence and produce a square of each value to generate a new sequence, as shown by the bottom line.

The vertical line at the end indicates that a sequence has terminated normally via a completed event. Don't worry if all these concepts don't click at the moment; we will revisit each one of them in much more detail as we go along in this book.

Let's take another example—the following image describes a merge operator; the functionality depicts that elements emitted from two observable sequences will be merged together in one sequence:

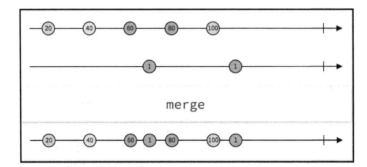

Moving any of the elements along the sequence reveals that merge will produce the merged sequence in the order they are emitted. You can see this in the following diagram:

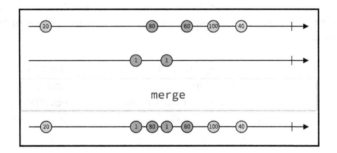

Merge happens as the elements are emitted from the observable sequences. Marble diagrams are also displayed on the ReactiveX website, although some of them are not interactive.

Here's an example of the catch operator from the website:

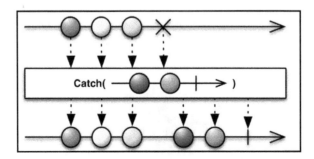

It is actually called the catch error operator in RxSwift, but the functionality is the same. The 'X' represents that the observable sequence terminated with an error. In this example, the sequence terminates with an error, but the catch operator introduces a new sequence that will take over and begin emitting its own events in place of the terminated one. If you want to explore more with marble diagrams using an IOS app, you're in luck. Head to the app store and search for RxMarbles; the app is built in RxSwift, and the most astonishing part is that it is open source and you can find the source code of this app on Github.

Homework: Find the link to the Github repository for this application. So put on your googler hats and start searching!

Once you have found the library, you can download the project, check the code for yourself, and run the app in the IOS simulator as well. After a quick introduction, you can browse through all the operators. The operators mentioned earlier in this section can be found too. Do play with the app, it is a fun way to learn this important concept. You can edit these diagrams to add an event or error element and observe how the operators are affected. This app is indispensable in learning Rx.

Schedulers

An observable and the operators you use on it will execute and notify observers on the same thread on which the subscribe operator is being used.

Schedulers are an abstraction that let you specify distinct queues on which to perform work. It is always a good idea to move all the intensive work off the main thread to keep it as responsive as possible for users, and schedulers make it easy to do this. They can be Serial or Concurrent.

You will use a serial scheduler if you want to ensure that work is carried out on that queue in the order it was added to the queue, otherwise you will typically just use a concurrent queue.

There are **built-in scheduler types** that work with **Grand Central Dispatch (GCD)** queues and `NSOperationQueues`. These are as listed:

- `SerialDispatchQueueScheduler`, which will dispatch work on a specified serial dispatch queue
- `ConcurrentDispatchQueueScheduler`, which will dispatch work on a concurrent dispatch queue
- `OperationQueueScheduler`, which will perform the work on a specified NSOperations queue

You can also create your own custom schedulers by conforming to the `ImmediateScheduler` protocol.

You also have access to a couple of helpful singletons that can be useful for common needs, such as the following:

`CurrentThreadScheduler`, which represents the current thread and is the default scheduler, and `MainScheduler`, which represents the main thread typically used for all UI-related work.

To specify a scheduler on which a subscription is created, it's handled or executed and is disposed of using the `suscribeOn` operator. This operator is not used normally, instead `observeOn` is used most of the time; it specifies the scheduler about the `next`, `error`, and `completed` events. The important thing to remember is that `subscribeOn` will direct which subscription is running on which scheduler, whereas `observeOn` only directs which scheduler to use after or below where `observeOn` is used in a chain. We will work with more marble diagrams and code blocks to revisit these concepts in the upcoming sections.

Railway-oriented programming

Railway-oriented programming comes into the picture when we need to bring functional concepts in error handling within our code base.

In general programming, a developer spends most of their time thinking about "the happy path," that is, when everything goes according to plan and is just done right, and they don't spend enough time thinking what will happen if things go wrong; that's what railway-oriented programming is all about. In an imperative world, when things go wrong, or in other words the code throws some kind of error, there is a certain way of handling those errors and the process is called exception handling. In this section, we will cover how to handle errors and exceptions in a functional way.

Let's take the example of a use case where a user wants to update their information and the steps involved in the overall process are listed in the following diagram:

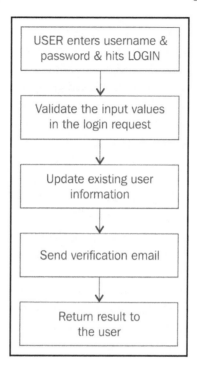

As you can see, the user wants to update their information, and they have to go through the following request and deal with the responses as mentioned in the flowchart. So the user enters their information, for example the user Id and password, and issues the request. We then need to run some validations on the data; for instance, the user Id should not be negative and the password cannot be nil, strip out the spaces from the data strings, and so on.

Then, we update the user data in the database by hitting an API and get a response from the server; some more operations that might be a side effect of the user credentials update, like an email telling you about the update.

So all those steps executed one after the other without any errors become the happy path, but wait, are we missing something? As most of you would agree, the world is full of errors, and smart developers keep this in mind all the time and have a plan to tackle error scenarios whenever or wherever they occur during program execution. The preceding functionality can throw one or more errors on each level; we can identify them with * in the following diagram:

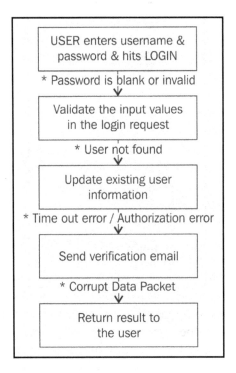

There are hundreds of other things that can go wrong with the functionality, and we have just highlighted a few just to scratch the surface and introduce the concept.

Now imagine writing all the error handling code for all those cases; won't that bloat your classes and make them look ugly? What percentage of code might be written just to handle possible errors? What about code readability? With error handling code sprinkled throughout my classes, wouldn't it be difficult to understand the underlying logic about what a class is supposed to do?

The following diagram separates the happy path from the unhappy path; note the error handling code that you have to write in order to handle all the errors that might spring up:

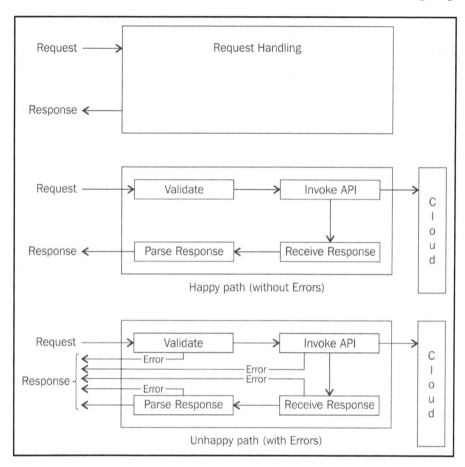

In short, if something fails, the program returns and further execution is halted. If the **Validate** operation fails -> return, if **Invoke API** fails -> return, and so on; as a result, the code base gets clumsy and difficult to manage, as discussed earlier.

So what's the solution?

Let's try to tackle the same situation in the functional way. In the functional model, you don't call a method and get a response; rather, you have a function, and the function has an input and an output. The function acts like a black box, and every function has exactly one input and exactly one output. So in this whole use case, we will have one function that will have just one input and will produce just one output.

In the happy path, a single function will consist of smaller functions that are connected together in a pipeline so that the output of the first function becomes the input to the other function and so on. That's fine when everything goes well, but what happens when everything breaks down or things don't go as planned?

In error scenarios, you cannot do an early return; that's an issue with functional programming, and this scenario is evident in the next diagram; you have to keep going all the way up to the end:

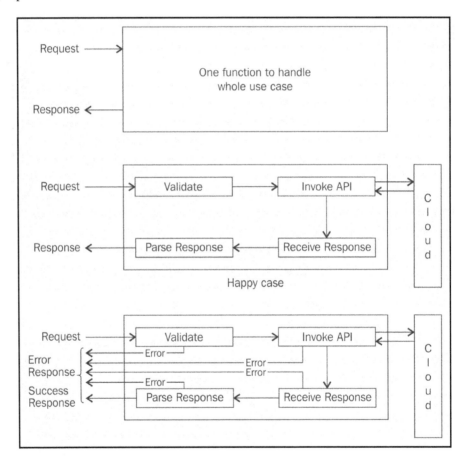

Some of you might have some questions regarding the preceding implementation:

- How can I return early?
- How can a function have two or more outputs, as you can see in the diagram: one for separate errors and the other that of a successful response type?

Let's try to answer the second question first—we can bring all the error types together and bridge them together under an umbrella called **Failure** and successful response to be success. You can declare an enumeration to have different names for different errors accordingly and success for successful response and now generate output of the result type. We can further parameterize the success type using Generics to have access to the type of the successful response.

So to sum things up, the overall internals of the function look something like the following diagram, where smaller components of the larger function produce errors, and the errors are aggregated under a bigger domain to join the output together in one single output:

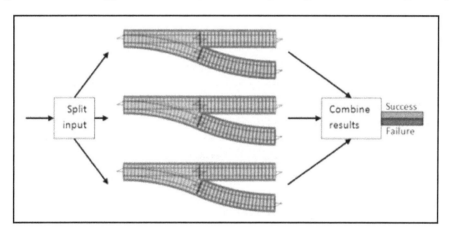

Since you get access to errors and a successful response in the output, you can take your own path in handling the error on its own and, in case you received a successful response, follow the correct rail and there is no need to digress, as shown in the diagram.

Summary

This chapter covered the gist of the concepts that form the basics of functional reactive programming paradigm. In the coming chapters, we will see all the components that were discussed in this chapter in action. We will start with unique implementations and then gradually bundle them together to make a full-blown app. So stay tuned, we are about to write a lot of code and this time, in declarative style!

3

Set up RxSwift and Convert a Basic Login App to its RxSwift Counterpart

In this chapter, we will start writing code to work with the concepts we have touched on in previous chapters. We will start with environment setup and then start working towards a very basic application. While we do so, we will revisit some important concepts that we discussed earlier, while expressing the functionality in code.

The main topics covered in this chapter are as follows:

- Setting up an RxSwift environment
- CocoaPods and Carthage
- Writing a singe view login app in RxSwift

RxSwift in action

RxSwift is a library, and we need to import it to our code base in order to invoke the functionality on offer and implement reactive components in our code. There are different ways to set up the environment to develop Rx code in Swift, and we will cover all of them in this chapter, but we will pick one out of the discussed methods and use that in the rest of the book. You are free to pick your implementations as each one serves the same primary requirement.

Once the environment is set up, we will start writing the code and from here onward, you will realize that we will work with code comparatively. Less theory and more hands on!

Let's build the environment first

`RxSwift` is the reactive extension for Swift and can be found for free at `https://github. com/ReactiveX/RxSwift`. Since the library is distributed under the MIT license, you are free to use it in your commercial apps on an as-is basis like any other MIT-licensed software provided to you, which includes a copyright notice in your apps during distribution.

The RxSwift repository includes the `RxSwift`, `RxCocoa`, `RxTest`, and `RxBlocking` libraries. The latter two will allow you to write `Rxtests`, whereas `RxCocoa` provides Rx features to UI controls. We will explore all these libraries in this book, starting in this chapter.

To get started with the concepts, the repository comes bundled with `Rx.playground` and `RxExample`. You can work with `Rx.playground` to play with most of the operators, whereas `RxExample` is an example app that showcases the use of `RxSwift` in an iOS application. So they're definitely worth working with; do take a look into these in your own time.

Setting up the environment

`Carthage` and `CocoaPods` are the easiest ways to include `RxSwift/RxCocoa` in your projects. You can also use the Swift package manager, but in this book we will use `CocoaPods` to set up the `RxSwift` environment, so ensure that you use `CocoaPods` while working with sample projects and other examples in this book.

Most developers are used to command and click when they need to jump over to the source code of the method they are working with; in order to facilitate similar behavior, it makes more sense to work with `CocoaPods` while you are in the learning phase. When it comes to your projects, feel free to use any method discussed earlier and the one that suits your workflow the best.

RxSwift with CocoaPods

It is very easy to work with `CocoaPods`; you can install `RxSwift` like any other library by making use of a `pod` file. A simple example of a `pod` file is as follows:

```
use_frameworks!
target 'YOUR_TARGET_NAME' do
pod 'RxSwift'
pod 'RxCocoa'
end
```

`RxTests` and `RxBlocking` make the most sense in the context of unit/integration tests:

```
target 'YOUR_TESTING_TARGET' do
    pod 'RxBlocking'
    pod 'RxTest'
end
```

It's totally up to you to include any number of libraries with the `RxSwift` library, depending on your requirements. Of course, you can choose just one, a combination of `RxSwift` and `RxCocoa`, or all of them.

Installing RxSwift

Install the latest and greatest version of `CocoaPods` before starting to work with chapters and code in this book. Executing the following command in the terminal will be enough to get you going:

```
sudo gem install cocoapods
```

To know more, visit the `CocoaPods` website at `https://guides.cocoapods.org/using/getting-started.html`.

You will be required to open the starter project and install `RxSwift` in the starter project at the start of each chapter. Perform the following steps in order to install `RxSwift` in the respective project associated to the chapter you are currently working with:

1. In the chapter that you are currently working with, in the requirements section for the chapter right after the introduction, find the `podfile` code.
2. Open `Terminal` and navigate to the project folder. Create a `pod` file inside your Xcode projects folder by executing the `pod init` command.

3. Open the created `podfile` and paste the `podfile` code copied in the first step.
4. Enter the command `pod install` to fetch all the listed libraries from GitHub and install all of them in the project.
5. As a result of the installation, you will find a newly created workspace called `.xcworkspace`. Launch this file, and you are ready to work with the reactive components that will be introduced in the chapter.

Type `cd /users/yourname/path/projectname` to reach the `podfile` that you have created:

```
use_frameworks!
target 'YOUR_TESTING_TARGET(Name of your target)' do
pod 'RxSwift', '~> 3.6'
end
```

If you receive any error while trying to work with `CocoaPods`, for example, you can't find `RxSwift`, try to update the pod by typing pod update so that it fixes the indexing.

Installing RxSwift with Carthage

Using `Carthage` is pretty much similar to working with `CocoaPods`. Install the latest version of `Carthage` by following the steps mentioned at `https://github.com/Carthage/Carthage#installing-carthage`.

Create a new file in your project named `CartFile` and add the following code to this file:

```
github "ReactiveX/RxSwift" ~> 3.6
```

Use the `Terminal.app` to execute the Carthage `update` command from the folder containing the newly created `CartFile`.

Once this command is executed, you will see framework files in the `Carthage` folder present inside the current folder. All the libraries mentioned on the `CartFile` are downloaded and built to form a framework file in this step and hence it might take some time. Include the framework in your project and build the project once again so that `Xcode` finds the newly added framework files. You are ready to go now.

As mentioned earlier in the chapter, we will use `CocoaPods` throughout this book and we recommend using it.

In the next sections, we will create a simple single view application where we will validate login credentials entered by the user and then decide whether they are allowed to log in or not.

Let's get started – The Login page

After setting up the environment for RxSwift, ensure that you build the Xcode project once before starting to code.

We will build a very simple login validation as mentioned earlier where the **username** and **password** fields have to be four or more letters before the **Login** button becomes enabled, as shown:

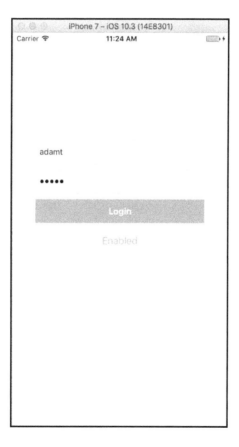

Also, if the validation fails, the **Login** button should stay disabled, as illustrated:

Setting up

We will create a single view application and add a couple of libraries:

- RxSwift
- RxCocoa, which will help us bind our viewModel to the input text fields and the **Login** button, as shown in the preceding screenshots

Steps to set up

1. Launch Xcode and create a single view application, as shown:

2. Launch Terminal app and navigate to the project directory.
3. Initialize the podfile by executing pod init in the terminal and then open the created podfile in any text editor:

4. Add the following code to the `podfile`:

```
# Uncomment the next line to define a global platform for your
project
# platform :ios, '9.0'
target 'RxSwiftLoginView' do
# Comment the next line if you're not using Swift and don't want to
use dynamic frameworks
use_frameworks!
pod 'RxSwift', '~> 3.6'
pod 'RxCocoa', '~> 3.6'
# Pods for RxSwiftLoginView
end
```

5. Execute `pod install` after saving the `podfile`.
6. Open the `.xcworkspace` created as a result of execution, and we are good to go.

Compare the difference in the project navigator before and after running the pod installation; after installation, you should see something like this:

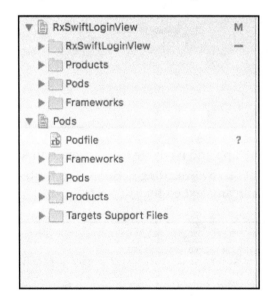

Since the libraries that we want are now available to us, we can start making use of their functionalities.

The Login page:

Open up your storyboard and create a simple layout; two text fields, one button, and one label, as follows:

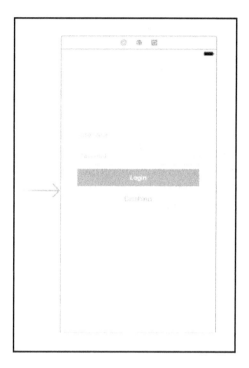

Then, we will link the UI elements to the view controller by making use of the assistant editor. *Ctrl* + click and drag over to the view controller for the username text field, and Xcode will give you an option to create an outlet or an action; enter the desired name for each field and press *Enter*. Repeat the same process for all the view elements; at the end, you will have the following code structure in your ViewController:

```
import UIKit
class ViewController: UIViewController {
    @IBOutlet weak var usernameTextField: UITextField!
    @IBOutlet weak var passwordTextField: UITextField!
    @IBOutlet weak var loginButton: UIButton!
    @IBOutlet weak var validationsLabel: UILabel!


    override func viewDidLoad() {
        super.viewDidLoad()
        // Do any additional setup after loading the view, typically
```

```
                                                    from a nib

    }
    override func didReceiveMemoryWarning() {
        super.didReceiveMemoryWarning()
        // Dispose of any resources that can be recreated.
    }
}
```

Follow proper naming conventions while writing the code; this book deals with advanced concepts, so we will not delve deeper into those concepts; however, naming conventions and proper indentation play a very important role in writing clean code.

In this project and many to follow, we will follow MVVM as the design pattern. We will dig deeper into design patterns including MVVM later in this book and for now, just take it in your stride and follow along. To give a brief introduction about the **Model View View Model** (**MVVM**) design pattern, we will separate logical concerns from ViewController by implementing a special class called a ViewModel, which will take care of UI formatting, interacting with Models, and such so that our ViewController does not bloat up unnecessarily and violate the single-responsibility principle of programming practice.

So, the next step in our project will be to add a ViewModel class to the project, and we will call it LoginViewModel. Create a new Swift file, as shown:

Then, import `RxSwift` to the newly generated file:

```
//  LoginViewModel.swift
//  RxSwiftLoginView
//
//  Created by Navdeep on 28/9/17.
//  Copyright © 2017 Navdeep. All rights reserved.
//
import Foundation
import RxSwift
```

From our previous life as a traditional Swift developer, we all know that Swift encourages developers to use `struct` as much as possible in their code; we will carry that knowledge forward and declare a `struct` in the newly generated `ViewModel` class:

```
//  LoginViewModel.swift
//  RxSwiftLoginView
//
//  Created by Navdeep on 28/9/17.
//  Copyright © 2017 Navdeep. All rights reserved.
//
import Foundation
import RxSwift
struct LoginViewModel {
    var username = Variable<String>("")
    var password = Variable<String>("")
}
```

As we can see, this structure includes two variables mapping the values returned from text fields on our `ViewController`. The `username` variable will represent the text in the username text field; as you might have already noted the type of the variable is quite unique. `Variable<String>("")` means that `username` is an `RxSwift` variable of type `String` with the default value of an empty string. Similarly, `password` is also declared as an `RxSwift` string variable with a default value of an empty string.

Our `ViewModel` will be responsible for performing all the validations, as mentioned earlier in the section, and return the result to `ViewController` so that the `ViewController` can reflect the result of these validations on the View to the user. Next, we will add a computed property to compute whether the text entered in both text fields fulfills the validation criteria or not:

```
var isValid : Observable <Bool> {
        return Observable.combineLatest(username.asObservable(),
password.asObservable()){                    usernameString, passwordString in
usernameString.characters.count >= 4
```

```
passwordString.characters.count >= 4
        }
    }
```

`isValid` is an `Observable` property of the `Bool` type, which makes use of the `combineLatest` operator to check both the values returned from both the text fields once the user starts typing. Here, the `combineLatest` operator is listening for the changes to the values passed as parameters to this operator, that is, `username` and `password`; if either of these values changes, we have to recalculate the validations.

`username.asObservable()` and `password.asObservable()` basically say that we want to know which one of them has a changed value. The condition in the closure then validates the logic as expected and returns true or false based on the condition expressed in the code.

Finally, `LoginViewModel` is complete:

```
//  LoginViewModel.swift
//  RxSwiftLoginView
//
//  Created by Navdeep on 28/9/17.
//  Copyright © 2017 Navdeep. All rights reserved.
//
import Foundation
import RxSwift
struct LoginViewModel {


    var username = Variable<String>("")
    var password = Variable<String>("")


    // Computed property to return the result of expected validation
    var isValid : Observable <Bool> {
        return Observable.combineLatest(username.asObservable(),
password.asObservable()){ usernameString, passwordString in
            usernameString.characters.count >= 4
passwordString.characters.count >= 4
        }
    }
}
```

Ultimately, we need to bind the result returned by the `isValid` property to our View in order to enable or disable the `Login` action.

To do this, switch to `ViewController` and import the `RxSwift` and `RxCocoa` libraries in the file; now we will write some code in the `viewDidLoad()` method to bind the text fields to our `ViewModel`:

```
var loginViewModel = LoginViewModel()
    override func viewDidLoad() {
        super.viewDidLoad()


        // Bind UI textFields to properties in ViewModel


        _ = usernameTextField.rx.text.map { $0 ?? "" }
        .bind(to: loginViewModel.username)
        _ = passwordTextField.rx.text.map {$0 ?? "" }
        .bind(to: loginViewModel.password)
    }
```

In order to bind the view elements to `ViewModel` variables, we need to declare a variable property in the `ViewController` to link `LoginViewMode`—`var loginViewModel = LoginViewModel()`. `RxCocoa` enables traditional UI elements to behave as reactive UI elements, and we can access the values returned from these newly transformed UI elements using `.rx` extensions on the UI elements. The `usernameTextField.rx.text` statement will return a control property that will be of type optional `String`, and we want to ensure that it is not optional so that we can use it for validations.

Functional programming to the rescue

We will use the `map` function on the control property to filter out values as follows:

```
usernameTextField.rx.text.map { $0 ?? "" }
```

`$0` represents the first variable, and if this is nil, we will return an empty string and pass that through to bind the returned value to the ViewModel's variable as desired by making use of the `bindTo` operator:

```
usernameTextField.rx.text.map { $0 ?? ""
        .bind(to: loginViewModel.username)
```

This will simply tell the `ViewModel` that the input of this text field has changed. The preceding line of code might throw a warning about an unused value.

To silence the warning, add _ =.

This can be resolved as follows:

```
_ = usernameTextField.rx.text.map { $0 ?? "" }
        .bind(to: loginViewModel.username)
```

That should remove the warning. Similarly, bind the password text field to ViewModel's password variable:

```
_ = passwordTextField.rx.text.map {$0 ?? "" }
        .bind(to: loginViewModel.password)
```

We can also bind the `isValid` result to our `loginButton` so that, if its not valid, we can ensure that the `login` button is not enabled; we can do this by making use of the library again, as follows:

```
_ = loginViewModel.isValid.bind(to: loginButton.rx.isEnabled)
```

This code line will bind the Boolean `Observable` to the `isEnabled` property of `loginButton`.

Finally, we want to control the state of the app by listening to the `isValid` property of the `ViewModel`. Let's do it in a slightly different way just to see how we can do this without making use of the bindings:

```
_ = loginViewModel.isValid.subscribe(onNext: {[unowned self] isValid in
        self.validationsLabel.text = isValid ? "Enabled" : "Disabled"
        self.validationsLabel.textColor = isValid ? .green : .red
    })
```

Let's segregate and explore the code in the code block—`loginViewModel.isValid.subscribe` allows you to subscribe to any change in the `isValid` property's value. Since `isValid` is declared as an `Observable`, we can subscribe to the events that `isValid Observable` will emit. We can subscribe to three different types of event emitted by an Observable: next, error, and completed. Dig into the `Event` definition, and you will come across the following:

```
/// Represents a sequence event.
///
```

```
/// Sequence grammar:
/// **next\* (error | completed)**
public enum Event<Element> {
    /// Next element is produced.
    case next(Element)
    /// Sequence terminated with an error.
    case error(Error)
    /// Sequence completed successfully.
    case completed
}
```

Don't worry if you can't fully comprehend the preceding code. We will cover all the topics touched on in the code that we wrote in this chapter in full detail in upcoming chapters. This chapter aims to give the reader a feel for how convenient and clear your code can look (and work) if you use RxSwift concepts.

Coming back to subscribe() as used in the preceding code:

```
loginViewModel.isValid.subscribe(onNext: { isValid in
        })
```

We are listening only for next events emitted by isValid, and this subscription will pick up anything that is emitted by the isValid Observable. Inside the closure, we want to react to the events emitted by the isValid Observable. As per our validation logic, we want to make the login button enabled or disabled, depending upon the number of characters inside the username and password text fields. Let's start by making the validationLabel react to emitted events:

```
loginViewModel.isValid.subscribe(onNext: {[unowned self] isValid in
            self.validationsLabel.text = isValid ? "Enabled" : "Disabled"
            self.validationsLabel.textColor = isValid ? .green : .red
        })
```

If isValid returns true, then validationsLabel will display enabled; if isValid returns false, then validationsLabel will display disabled. Similarly, the color of the label will change depending on the boolean value of the isValid variable.

Run the app on a device or simulator and play with the app; you will notice the desired behavior.

We can now extend the validations to involve the **Login** button as well. Let's modify the requirements a bit. Let's keep the **Login** button disabled and inactive until the user enters four or more letters in each text field; if the validations fail, the view should look like this:

Once validations pass, the view should transform to enable the **Login** button and validationsLabel will say enabled in green , as follows:

We can achieve the aforementioned behavior by making small changes to the code written in the `viewDidLoad()` method of the `ViewController`. Firstly, we have to disable the Login button and change the background color in `viewDidLoad()`:

```
loginButton.isEnabled = false
loginButton.backgroundColor = UIColor.lightGray
```

We can avoid the preceding step if we keep the default state of the `login` button at `disabled`. Now we want to change the state of the `login` button as soon as the validation rule returns true, that is, the `isValid` variable of `ViewModel` returns true, and we can achieve this by refactoring the subscription as follows:

```
_ = loginViewModel.isValid.subscribe(onNext: { [unowned self] isValid in


        self.validationsLabel.text = isValid ? "Enabled" :
                                        "Disabled"
        self.validationsLabel.textColor = isValid ? .green : .red


        //Making changes to the login button
        self.loginButton.isEnabled = isValid ? true : false
        self.loginButton.backgroundColor = isValid ? UIColor.orange
                                        :UIColor.lightGray
    })
```

We are changing the state of the Login button depending on the value of the `isValid` property. Right now, we are handling all the events emitted by the `isValid` observer, and we can validate by logging in values returned by `isValue` in the subscription code:

```
_ = loginViewModel.isValid.subscribe(onNext: { [unowned self] isValid in


    self.validationsLabel.text = isValid ? "Enabled" : "Disabled"
    self.validationsLabel.textColor = isValid ? .green : .red


    //Log the values with each key in event
    print(isValid)


    //Making changes to the login button
    self.loginButton.isEnabled = isValid ? true : false
    self.loginButton.backgroundColor = isValid ? UIColor.orange :
                                        UIColor.lightGray
})
```

Build and run the app once again and note the value of the `isValid` variable in the console. Finally, the `ViewController` file will look like the following:

```swift
// ViewController.swift
// RxSwiftLoginView
//
// Created by Navdeep on 27/9/17.
// Copyright © 2017 Navdeep. All rights reserved.
//
import UIKit
import RxSwift
import RxCocoa
class ViewController: UIViewController {
    @IBOutlet weak var usernameTextField: UITextField!
    @IBOutlet weak var passwordTextField: UITextField!
    @IBOutlet weak var loginButton: UIButton!
    @IBOutlet weak var validationsLabel: UILabel!


    var loginViewModel = LoginViewModel()


    override func viewDidLoad() {
        super.viewDidLoad()
        loginButton.isEnabled = false
        loginButton.backgroundColor = UIColor.lightGray

      //Bind UI textFields to properties in ViewModel


        _ = usernameTextField.rx.text.map { $0 ?? "" }
        .bind(to: loginViewModel.username)
        _ = passwordTextField.rx.text.map {$0 ?? "" }
        .bind(to: loginViewModel.password)


        _ = loginViewModel.isValid.bind(to: loginButton.rx.isEnabled)


        _ = loginViewModel.isValid.subscribe(onNext: {[unowned self]
                                                    isValid in


            self.validationsLabel.text = isValid ? "Enabled" :
                                                "Disabled"
            self.validationsLabel.textColor = isValid ? .green : .red
```

```
            //Log the values with each key in event
            print(isValid)

        //Making changes to the login button
            self.loginButton.isEnabled = isValid ? true : false
            self.loginButton.backgroundColor = isValid ? UIColor.orange
                                                        :UIColor.lightGray
        })
    }
}
```

Summary

In this chapter, you got a feel for working with RxSwift code and were introduced to the RxCocoa library as well. You converted your traditional UI elements to Rx components, created a computed property, and made it an Observable. Later, you subscribed to events emitted by the computed property to reflect the state of validations in the main View. We achieved a lot in terms of writing code with RxSwift and a number of things might be unclear at this point—you might have a number of questions regarding Observables, Events, subscribing, subjects, and more. If that's right, then stay tuned, because we will enlarge on all those concepts individually and dissect each in order to acquire a complete understanding.

4
When to Become Reactive?

In `Chapter 2`, *FRP Fundamentals, Terminology, and Basic Building Blocks*, we introduced a number of concepts and called them the basic building blocks of functional reactive programming. In `Chapter 3`, *Set up RxSwift and Convert a Basic Login App to its RxSwift Counterpart*, we worked with a sample application to get a feel of `RxSwift` code base, and we also brushed up on some code concepts. In this chapter, we will take a step back and dive deeper into the concepts that were introduced in `Chapter 2`, *FRP Fundamentals, Terminology, and Basic Building Blocks*, and work with code to reiterate over the concepts in a different manner. We worked with a basic `RxSwift` application in the previous chapter and made use of Observables, subjects, and so on to get our work done without knowing the functional details of these individual concepts. Due to that, some of you might have developed a gap in your understanding of how things actually work in `RxSwift`. Well, here's the good news!

This chapter will cover those topics in detail and lay down a solid foundation for the upcoming chapters. This chapter will cover the following topics:

- Observable sequences—Creating and subscribing
- Different types of subjects
- Introduction to traits—Single, completable, and maybe

Once the understanding of these concepts is clear, you will be able to take an informed decision of when, where, and how to go Reactive. This chapter will lay down the foundation based on which you can start visualizing your code conversion from traditional to `RxSwift`. Remember that at the end of the day, it is your decision to choose between traditional and Rx concepts, and this book will help you make this decision wisely.

Creating and subscribing to Observables

In the upcoming sections, we will work with a sample project and see how can we create and subscribe to Observables in code.

Project setup

As discussed earlier, we need to set up a workspace to work with RxSwift:

1. Create a single view application project and name it RxBasics.
2. Open Terminal and navigate to the project folder. Create a pod file inside your Xcode projects folder by executing the pod init command.
3. Open the created pod file and paste the pod file's code:

    ```
    # Uncomment the next line to define a global platform for your
    project
        target 'RxBasics' do
     # Comment the next line if you're not using Swift and don't want
    to use dynamic frameworks
     use_frameworks!
     pod 'RxSwift'
     # Pods for RxBasics                                            end
    ```

4. Enter the pod install command to fetch all the listed libraries from GitHub and install all of them in the project.
5. As a result of this installation, you will find a newly created workspace by the name .xcworkspace. Launch this file, and you are ready to work with the reactive components that will be introduced in the chapter.

We will work with playground in this chapter and as soon as we have the .xcworkspace ready, create a new playground file in the project and name it RxBasics. This is the easiest way to get things going. Working only with Playgrounds and third-party libraries is a gray area when it comes to Apple documentation. Next, Import RxSwift in this newly created RxBasics.playground file and build the project to get rid of any possible errors.

Getting started

Let's create a helper function called `executeProcedure(with description:String, procedure: () -> Void)`. The function takes two params: a string description and a procedure closure. It will print the description and will execute the procedure. We will use this function to encapsulate each procedure and make it easier to determine what each procedure is printing to the console:

```swift
import UIKit
import RxSwift
public func executeProcedure(for description:String, procedure: () ->
Void){
    print("Procedure executed for:", description)
    procedure()
}
```

Firstly, we will cut and paste this function to a separate file in the `Sources` folder for this playground. By twisting down the playground page in the project navigator, right-click on the `Sources` folder and select a new file; name it `Helper`. Now select the playground file again, cut the `executeProcedure(with description:String, procedure: () -> Void)` function, and paste it into the support code file. The project structure in the project navigator will look something like this:

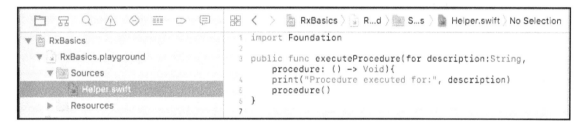

Build the project once again to make the function available to the main playground file.

Previously, we explained that events are emitted by an Observable sequence. So now, we will create a few examples of observable sequences, and we will observe them emitting some events.

Let's start by creating the simplest of Observables, a single element sequence using the `just` operator:

```
executeProcedure(for:  "just"){
    let observable = Observable.just("Example of Just Operator!")
}
```

```
6  executeProcedure(for:  "just"){
7      let observable = Observable.just("Example of Just Operator!")
       1

       Declaration  static func just(_ element: String) ->
                    Observable<String>

       Description  Returns an observable sequence that contains a single element.

       Parameters   element   Single element in the resulting observable sequence.

       Returns  An observable sequence containing the single specified element.

       Declared In  RxSwift
```

By clicking the option on the `just` operator, you can see that it returns an Observable sequence of a single element of a String type.

 Rx functions or methods are referred to as operators in Rx. Whenever we say operators in Rx, you can think of methods in traditional Swift.

Now we will look at the `subscribe` operator to subscribe to events being emitted by an Observable and print each event as it is emitted:

```
executeProcedure(for:  "just"){
    let observable = Observable.just("Example of Just Operator!")
    observable.subscribe({ (event: Event<String>) in
        print(event)
    })
}
```

`subscribe` takes a closure that receives the emitted event and will execute this closure each time an event is emitted. We manually define the event argument that is passed to subscribe's closure as being an event of the String type, and then we print each event as it is emitted. The result is the single next event that we created with the String **Example of Just Operator!** followed by the **completed** event:

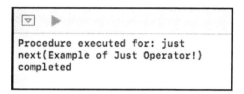

```
Procedure executed for: just
next(Example of Just Operator!)
completed
```

Remember that we have three types of Observable events:

- next
- error
- completed

Also, once an error or a completed event is emitted, the Observable sequence is terminated and cannot emit additional events. The event param is an enumeration of the type event of `Element`:

```
/// Represents a sequence event.
///
/// Sequence grammar:
/// **next\* (error | completed)**
public enum Event<Element> {
    /// Next element is produced.
    case next(Element)
    /// Sequence terminated with an error.
    case error(Swift.Error)
  /// Sequence completed successfully.
    case completed
}
```

Element is a generic placeholder for the Observable's type, a String in this example. We explicitly specified String, but if we hadn't, it could also be inferred by the type the observable instance's `subscribe` is called on.

Next, we will create an Observable sequence with multiple elements using the `of` operator:

```
executeProcedure(for: "of"){
        let observable = Observable.of(10, 20, 30)
        observable.subscribe({
        print($0)
    })
}
```

We created an Observable with elements `10, 20, 30` and subscribed to this sequence to print out the sequence, just like the previous example, except that this time we used the `$0` shorthand argument name instead of explicitly declaring an argument name. Each next event is printed followed by the completed event:

```
Procedure executed for: just
next(Example of Just Operator!)
completed
Procedure executed for: of
next(10)
next(20)
next(30)
completed
```

Let's create an observable sequence from an array using the `from` operator:

```
executeProcedure(for: "from"){
    Observable.from([10, 20,30])
        .subscribe{
            print($0)
    }
}
```

As you can see, we have not declared a variable to assign the returned value as we did in the previous examples. We then chained the subscription onto the Observable sequence returned and wrapped the subscription onto the next line to improve readability. The output of the preceding method will be as follows:

```
Procedure executed for: from
next(10)
next(20)
next(30)
completed
```

This is how you will typically see chained operators. Let's *command* + click and see the `subscribe` operator's source:

```
/**
    Subscribes an event handler to an observable sequence.

    - parameter on: Action to invoke for each event in the observable sequence.
    - returns: Subscription object used to unsubscribe from the observable sequence.
    */
public func subscribe(_ on: @escaping (RxSwift.Event<Self.E>) -> Swift.Void) -> Disposable
```

As you can see, subscribe returns **Subscription object used to unsubscribe from the observable sequence**. This subscription object is of the type that confirms to the `Disposable` protocol that represents any disposable resource. After we *command* + click on the `Disposable` protocol, we find that it requires a `dispose()` method to be implemented:

```
/// Respresents a disposable resource.
public protocol Disposable {
    /// Dispose resource.
    func dispose()
}
```

Digging into the source like this can really help you understand how `RxSwift` works. Let's go back to the playground and assign the result we returned from subscribe to a local variable `subscribed`, which is of the `Disposable` type:

```
25  executeProcedure(for: "from"){
26      let subscribed = Observable.from([10, 20,30])
27          .sub  ibe{

     Declaration  let subscribed: Disposable

     Declared In  RxBasics.playground
```

Disposing of a subscription will cause the underlying Observable sequence to emit a completed event and terminate. In these basic examples, we have explicitly defined all the Observable sequence elements ahead of time, and they will automatically emit a completed event after emitting the last next event. More often than not though, an Observable sequence can continue to emit events, and they must be manually terminated or else you will leak that memory. So the right thing to do here is to ensure that subscription is disposed of when we are done with it. One way to do that is by calling `dispose()`:

```
executeProcedure(for: "from"){
    let subscribed = Observable.from([10, 20,30])
            .subscribe{
```

```
            print ($0)
    }
    subscribed.dispose ()
}
```

That's actually not done in practice though; the more conventional approach is to add subscriptions to a container that holds disposables and will call `dispose()` on its contents on its `deInit`. That container is called a `DisposeBag`. We will create a `DisposeBag` instance before the subscription:

```
executeProcedure (for:  "from") {
    let disposeBag = DisposeBag()
    let subscribed = Observable.from([10, 20,30])
     .subscribe (onNext:{
            print ($0)
    })
    subscribed.disposed (by:  disposeBag)
}
```

Then, we add the subscription to `disposeBag` using the `disposed(by:)` method.

If you just want to get the next event elements, instead of getting each next event containing an element, you can use the `subscribe(onNext:)` operator instead, as done in the preceding code. The output of the code will be this:

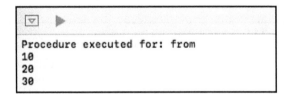

```
Procedure executed for: from
10
20
30
```

As you can see, only the next event elements are printed and the completed event is ignored. The following points are worthy to be noted:

- If an error event was emitted, it will be ignored too, because we have subscribed to next events only
- We can actually subscribe to get next, completed and/or error events and react when the subscription is terminated and disposed of for any reason

For example, let's create a sequence from another array of `Int` values:

```
Observable.from([1, 2, 3])
```

This time, we will choose subscribe on all the possible events, as follows:

```
.subscribe(onNext: nil, onError: nil, onCompleted: nil, onDisposed: nil)
// nil is written in this case just to shorten the format
```

Note that each of these parameters is an option, so you can skip one or more of them if you want to. For example, let's remove `onError` from the function:

```
.subscribe(onNext: nil, onCompleted: nil, onDisposed: nil)
```

We are now just subscribing to `onNext`, `onCompletion` and `onDisposed` events. Let's print the elements from the `next` events, and print completion message `onCompleted` event and the `Disposed` message as soon as the sequence terminates:

```
Observable.from([1, 2, 3])
        .subscribe(onNext: {print($0)},
                    onCompleted:
{print("Completed the events")},
                    onDisposed: {print("Sequence terminated hence
Disposed")}
    )
```

Finally, we will add the subscription to `DisposeBag`:

```
Observable.from([1, 2, 3])
        .subscribe(onNext: {print($0)},
                    onCompleted: {print("Completed the events")},
                    onDisposed: {print("Sequence terminated hence
Disposed")}
        )
    .disposed(by: disposeBag)
```

Sometimes we have to manually indent `RxSwift` code, and we can do so by selecting the code block and pressing *control* + *I*. Try this activity and note the difference. Meanwhile, check the output:

```
Procedure executed for: from
10
20
30
1
2
3
Completed the events
Sequence terminated hence Disposed
```

As expected, all the next events are printed, followed by the completed event and finally disposed is called.

As we are working with finite Observable sequences here, they automatically emit completed events and terminate after the last element. It's better to be safe than sorry, so just get into the habit of always adding subscriptions to a `disposeBag`, and you will avoid potentially leaking memory. Let's look at an example of subscribing to an error event at this point:

```
executeProcedure(for: "error"){
    enum CustomError: Error{
        case defaultError
    }
    let disposeBag = DisposeBag()
Observable<Void>.error(CustomError.defaultError)
        .subscribe(onError: {print($0)})
        .disposed(by: disposeBag)
}
```

First, we created a `CustomError` enum with a single case of `defaultError` and then we have created an Observable sequence that terminates with an error using the error operator that takes an error as a parameter. It's necessary to specify the type to the observable sequence here, so we just used `Void`; then we subscribed on the `error` operator to print the `error`. Lastly, we disposed of the subscription by adding it to a `dispose bag`. You can see the output:

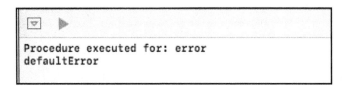

```
Procedure executed for: error
defaultError
```

This was just a small example; we will work with errors in more detail in the upcoming chapters. In the next sections, we will go over some special kinds of Observable called `subjects` that can continue to emit new events to subscribers. In `Chapter 2`, *FRP Fundamentals, Terminology, and Basic Building Blocks*, we described a `subject` and various types of subject in theory, and now we will work with all those concepts in code, starting with `PublishSubject`.

Different types of subject

There are four different types of subject: `PublishSubject`, `BehaviorSubject`, `ReplaySubject`, and `Variable`, as discussed earlier. In this section, we will work with all of them in code, starting with `PublishSubject`, and gradually work our way to explain other subjects as well. You will understand when to use any particular type of subject while working with Observables and subscriptions depending on the respective requirements.

PublishSubject in action

We can continue to work with the same project that we set up earlier in the chapter. Just use multiline comments to comment out the earlier code to differentiate between outputs from the current sections and the previous ones.

A `PublishSubject` emits only new items to its subscriber, that is, it does not replay events. We will create a `PublishSubject` instance named `pubSubject`:

```
let pubSubject = PublishSubject<String>()
```

Note that the `PublishSubject` initializer is empty, but we need to declare a type that is String in our case. Next, we will subscribe to it and print each emitted event. Subject is empty at this point, so the subscription will not yield anything:

```
pubSubject.subscribe {
        print($0)
    }
```

We will now use the `on` operator to add a new next event, an element, onto `pubSubject`:

```
pubSubject.on(.next("First Event"))
```

The `on` operator will notify all subscribers about the new event. Using the `on` operator and passing a next event causes the subscription to emit that event. The `on` operator has convenience methods to simplify the syntax. For example, instead of writing an `on` and passing a next event to it, we can just write `onNext` and pass the value you want to emit in the next event to observers. In the code, we can create an `onNext` event, as follows:

```
pubSubject.onNext("Second Event")
```

The overall code till now is this:

```
executeProcedure(for: "PublishSubject"){
    let pubSubject = PublishSubject<String>()
    pubSubject.subscribe {
        print($0)
    }
    pubSubject.on(.next("First Event"))
    pubSubject.onNext("Second Event")
}
```

It will produce the following output:

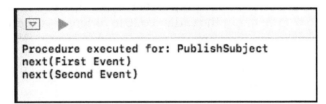

```
Procedure executed for: PublishSubject
next(First Event)
next(Second Event)
```

Let's try to tweak the events a bit and see what would happen if we added a completed event to the subject before Second Event:

```
executeProcedure(for: "PublishSubject"){
    let pubSubject = PublishSubject<String>()
    pubSubject.subscribe {
        print($0)
    }
    pubSubject.on(.next("First Event"))
    pubSubject.onCompleted()
    pubSubject.onNext("Second Event")
}
```

In this case, the sequence will end while the completion event is emitted, and the subject will not emit any more events, that is, Second event will not be emitted; you can see this behavior in the output:

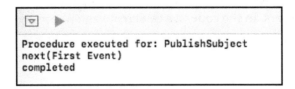

```
Procedure executed for: PublishSubject
next(First Event)
completed
```

Let's comment out the completion event and add an error event to the subject. Adding an error event will cause the subject to emit an error event before it terminates. First, we will create an enum of the CustomError type, as earlier, and register a defaultError case:

```
executeProcedure(for: "PublishSubject"){
    enum CustomError: Error{
        case defaultError
        }
        let pubSubject = PublishSubject<String>()
        pubSubject.subscribe {
            print($0)
        }
    pubSubject.on(.next("First Event"))
    pubSubject.onError(CustomError.defaultError)
    //pubSubject.onCompleted()
    pubSubject.onNext("Second Event")
}
```

You will note that the subject stops emitting any more events after the error event in the output, which means the subject terminated with an error event:

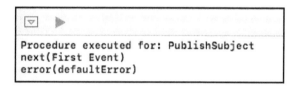

These are pretty much the basics of Rx; everything else is icing on the cake. Let's play a bit more with PublishSubjects.

We will now create a new subscription to the subject in order to subscribe on next events and monitor the output in the console:

```
executeProcedure(for: "PublishSubject"){
    enum CustomError: Error{
        case defaultError
        }
        let pubSubject = PublishSubject<String>()
        pubSubject.subscribe {
            print($0)
        }
    pubSubject.on(.next("First Event"))

    //pubSubject.onError(CustomError.defaultError)
    //pubSubject.onCompleted()
    pubSubject.onNext("Second Event")
```

```
        let newSubcription = pubSubject.subscribe(onNext: {
            print("New Subscription", $0)
        })
    }
```

As you can see, we want to print the next element prefixed with New Subscription to distinguish it from the first subscription. Let's monitor the output:

```
┌─────────────────────────────────────────────────────┐
│  ▽   ▶                                                │
├─────────────────────────────────────────────────────┤
│  Procedure executed for: PublishSubject               │
│  next(First Event)                                    │
│  next(Second Event)                                   │
│                                                       │
└─────────────────────────────────────────────────────┘
```

Nothing happens because the new subscription will only get new events and not previous ones, so we will add a new element to the subject right after the declaration of the new subscription:

```
        let newSubcription = pubSubject.subscribe(onNext: {
            print("New Subscription", $0)
        })
        pubSubject.onNext("I am New!")
```

Then, we will monitor the output once again:

```
┌─────────────────────────────────────────────────────┐
│  ▽   ▶                                                │
├─────────────────────────────────────────────────────┤
│  Procedure executed for: PublishSubject               │
│  next(First Event)                                    │
│  next(Second Event)                                   │
│  next(I am New!)                                      │
│  New Subscription I am New!                           │
└─────────────────────────────────────────────────────┘
```

We can see that both the subscriptions print out the newly added event. Let's call dispose() on the new subscription and then add one more event on the subject:

```
    let newSubcription = pubSubject.subscribe(onNext: {
            print("New Subscription", $0)
        })
        pubSubject.onNext("I am New!")
        newSubcription.dispose()
        pubSubject.onNext("Fourth Event")
```

You might have guessed it already; if we monitor the output now, we will see that only the first subscription will print out the **Fourth Event**:

```
Procedure executed for: PublishSubject
next(First Event)
next(Second Event)
next(I am New!)
New Subscription I am New!
next(Fourth Event)
```

As we mentioned earlier, a good programmer always keeps track of memory and as per our implementation, you might have noticed an issue that might lead to a memory leak. Let's go ahead and fix the issue and take a look at the final code:

```
executeProcedure(for: "PublishSubject"){
    enum CustomError: Error{
        case defaultError
        }
    let pubSubject = PublishSubject<String>()
    let disposeBag = DisposeBag()
    pubSubject.subscribe {
        print($0)
    }
    .disposed(by: disposeBag)
    pubSubject.on(.next("First Event"))
    //pubSubject.onError(CustomError.defaultError)
    //pubSubject.onCompleted()
    pubSubject.onNext("Second Event")
    let newSubcription = pubSubject.subscribe(onNext: {
        print("New Subscription", $0)
        })
    pubSubject.onNext("I am New!")
    newSubcription.dispose()
    pubSubject.onNext("Fourth Event")
}
```

BehaviorSubject in action

A `BehaviorSubject` will replay the latest or initial value in a next event to new subscribers. We will create a `BehaviorSubject` instance with an initial value of `Test`. We will start this section with a basic code setup and build on top of the previous example by just commenting out the sample code for `PublishSubject`:

```
executeProcedure(for: "BehaviorSubject"){
    let disposeBag = DisposeBag()
}
```

Then, we will create a subscription on it using `subscribe(onNext:)`:

```
let behSubject = BehaviorSubject(value: "Test")
    let initialSubscripton = behSubject.subscribe(onNext: {
        print("Line number is \(#line) and value is" , $0)
    })
```

We have used the line debugging identifier as an easy way to distinguish this printout in the console by printing the line number. Note that the initial value is printed on subscription:

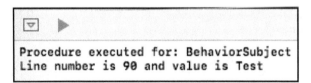

```
Procedure executed for: BehaviorSubject
Line number is 90 and value is Test
```

Next, we will add a new `"Second Event"` element onto the subject:

```
let behSubject = BehaviorSubject(value: "Test")
    let initialSubscripton = behSubject.subscribe(onNext: {
        print("Line number is \(#line) and value is" , $0)
    })
    behSubject.onNext("Second Event")
```

As expected, this element is emitted and printed:

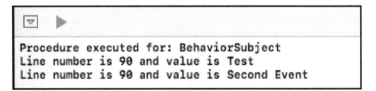

```
Procedure executed for: BehaviorSubject
Line number is 90 and value is Test
Line number is 90 and value is Second Event
```

Now, let's create a subsequent subscription to explore more about the nature of
BehaviorSubjects:

```
let subsequentSubscription = behSubject.subscribe(onNext: {
    print("Line number is \(#line) and value is" , $0)
})
```

Note that the subsequent subscription only emits and prints the most recent element on the
subject sequence, that is, Second Event in this case:

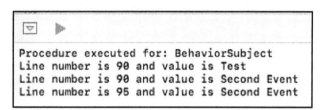

Finally, don't forget to add these subscriptions to the dispose bag so that they are properly
disposed off. The final code after adding the subscriptions to the dispose bag will look like
this:

```
executeProcedure(for: "BehaviorSubject"){
    let disposeBag = DisposeBag()
    let behSubject = BehaviorSubject(value: "Test")
    let initialSubscripton = behSubject.subscribe(onNext: {
        print("Line number is \(#line) and value is" , $0)
    })
    behSubject.onNext("Second Event")
    let subsequentSubscription = behSubject.subscribe(onNext: {
        print("Line number is \(#line) and value is" , $0)
    })
    initialSubscripton.disposed(by: disposeBag)
    subsequentSubscription.disposed(by: disposeBag)
}
```

ReplaySubject in action

`ReplaySubject` will maintain and replay a buffer of the size you specify of the latest next events in the order they were emitted. To create a `ReplaySubject`, you need to explicitly declare a type because the initializer does not take an initial value, so it can't infer the type and use the `create(bufferSize:)` static convenience method to pass the number of elements you want replayed to new subscribers for the `bufferSize` parameter. Similar to the last section, we will start this section with a basic code setup and build on top of the previous example by just commenting out the sample code for `BehaviorSubject`:

```
executeProcedure(for: "ReplaySubject"){
    let disposeBag = DisposeBag()
}
```

Then, to this basic implementation we will add the instance of `ReplaySubject`, as follows:

```
let repSubject = ReplaySubject<String>.create(bufferSize: 3)
```

This subject will replay the last three elements. Next, we will add three elements onto the subject:

```
repSubject.onNext("First")
repSubject.onNext("Second")
repSubject.onNext("Third")
```

Then, we will create the `onNext` subscription, printing out each element as it is emitted:

```
repSubject.subscribe(onNext: {
        print($0)
    })
        .disposed(by: disposeBag)
```

On monitoring the output in console, we will see that all three elements are printed:

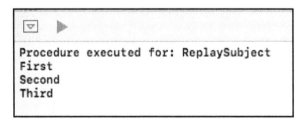

Now we will add another element to the subject before the subscription:

```
repSubject.onNext("First")
    repSubject.onNext("Second")
    repSubject.onNext("Third")
    repSubject.onNext("Fourth")
    repSubject.subscribe(onNext: {
        print($0)
    })
        .disposed(by: disposeBag)
```

Check the output; you will see that still only the last three next elements are replayed and hence printed:

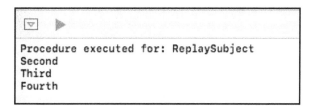

```
Procedure executed for: ReplaySubject
Second
Third
Fourth
```

Now add another value, this time after the subscription; that element is emitted and printed by itself after the buffer that was printed upon subscription:

```
repSubject.subscribe(onNext: {
        print($0)
    })
        .disposed(by: disposeBag)
    repSubject.onNext("Fifth")
```

It will give the following output:

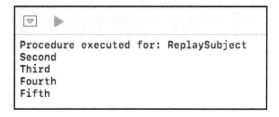

```
Procedure executed for: ReplaySubject
Second
Third
Fourth
Fifth
```

A `ReplaySubject` will emit each element as it's added on to the `sequence` after subscription. It only replays its whole buffer to its new subscribers.

Let's create a new subscription, once again differentiating it by prefixing New Subscription in the print statement:

```
repSubject.subscribe(onNext: {
    print("New Subscription: ", $0)
})
    .disposed(by: disposeBag)
```

The new subscription only gets the last three buffered elements that are replayed, which you can see in the output:

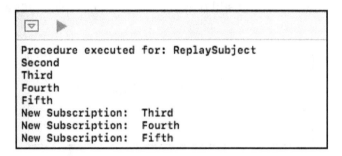

```
Procedure executed for: ReplaySubject
Second
Third
Fourth
Fifth
New Subscription:   Third
New Subscription:   Fourth
New Subscription:   Fifth
```

Consolidated code for the ReplaySubject in this example will be as follows:

```
executeProcedure(for: "ReplaySubject"){
    let disposeBag = DisposeBag()
    let repSubject = ReplaySubject<String>.create(bufferSize: 3)
    repSubject.onNext("First")
    repSubject.onNext("Second")
    repSubject.onNext("Third")
    repSubject.onNext("Fourth")
    repSubject.subscribe(onNext: {
        print($0)
    })
        .disposed(by: disposeBag)
    repSubject.onNext("Fifth")
    repSubject.subscribe(onNext: {
        print("New Subscription: ", $0)
    })
        .disposed(by: disposeBag)
}
```

Variable in action

The last of the subject types, and by no means the least, is `variable`. Remember that it's a wrapper around the `BehaviorSubject` that won't `error` out; it automatically completes and uses the dot " . " syntax to get and set its values. Similar to the last section, we will start this section with a basic code setup and build on top of the previous example by just commenting out the sample code for `ReplaySubject`:

```
executeProcedure(for: "Variable") {
let disposeBag = DisposeBag()
}
```

We will create a variable by passing an initial value to its initializer. The `type` is inferred by the value passed, a `variable` of the `Int` type in this case:

```
let variable = Variable(1)
```

We will create a subscription to this variable and print out the emitted event:

```
variable.asObservable()
        .subscribe{
            print($0)
        }
        .disposed(by: disposeBag)
```

Don't forget to press *control* + *I* in order to correct the indentation. As `variable` is a wrapper around `BehaviorSubject`; it will automatically replay the latest or initial value to new subscribers, and `variable` will automatically emit a completed event before it's deallocated. We can see this by checking the output in the console:

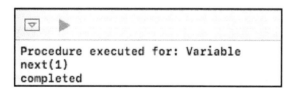

```
Procedure executed for: Variable
next(1)
completed
```

Some of you may be wondering why we called `asObservable()` on variable before subscribing to it. This is a good question! Let's *command* + click on `variable` to check its source. We will see that a `Variable` has a `_subject` private property that holds its `BehaviorSubject` value:

```
public final class Variable<Element> {
    public typealias E = Element
    private let _subject: BehaviorSubject<Element>
```

```
        private var _lock = SpinLock()
... so on
```

That is exposed via the `asObservable()` method:

```
/// - returns: Canonical interface for push style sequence
    public func asObservable() -> Observable<E> {
        return _subject
    }
```

Unlike other subjects, you can access the latest value of a `Variable` using the dot `"."` syntax:

```
executeProcedure(for: "Variable") {
    let disposeBag = DisposeBag()

    let variable = Variable(1)
    variable.asObservable()
        .subscribe{
            print($0)
        }
        .disposed(by: disposeBag)
    variable.value



                    1


}
```

Now we will add a new value onto variable:

```
variable.value = 2
```

We can see the added event in the console:

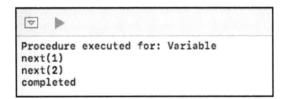

```
Procedure executed for: Variable
next(1)
next(2)
completed
```

Be cautious while trying to do that; while this appears to just mutate the property named value, appearances are deceptive. *command* + click on the `value` property, and you will see that in the `setter` for value, the `newValue` is set on the `_value` private property:

```
/// Gets or sets current value of variable.
    ///
```

```
    /// Whenever a new value is set, all the observers are notified of the
change.
    ///
    /// Even if the newly set value is same as the old value, observers are
still notified for change.
    public var value: E {
        get {
            _lock.lock(); defer { _lock.unlock() }
            return _value
        }
        set(newValue) {
            #if DEBUG
_synchronizationTracker.register(synchronizationErrorMessage: .variable)
            defer { _synchronizationTracker.unregister() }
            #endif
            _lock.lock()
            _value = newValue
            _lock.unlock()
            _subject.on(.next(newValue))
        }
    }
}
```

The getter simply returns the _value, as you can see in the preceding code block. The setter also adds the newValue onto the private BehaviorSubject property, and doing that is what causes the subscribers to receive a next event with that element.

Now that we have gone over how to create and subscribe to observable sequences and subjects, we can get into how to use Rx operators to work with those Observable sequences. However, first we want to uncover a new addition to the RxSwift library called traits.

Understanding traits and its types

As mentioned earlier, traits are a new addition to the RxSwift library and their use is optional. Since we are just getting started with RxSwift, we might just want to skip this concept, but it makes more sense to at least glance the topic so that it becomes easier to dig deep into details as and when required.

What are traits?

Traits are intended to help provide clarity of intention. We write code once, but this code might potentially be read many times by us during the course of development and others while trying to maintain it. So we should make as much effort as possible to reduce the cognitive load in understanding what a block of code does, or help make the overall code base that much easier to maintain, adapt, and extend. This is why we should use traits in our code. Fundamentally, traits are just structures that wrap Observable sequences. To access a trait's Observable sequence, we need to call `asObservable()` on it. It might seem very similar to the usage of the `Variable` type that we discussed in the last section.

Different types of trait

There are three types of trait in `RxSwift` and they are as listed:

- Single trait
- Completable trait
- Maybe trait

We will discuss each one of these in detail now, starting with Single traits.

The single trait

A single trait will only emit either a single next event containing an element, or it will emit an error event containing an error. It will not replay its single emitted error or next event to new subscribers. We can convert a raw Observable sequence to single by calling `asSingle()` on it. There are a number of places where you might use a single, such as retrieving data from local disk or from a networking operation. They will either deliver the data that is expected or fail with an error.

The completable trait

A completable trait will either only emit a completed event, or it will emit an error event containing an error. It cannot emit next events. It also does not replay its completed or error events. We can convert a raw Observable sequence to Completable by calling `asCompletable()` on it. We will use a Completable when we only care if some operation has completed, such as a file read or some other complex operation that can fail.

The maybe trait

Maybe is a mix of single and completable. It can emit a single next event, a completed event, or an error event. In other words, it can either emit an element or error and be done or emit a completed event without emitting anything else. Like single and completable, it does not replay, and we can convert a raw Observable sequence to a maybe by calling `asMaybe()` on it. A maybe can be used just like a single in places where it might be possible that it won't emit an element or an error and could just complete.

Summary

This chapter gave us a perspective on how you can change your programming approach from traditional to reactive. Reactive or traditional: this chapter explored some options and solutions that can be addressed in a Reactive way. We learned how to work with Observables and subjects; how to create and react to Observable sequences to give a perspective on how we can convert our regular data types like arrays to sequences and control execution based on the subscription.

This chapter laid down foundation, and the next two chapters will completely transform the way you think about your logic. We will learn how to operate on the events that we learned to create in this chapter. More goodies to collect, stay tuned :)

5
Filter, Transform, and Simplify

When an Observable sequence emits a next event, you will typically want to work with that element, such as transforming it in some way or the other. For example, consider that the element is a date instance, and you want to format it as a String representation before displaying it in a UILabel. In this chapter, we will start with operators that will enable you to perform tasks similar to the one mentioned in the example that we covered in the previous chapter. In this chapter, you will learn the following:

- Working with transform operators
- Working with marble diagrams to see the operator in action
- Knowing how to filter events using the Filter operator
- Simplifying the traditional coding practices by making use of reactive paradigms

Working with events using operators

RxSwift offers a range of operators that provide immense control over how you want to work with the data and events in your application. In subsequent sections, we will cover different operators in theory and then write some code to exercise the knowledge. In the coming chapters, we will learn how to combine these operators to maximize their use to our benefit.

One of the most important categories of operators is transforming operators and in the next section we will learn how to work with this category of operators.

Environment setup

Before we go ahead and start working with code, we need to set up the project for this chapter. This process is similar to the one we followed in earlier chapters with a small difference—follow the steps in order to get started:

1. Create a single view application project and name it RxOperators.
2. Open `Terminal.app` and navigate to the project folder. Create a `podfile` inside your Xcode projects folder by executing the `pod init` command.
3. Open the created `podfile` and paste the code of the `podfile`:

   ```
   # Uncomment the next line to define a global platform for your
   project
    target 'RxOperators' do
    # Comment the next line if you're not using Swift and don't want
   to use dynamic frameworks
    use_frameworks!
    pod 'RxSwift'
    # Pods for RxOperators                                         end
   ```

4. Enter the `pod install` command to fetch all the listed libraries from GitHub and install all of them in the project.
5. As a result of the installation, you will find a newly created workspace by the name `.xcworkspace`. Launch this file, and you are ready to work with the reactive components that will be introduced in this chapter.

We will work with a playground in this chapter and, as soon as we have the `.xcworkspace` ready, we will create a new playground file in the project and name it RxOperators.

Next, we will import `RxSwift` in this newly created `RxOperators` playground file and build the project to get rid of any possible errors. After the setup is complete, the project will look something like this:

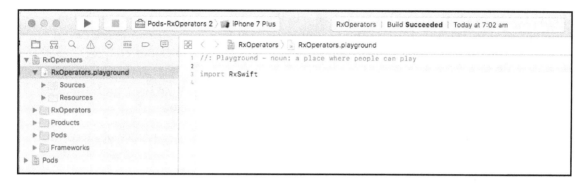

 Sometimes Xcode stops responding as soon as you open the
`.xcworkspace` file or might give unexpected error messages. The easiest
fix for this problem is to close all the instances of Xcode and then start
fresh. That works like magic sometimes!

Transforming operators

Transforming operators are used when you want to model the data coming from a sequence
to suit your requirements; in other words, prepare the data to match the requirements of a
subscriber. For example, to transform elements emitted from an Observable sequence, you
use the `map` operator; `map` will transform each element as it is emitted from the source
Observable sequence. This is similar to the `map (_:)` method in the standard Swift library,
except that this map works with Observable sequence elements. A marble diagram
representation of the `map` operator will look like this:

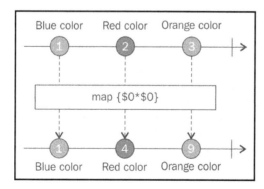

We will go through an example of using `map` in the `playground` that we set up in the previous section. We will need our helper function, that is, `executeProcedure(with description:String, procedure: () -> Void)` from the previous chapter. Remember that the function takes two params: a string `description` and a `procedure closure`. It then prints the description, followed by the execution of the procedure. We will move this to another file as earlier, and we are then good to go.

Coming back to the playground file, we will create an Observable sequence of integers using the `of` operator:

```
executeProcedure(for: "map") {
    Observable.of(10, 20, 30)
}
```

Then, we will use map operator to multiply each integer element by itself:

```
Observable.of(10, 20, 30)
        .map{ $0 * $0 }
```

Then, we will subscribe `onNext` to print each transformed element:

```
Observable.of(10, 20, 30)
        .map{ $0 * $0 }
        .subscribe(onNext:{
            print($0)
        })
```

After that, we call `dispose()` on the return value from `subscribe(onNext:)`. Remember that subscriptions return a `Disposable`. The overall code for the function becomes this:

```
executeProcedure(for: "map") {
    Observable.of(10, 20, 30)
        .map{ $0 * $0 }
        .subscribe(onNext:{
            print($0)
        })
        .dispose()
}
```

This prints the expected result, which you can check in the console:

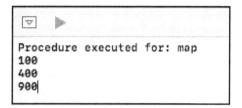

An Observable sequence can itself have Observable properties that you want to subscribe to; `flatMap` can be used to reach into an Observable sequence to work with its Observable sequences. In the following example, 01, 02, 03 are Observable sequences; `flatMap` will flatten emissions from each of those sequences into a single sequence, applying a transform to each element:

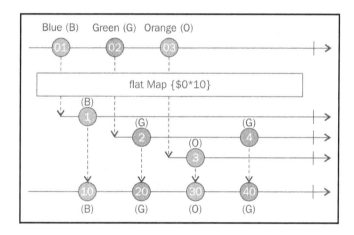

There is also a `flatMapLatest` operator. This is the one that you want to know about since you will use this operator a lot. The difference between `flatMap` and `flatMapLatest` is that `flatMapLatest` will only produce elements from the most recent Observable sequence, so as the Observable sequence emits new Observable sequence, `flatMapLatest` switches to that new Observable sequence and ignores emissions from the previous sequence.

In the example shown in the following diagram, when the **02** sequence emits the `element` `"2"`, **01** will now be ignored because **02** is the latest sequence. As a result, when **01** emits `element` `"3"`, it is ignored. Similarly, when **03** starts emitting, starting with `element` `"4"`, it becomes the active sequence and **02** is ignored. So, when **02** emits `element` `"5"`, it is ignored:

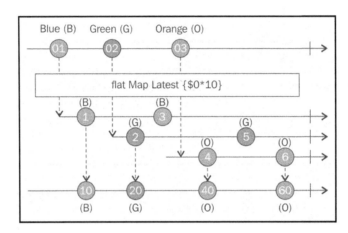

`flatMapLatest` is quite commonly used with asynchronous operations such as networking. We will work with `flatMapLatest` and networking when we work with networking code in subsequent sections.

flatMap and flatMapLatest in action

In the previous section, we read about three transforming operators and saw the `map` operator in action. In this subsection, we will work with `flatMap` and `flatMapLatest` and see how we can implement these operators in a code base. Let's start with `flatMap`.

Switch over to the playground and comment out the code that we wrote so far in order to segregate the outputs of these operators from `map` which was implemented earlier.

First, we will declare a `GamePlayer` struct with a `playerScore` property that is a `Variable` event of the `Int` type. We will also declare a `disposeBag`, as follows:

```
executeProcedure(for: "flatMap and flatMapLatest") {
    struct GamePlayer {
        let playerScore: Variable<Int>
    }
    let disposeBag = DisposeBag()
}
```

Next, let's declare a couple of `GamePlayer` instances, `alex` and `gemma`, and a current player that is also a `Variable`, with an initial value of `alex`:

```
let alex = GamePlayer(playerScore: Variable(70))
let gemma = GamePlayer(playerScore: Variable(85))
var currentPlayer = Variable(alex)
```

We should point out that `currentPlayer` is of the `Variable<Player>` type; you can see this by *Option* + clicking on the `currentPlayer` instance, as follows:

```
25
26       var currentPlayer = Variable(alex)

    Declaration  var currentPlayer: Variable<GamePlayer>

    Declared In  RxOperators.playground
```

The `dataType` of the `currentplayer` variable can be inferred from its initial value. So, `currentPlayer` is an Observable of a `GamePlayer`, which has a `playerScore` Observable property. We want to subscribe to the `playerScore` of the `currentplayer`. Remember that we will need to first call `asObservable()` to work with the observable `subject` value of `Variable`, because a `Variable` is a wrapper around `BehaviorSubject`. A moment ago, we mentioned that a `flatMap` and `flatMapLatest` allow us to reach into an `Observable` to access its observable properties. Let's see this in action; we will use `flatMap` first. We will reach into the element, a `GamePlayer` instance, access its `playerScore` Variable, and get its Observable `subject` value:

```
currentPlayer.asObservable()
        .flatMap{ $0.playerScore.asObservable() }
```

Now, subscribe to that observable and print it out:

```
currentPlayer.asObservable()
        .flatMap{ $0.playerScore.asObservable() }
        .subscribe(onNext:{
            print($0)
        })
```

At the end, add the subscription to the `disposeBag`:

```
currentPlayer.asObservable()
        .flatMap{ $0.playerScore.asObservable() }
        .subscribe(onNext:{
            print($0)
```

```
})
.disposed(by: disposeBag)
```

As `Variable` wraps a `BehaviorSubject` that replays its most recent or initial element to new subscribers, that value is printed out:

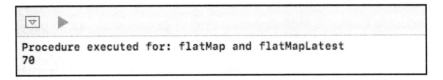

We will update the value of the `playerScore` of `currentplayer`:

```
currentPlayer.value.playerScore.value = 90
```

Then, that value is printed out:

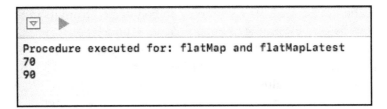

It is important to realize that what we are specifically subscribed to the score of `alex` because the value of `currentPlayer` is currently `alex`. So we can also just add a new value to `alex.playerScore`:

```
alex.playerScore.value = 95
```

Our subscription will print out that value, as follows:

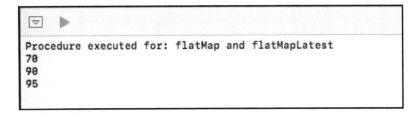

Let's add `gemma` to our `currentPlayer` instance and monitor the changes:

```
currentPlayer.value = gemma
```

You will note that the subscription will now print the values accordingly; that is, gemma's score will be printed:

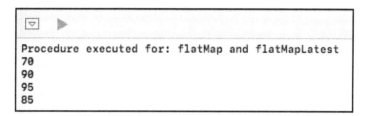

Can you guess what happened to our subscription to alex's `playerScore`? Let's find out; we will add a new value to `alex.playerScore.value` directly:

```
alex.playerScore.value = 96
```

Then, you will note that it is also printed in the console:

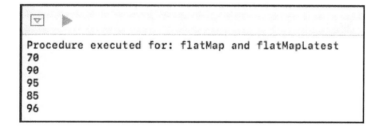

This is because `flatMap` does not unsubscribe from the previous sequence. So be watchful while using `flatMap`. If you use `flatMap`, you could be keeping a bunch of subscriptions around that you don't need anymore, and those `nextEvent` handlers will do things that you don't mean to do or you no longer want to do.

On the other hand, `flatMapLatest` will unsubscribe from the previous sequence, subscribe to the new one, and only produce values from the most recent sequence. Let's take a look at the code that we have written for `flapMap` till now:

```
executeProcedure(for: "flatMap and flatMapLatest") {
    struct GamePlayer {
        let playerScore: Variable<Int>
    }
    let disposeBag = DisposeBag()
    let alex = GamePlayer(playerScore: Variable(70))
    let gemma = GamePlayer(playerScore: Variable(85))
    var currentPlayer = Variable(alex)
    currentPlayer.asObservable()
        .flatMap{ $0.playerScore.asObservable() }
        .subscribe(onNext:{
            print($0)
        })
        .disposed(by: disposeBag)
    currentPlayer.value.playerScore.value = 90
    alex.playerScore.value = 95
    currentPlayer.value = gemma
    alex.playerScore.value = 96
}
```

The output of the code is this:

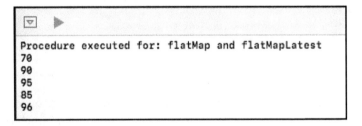

Now, let's change `flatMap` to `flatMapLatest` in the preceding code:

```
executeProcedure(for: "flatMap and flatMapLatest") {

    struct GamePlayer {
        let playerScore: Variable<Int>
    }
    let disposeBag = DisposeBag()
    let alex = GamePlayer(playerScore: Variable(70))
    let gemma = GamePlayer(playerScore: Variable(85))
    var currentPlayer = Variable(alex)
    currentPlayer.asObservable()
```

```
        .flatMapLatest{ $0.playerScore.asObservable() }
        .subscribe(onNext:{
            print($0)
        })
        .disposed(by: disposeBag)
    currentPlayer.value.playerScore.value = 90
    alex.playerScore.value = 95
    currentPlayer.value = gemma
    alex.playerScore.value = 96
}
```

Note that we no longer receive new events on `alex`. So the `96` we added to `alex.playerScore.value` is not printed:

```
 ▽   ▶

Procedure executed for: flatMap and flatMapLatest
70
90
95
85
```

There are a few more transforming operators in `RxSwift`, and we will cover them in the coming sections.

Scan, reduce, and buffer

Some operators that we come across in `RxSwift` are similar to the ones we use in Swift standard libraries. We will cover some of these operators in the following sections. If you follow closely, you will find that scan, reduce, and buffer exhibit some qualities of standard Swift functions. Which ones? Well, read on to find out more.

Scan

Sometimes you want to pick up each value from an array, apply a specified operation on each element, and return a new array with new elements generated after the application of a specified operation. RxSwift offers the scan operator, which enables you to perform such actions. If you are familiar with the reduce (_:_:) Swift standard library method, you will find scan to be similar; scan starts with an initial seed value and is used to aggregate values just like reduce (_:_:), but there is a small difference—unlike reduce (_:_:), which only returns the final value, scan will return an Observable for each intermediate result along the way:

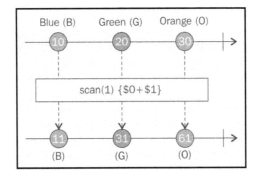

There is also a reduce operator in RxSwift that works just like the standard library reduce (_:_:) and returns an Observable sequence of the final aggregated value. This can be useful for working with finite Observable sequences:

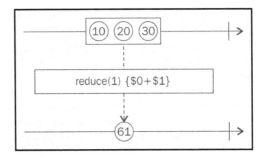

You might find scan useful in case you are developing systems similar to a scoring system for games such as darts. Let's implement the code using the scan operator to understand the concept better.

Open the playground for this chapter, and in order to keep the output console clean so that you don't see outputs from previous implementations, comment out code that corresponds to the previous sections.

Start by creating a `disposeBag` and a `gameScore` as `PublishSubject`:

```
executeProcedure(for: "scan and buffer") {
    let disposeBag = DisposeBag()
    let gameScore = PublishSubject<Int>()
}
```

Now, let's use the `scan` operator and pass an initial seed value of `501`. Instead of passing a trailing closure for the `accumulator` parameter, we pass an operator directly as the parameter. We can do this because the operator matches the function type. In darts, each player starts with the `501` score, and the score for each dart is deducted from the total score. The first to zero wins the leg:

```
gameScore.scan(501, accumulator: -)
```

We will chain a map onto the result from `scan` to return the max of zero or the total:

```
gameScore.scan(501, accumulator: -)
        .map { max($0, 0) }
```

Then, we will subscribe to the next event and print out the new total:

```
gameScore.scan(501, accumulator: -)
        .map { max($0, 0) }
        .subscribe(onNext:{
            print($0)
        })
```

Next, we will dispose the subscription by adding it to the `disposeBag`:

```
gameScore.scan(501, accumulator: -)
        .map { max($0, 0) }
        .subscribe(onNext:{
            print($0)
        })
        .disposed(by: disposeBag)
```

Let's say that the player throws three darts in the first turn, and they score 60, which is the highest achievable score, a 13, and a bullseye for another 50 points:

```
gameScore.scan(501, accumulator: -)
        .map { max($0, 0) }
        .subscribe(onNext:{
```

```
        print ($0)
    })
    .disposed (by: disposeBag)
gameScore.onNext (60)
gameScore.onNext (13)
gameScore.onNext (50)
```

You will see the score reduced by each dart score and printed in the console:

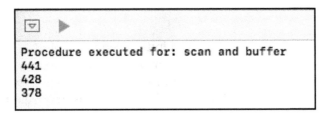

```
Procedure executed for: scan and buffer
441
428
378
```

Let's say that we wanted to print each dart score and the result in the total score for each turn. To achieve this, we can use the `buffer` operator to group emissions.

Buffer

`Buffer` will hold on to events emitted by the source observable sequence until the specified time span in seconds has passed or the count of buffered items has been reached, whichever happens first. Then, it will emit an observable array of the buffered events. Passing zero for the `timeSpan` argument and specifying the time span and passing zero for count; ignores count, that is, we are trying to do this:

```
buffer(timeSpan: 0.0, count: 0, scheduler: scheduler)
```

In this case, count will be ignored. We will cover schedulers later in detail:

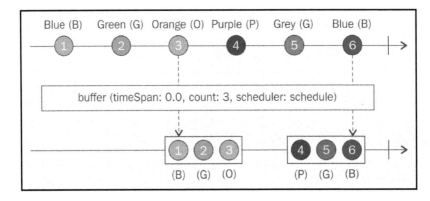

We will insert a `buffer` before `scan`. In this example, we are not concerned with time elapsing, so we will just pass zero for the `timeSpan`, and we will pass 3 for `count`. As a result, this will buffer three emissions from `gameScore` and then emit an observable array of the three scores. We have entered `MainScheduler.instance` for the scheduler, which will cause this buffer to be executed on the main thread. As we mentioned, we will discuss schedulers in detail later in the book:

```
gameScore
        .buffer(timeSpan: 0.0, count: 3,
                            scheduler:MainScheduler.instance)
        .scan(501, accumulator: -)
        .map { max($0, 0) }
        .subscribe(onNext:{
            print($0)
    })
        .disposed(by: disposeBag)
```

Next, we will use map to print the array, and we are using an empty `terminator` string because we will append this printout in the overall result and then return the result of using `reduce` to sum its values, which will be passed to `scan`:

```
gameScore
        .buffer(timeSpan: 0.0, count: 3, scheduler:
                                MainScheduler.instance)
        .map {
            print($0, "--> ", terminator: "")
            return $0.reduce(0, +)
    }
        .scan(501, accumulator: -)
        .map { max($0, 0) }
        .subscribe(onNext:{
            print($0)
    })
        .disposed(by: disposeBag)
```

Now, for each next event, the array of three dart scores and the total score will be printed; check this in the console output:

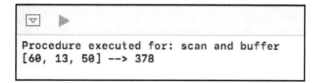

For pro dart players, this is a highly mellowed down version of the darts scoring system, a very simplified version.

The overall code provides a good example of how we can chain operators in RxSwift, where each operator is playing its part and passing on the result to the next operator:

```
executeProcedure(for: "scan and buffer") {
    let disposeBag = DisposeBag()
    let gameScore = PublishSubject<Int>()
    gameScore
        .buffer(timeSpan: 0.0, count: 3, scheduler:
                                        MainScheduler.instance)
        .map {
            print($0, "--> ", terminator: "")
            return $0.reduce(0, +)
        }
        .scan(501, accumulator: -)
        .map { max($0, 0) }
        .subscribe(onNext:{
            print($0)
        })
        .disposed(by: disposeBag)
    gameScore.onNext(60)
    gameScore.onNext(13)
    gameScore.onNext(50)
}
```

The print statement in the first map is this:

```
print($0, "--> ", terminator: "")
```

It is really a side effect; we will cover performing side effects in the next chapter. There are additional transforming operators available, which you can check out in the RxSwift repo. However, trying to memorize all the operators at once might be really overwhelming. We worked with some of the most useful operators and when you need something beyond their capabilities, then you might want to go ahead and explore these additional operators in the repo.

In addition to transforming Observable sequences, you will frequently want to filter sequences and only react to next events based on certain criteria. In the next section, we will learn about filtering operations and work with some code examples to apply the concepts.

Filtering operators

Filtering operators can be divided into separate categories depending on the type of filtering they provide. For instance, operators that ignore certain events, operators that skip events based on certain criteria, or the opposite of skipping, operators that allow you to take elements. Then come operators that allow us to work with distinct elements. In this section, we will cover some operators from these categories; we will cover those operators you will work with most often while working with RxSwift. In order to explore other filtering operators, feel free to check the RxSwift library. Let's start with our very first filtering operator, which is the filter operator.

The filter operator

The filter operator applies a predicate to each emitted element and only allows them through if they pass:

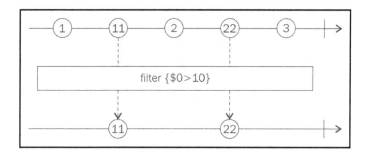

Let's say that we have a sequence of integers and we want to only work with prime integers, that is, the integer should be greater than one and only divisible by itself and **1**.

Let's add a helper extension to our Helper file in the playground. This will be an extension on the Int type to determine whether an integer is a prime number:

```
// Extension on Int to check if a number is prime or not
public extension Int {
    func isPrime() -> Bool {
        guard self > 1 else { return false }
        var isPrimeFlag = true
        for index in 2..<self {
            if self % index == 0 {
                isPrimeFlag = false
            }
        }
    }
```

```
            return isPrimeFlag
    }
}
```

The extension has an `isPrime()` function, which checks whether a given integer is a prime number or not.

First, it guards whether the element is greater than or else it returns false. Then, it iterates over a range from 2 to that number, setting `isPrimeFlag` to false if the number is an exact multiple of the divisor.

Switch back to the playground page and create a bare-bones method implementation where we want to work with the `operator` filter, as follows:

```
executeProcedure(for: "filter") {
    let disposeBag = DisposeBag()
}
```

We have declared a `disposeBag` and commented out the rest of the implementations so that the results in the console do not interfere with the results of the previous operator implementations.

Let's look at the overall structure of the commented section with this fresh implementation so that you have an idea about how to segregate the concerns:

```
//: Playground - noun: a place where people can play
import RxSwift
/*
executeProcedure(for: "map") {
    Observable.of(10, 20, 30)
        .map{ $0 * $0 }
        .subscribe(onNext:{
            print($0)
        })
        .dispose()
}
executeProcedure(for: "flatMap and flatMapLatest") {
    struct GamePlayer {
        let playerScore: Variable<Int>
    }
    let disposeBag = DisposeBag()
    //Rest of the implementation for flatMap and flatMapLatest..
....... continued


}
```

```
executeProcedure(for: "scan and buffer") {
    let disposeBag = DisposeBag()
    let gameScore = PublishSubject<Int>()
    gameScore
        .buffer(timeSpan: 0.0, count: 3, scheduler: MainScheduler.instance)
        .map {
            print($0, "--> ", terminator: "")
            return $0.reduce(0, +)
//Rest of the implementation for scan and buffer..
....... continued



}
*/
// fresh implementation from here
executeProcedure(for: "filter") {
    let disposeBag = DisposeBag()
}
```

As a result, you can see the following output in the console so far:

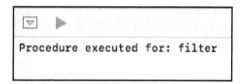

The importance of structuring code this way is that it enables us to keep all the implementations performed so far in one place, which makes it easier for you to refer to any example anytime you want, and commenting out the previous implementations allow us to focus on the output of current implementation only.

Coming back to the current implementation for the `filter` operator, first we will use the `generate` operator to create an Observable sequence of integers from 1 to 100. Generate takes `initialState`, a condition that will terminate the generation when it returns false, and a function that produces each `iterate` value:

```
Observable.generate(initialState: <Element>,
                    condition: <(Element) throws ->Bool>,
                    iterate: <(Element) throws -> Element>)
```

We will set the initial state to 1, set a condition that the value is less than 101, and increment the value by 1 in each iteration:

```
let integers = Observable.generate(initialState: 1,
                                    condition: { $0 < 101 },
                                    iterate: { $0 + 1 })
```

Let's print this out in a subscription to confirm that we do have a sequence from 1 to 100:

```
let integers = Observable.generate(initialState: 1,
                                    condition: { $0 < 101 },
                                    iterate: { $0 + 1 })
    integers.subscribe(onNext: {
        print( $0, terminator: " " )
    })
```

Check the output console to confirm that all the values are printed from 1 to 100; we used terminated as " ", because we did not want all the elements to be printed on a new line:

```
Procedure executed for: filter
1 2 3 4 5 6 7 8 9 10 11 12 13 14 15 16 17 18 19 20 21 22 23 24 25 26 27 28 29 30 31 32 33 34 35 36 37 38 39 40 41 42
43 44 45 46 47 48 49 50 51 52 53 54 55 56 57 58 59 60 61 62 63 64 65 66 67 68 69 70 71 72 73 74 75 76 77 78 79 80 81
82 83 84 85 86 87 88 89 90 91 92 93 94 95 96 97 98 99 100
```

Did we forget something? From our understanding so far, we know that all the subscriptions should be disposed. Hence, add the subscription to `dispose()`:

```
    integers.subscribe(onNext: {
        print( $0, terminator: " " )
    })
    .disposed(by: disposeBag)
```

 Don't forget to dispose the subscriptions; good developers make use of the memory judicially.

This print statement was required to ensure that the sequence is created successfully, so we can comment it out now.

We will use the filter operator with this Observable sequence. Filter takes a closure that will be applied to test each element, and it returns a bool, so we can use it to check whether each integer is prime:

```
integers
        .filter { $0.isPrime() }
```

Then, we will use the `toArray` operator to convert the sequence to a single Observable array:

```
integers
        .filter { $0.isPrime() }
        .toArray()
```

Subscribe to the array and print out each next event's element:

```
integers
        .filter { $0.isPrime() }
        .toArray()
        .subscribe({
            print( $0 )
        })
```

Check the output and see whether you have achieved the desired output:

```
Procedure executed for: filter
next([2, 3, 5, 7, 11, 13, 17, 19, 23, 29, 31, 37, 41, 43, 47, 53, 59, 61, 67, 71, 73, 79, 83, 89, 97])
completed
```

Finally, don't forget to dispose the subscription. The overall implementation for the filter operator will be as follows:

```
// Implementation for filter operator
executeProcedure(for: "filter") {
    let disposeBag = DisposeBag()
    let integers = Observable.generate(initialState: 1,
                                condition: { $0 < 101 },
                                iterate: { $0 + 1 }
    )
    integers
        .filter { $0.isPrime() }
        .toArray()
        .subscribe({
            print( $0 )
        })
```

```
        .disposed(by: disposeBag)
    }
```

The next filtering operator that we will discuss helps us work with distinct elements.

The distinctUntilChanged operator

The distinctUntilChanged() operator is also widely used. This operator will only allow unique contiguous elements to pass through; in other words, if the next element is equal to the previous one, it will not be allowed through:

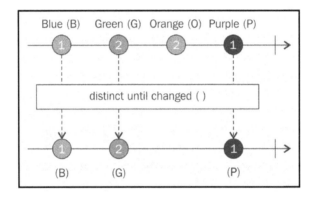

This can be used with search logic to prevent executing a search twice in a row on the same search string or even on an insert statement where you want to add the login status to the local storage, and you don't want to save the same state more than once if it is the same.

Let's see the operator in action; we need to create a similar bare-bones function implementation with a disposeBag instance after commenting out all the previous implementations:

```
// Implementation for distinctUntilChanged operator
executeProcedure(for: "distinctUntilChanged") {
    let disposeBag = DisposeBag()
}
```

Now we will create a stringToSearch as Variable. This will be treated as the Observable sequence for the subscription:

```
let stringToSearch = Variable("")
```

The first thing we will do right after the `Variable` declaration is to convert the `stringToSearch` to lowercase using the `map` operator:

```
let stringToSearch = Variable("")
    stringToSearch.asObservable()
        .map({
            $0.lowercased()
        })
```

Next, we will use `distinctUntilChanged` to prevent identical contiguous elements from passing through, and then we will subscribe and print out events as they are emitted:

```
stringToSearch.asObservable()
        .map({
            $0.lowercased()
        })
        .distinctUntilChanged()
            .subscribe({
                print($0)
            })
```

Don't forget to add the subscription to `disposeBag`:

```
stringToSearch.asObservable()
        .map({
            $0.lowercased()
        })
        .distinctUntilChanged()
            .subscribe({
                print($0)
            })
        .disposed(by: disposeBag)
```

At this point, only the empty string element we initialized as a `Variable` is printed, and you can check this in the console:

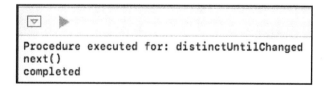

```
Procedure executed for: distinctUntilChanged
next()
completed
```

Now we will add a couple of values that are equal, except for letter casing, to the `stringToSearch`:

```
stringToSearch.asObservable()
        .map({
            $0.lowercased()
        })
        .distinctUntilChanged()
            .subscribe({
                print($0)
            })
        .disposed(by: disposeBag)
        stringToSearch.value = "TINTIN"
        stringToSearch.value = "tintin"
```

In the output, you will note that only the first element has passed through to the subscription and printed out:

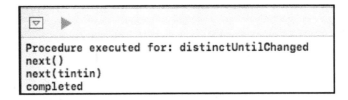

```
Procedure executed for: distinctUntilChanged
next()
next(tintin)
completed
```

We will add a different value to the `stringToSearch`:

```
stringToSearch.value = "TINTIN"
    stringToSearch.value = "tintin"
    stringToSearch.value = "noDDy"
```

Then we note the difference in the output console; the newly added element is printed out:

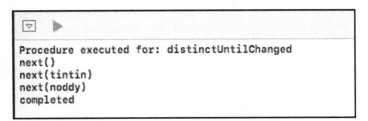

```
Procedure executed for: distinctUntilChanged
next()
next(tintin)
next(noddy)
completed
```

Then, we will add the same value as we did initially to `stringToSearch`:

```
stringToSearch.value = "TINTIN"
    stringToSearch.value = "tintin"
    stringToSearch.value = "noDDy"
    stringToSearch.value = "TINTIN"
```

Now, see what happens to the output; the element that we added finally gets printed to the console:

```
Procedure executed for: distinctUntilChanged
next()
next(tintin)
next(noddy)
next(tintin)
completed
```

Can you figure out why this was printed? The answer is in the definition of the operator we explained earlier; that is, only contiguous values are filtered out. The complete implementation of `distinctUntilChanged` is as follows:

```
// Implementation for distinctUntilChanged operator
executeProcedure(for: "distinctUntilChanged") {
    let disposeBag = DisposeBag()
    let stringToSearch = Variable("")
    stringToSearch.asObservable()
        .map({
            $0.lowercased()
        })
    .distinctUntilChanged()
        .subscribe({
            print($0)
        })
    .disposed(by: disposeBag)
    stringToSearch.value = "TINTIN"
    stringToSearch.value = "tintin"
    stringToSearch.value = "noDDy"
    stringToSearch.value = "TINTIN"
}
```

There are several more filtering operators. Let's work with one more filtering operator.

The takeWhile operator

Like `filter`, `takeWhile` also applies a predicate to elements emitted from observable sequences. However, `takeWhile` will terminate the sequence after the first time the specified condition is false, and all the remaining emitted element will be ignored. Think of `takeWhile` as a gate; once the gate is closed, nothing else gets through:

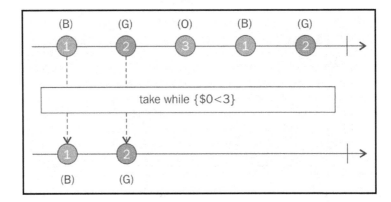

Let's make our playground ready for the implementation of `takeWhile` in a manner similar to what we did for all the other operators. Comment out all the previous implementations, create a bare-bones function implementation, and declare a `disposeBag` instance:

```
// Implementation for takeWhile operator
executeProcedure(for: "takeWhile") {
    let disposeBag = DisposeBag()
}
```

Next, we will add an observable sequence of integers:

```
executeProcedure(for: "takeWhile") {
    let disposeBag = DisposeBag()
    let integers = Observable.of(10, 20, 30, 40, 30, 20, 10)
}
```

Now we will use `takeWhile`, but note that there are several additional `take` operators:

```
116     let integers = Observable.of(10, 20, 30, 40, 30, 20, 10)
117     integers
118     .take
```

M		Observable<Int> **take**(count: Int)
M		Observable<Int> takeLast(count: Int)
M		Observable<Int> takeUntil(other: ObservableType)
M		Observable<Int> takeWhile(predicate: (Int) throws -> Bool)
M		Observable<Int> take(duration: RxTimeInterval, scheduler: SchedulerType)
M		Observable<Int> takeWhileWithIndex(predicate: (Int, Int) throws -> Bool)
M	ConnectableObservable<SubjectType.E>	multicast(makeSubject: () -> SubjectType)

We will use `takeWhile` for now, while the value is less than 40:

```
integers
    .takeWhile({
    $0 < 40
    })
```

Then, we will subscribe and print out those elements:

```
integers
        .takeWhile({
            $0 < 40
>       })
        .subscribe(onNext: {
            print( $0 )
        })
```

Note the output printed in the console:

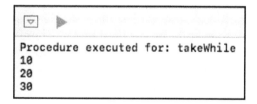

```
Procedure executed for: takeWhile
10
20
30
```

Only elements up to the failed test are tested. Don't forget to dispose the subscriptions once again. The overall completed code for this implementation is as follows:

```
// Implementation for takeWhile operator
executeProcedure(for: "takeWhile") {
    let disposeBag = DisposeBag()
    let integers = Observable.of(10, 20, 30, 40, 30, 20, 10)
    integers
        .takeWhile({
            $0 < 40
        })
        .subscribe(onNext: {
            print( $0 )          .disposed(by: disposeBag)
}
```

We discussed a few of the most most used filtering operators in this chapter that you can use with RxSwift, but there are more. You can check them out as the need arises.

Summary

In this chapter, we worked with transforming and filtering operators to model our Observable sequences. The chapter was majorly divided into two sections; in the first section, we learned how to transform the outputs from one Observable sequence to match the inputs as expected by other subscriptions, and in the second section, we learned how to select the elements from an array of elements that suit our requirements. We saw how we can chain a number of operators to perform a consolidated action and noted how this process improves the readability of code. You might have felt the difference while working with the declarative style of programming, since operators perform a major chunk of work under the hood without dishing out the implementation details. Moving on, we will get into how we can combine multiple Observables into a single Observable sequence. You will work with operator chaining to even more detailed levels. There's nothing to worry since we will follow the same stepwise approach of adding operators and explanations at each step while chaining the code so that you understand the code at each and every step. Finally, congratulations on making it so far! We are nearly halfway through. Kudos!

6
Reduce by Combining and Filtering and Common Trade Offs

Sometimes we want to work with multiple Observable sequences, reacting to new elements emitted from one or more of those sequences. There are a handful of operators that combine Observable sequences in a variety of ways. In this chapter, we will explore such operators that allow us to combine and filter Observable sequences.

In this chapter, we will cover the following topics:

- Concatenating and prefixing
- Merging
- Zipping
- Performing side effects
- Creating a demo application to cover all the topics covered so far

Combining and filtering Observable sequences

In the previous chapters, we learned how to create, transform, and filter Observable sequences. You would have found a lot of similarities between filtering of RxSwift, transforming operators, and traditional Swift's standard collection methods. You got acquainted with the true power of RxSwift while working with operators such as flatMap where you had to write very little code to get a great deal of work done.

This chapter will show you various techniques with which you can assemble and combine sequences to control data as desired. Before delving into the concepts, let's set up the project first.

Project setup

As discussed earlier, let's set up a workspace to work with RxSwift:

1. Create a single view application project and name it RxAdvancedOperators.
2. Open Terminal.app and navigate to the project folder. Create a podfile inside your Xcode projects folder by executing the pod init command. Once the command is executed, you will see a Podfile in the project folder:

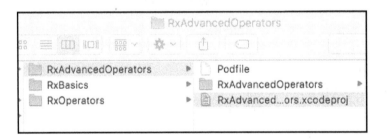

3. Open the created Podfile and paste the Podfile code:

   ```
   # Uncomment the next line to define a global platform for your
   project


   target 'RxAvancedOperators' do
   # Comment the next line if you're not using Swift and don't want to
   use dynamic frameworks
   ```

```
use_frameworks!

pod 'RxSwift'
# Pods for RxAvancedOperators

end
```

4. Enter the `pod install` command to fetch all listed libraries from GitHub and install all of them in the project. You will notice the following summary in the Terminal:

```
Sonar-MBP:RxAdvancedOperators sonar$ pod install
Analyzing dependencies
Downloading dependencies
Installing RxSwift (3.6.1)
Generating Pods project
Integrating client project

[!] Please close any current Xcode sessions and use `RxAdvancedOperators.xcworkspace` f
or this project from now on.
Sending stats
Pod installation complete! There is 1 dependency from the Podfile and 1 total pod insta
lled.

[!] Automatically assigning platform ios with version 10.3 on target RxAdvancedOperator
s because no platform was specified. Please specify a platform for this target in your
Podfile. See `https://guides.cocoapods.org/syntax/podfile.html#platform`.
Sonar-MBP:RxAdvancedOperators sonar$
```

As a result of the installation, you will find a newly created workspace by the name `.xcworkspace`:

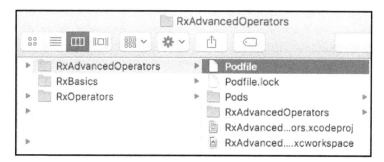

Launch this file, and you are ready to work with the reactive components that will be introduced in the chapter:

We will work with playgrounds in this chapter and, as soon as we have the `.xcworkspace` ready, we will create a new playground file in the project:

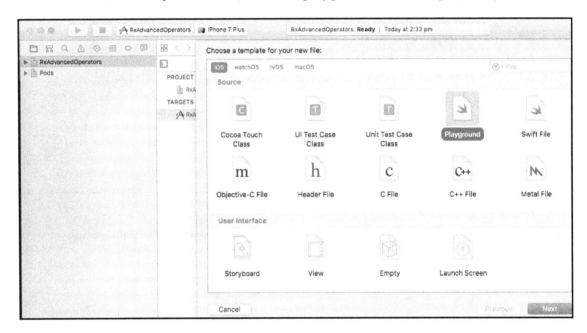

We will name it `RxAdvancedOperators`:

We will `import RxSwift` into this newly created `RxAdvancedOperators.playground` file and build the project to get rid of any possible errors:

Concatenating and prefixing

While working with Observables, one of the most obvious requirements is to provide an initial or starting value to an observer. Some examples of this use case come into use while working with locations service and network connectivity when it becomes essential to provide an initial state to the observer; startWith is one such operator that allows us to prefix an initial value.

Let's work with its implementation in detail—startWith will prepend or add an Observable sequence to the beginning of the source Observable sequence, and those elements will be emitted before beginning to emit elements from the source Observable sequence.

The following describes the functionality of startWith:

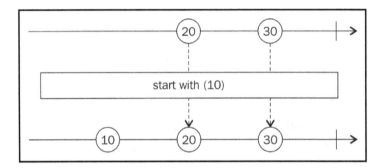

Let's work with startWith in a code example, as follows:

In the playground that was set up in the previous section, remember to add the Helper file to the sources folder in this playground with the following code, which we wrote for the previous chapter:

```
import Foundation
public func executeProcedure(for description:String, procedure: () ->
Void){
    print("Procedure executed for:", description)
    procedure()
}
```

The project structure with the code implementation will look like this:

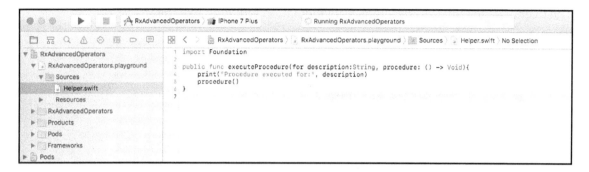

Then, we will declare a `disposeBag` inside a bare-bones implementation inside the playground file, as shown:

```
executeProcedure(for: "startWith") {
    let disposeBag = DisposeBag()
}
```

Next, we will create an Observable sequence of Strings, as illustrated:

```
executeProcedure(for: "startWith") {
    let disposeBag = DisposeBag()
    Observable.of("String 2", "String 3", "String 4")
}
```

Then, we will use `startWith` to prepend some elements:

```
Observable.of("String 2", "String 3", "String 4")
        .startWith("String 0", "String 1")
        .startWith("String -1")
        .startWith("String -2")
```

Note that we can do it multiple times and include multiple elements in a single call too. Once again, we will subscribe to next events and print them out, as depicted here:

```
Observable.of("String 2", "String 3", "String 4")
        .startWith("String 0", "String 1")
        .startWith("String -1")
        .startWith("String -2")
        .subscribe(onNext:{
            print($0)
        })
```

Also, once again, don't forget to add the subscription to the `disposeBag`.

The overall code with the complete implementation will look like this:

```
executeProcedure(for: "startWith") {
    let disposeBag = DisposeBag()
    Observable.of("String 2", "String 3", "String 4")
        .startWith("String 0", "String 1")
        .startWith("String -1")
        .startWith("String -2")
        .subscribe(onNext:{
            print($0)
        })
        .disposed(by: disposeBag)
}
```

Note that, when chaining multiple `startWith` operators, each sequence is emitted completely on a **last in first out** (**LIFO**) basis. The last `startWith` we used was to prepend **String -1** and **String -2**, so they will be the first ones to be emitted, then the **String 0** and **String 1**, and finally, **String2**, **String 3**, and **String 4**. You can check this in the output console:

```
Procedure executed for: startWith
String -2
String -1
String 0
String 1
String 2
String 3
String 4
```

Merging

In general terminology, merging can be defined as combining two or more sequences in the simplest way possible. In this section, we will go through the `merge` operator. Merge will combine emissions by multiple Observable sequences into a single new Observable sequence and emit each event in the order it is emitted by each source sequence. The following diagram of the `merge` operator will clear a few errands:

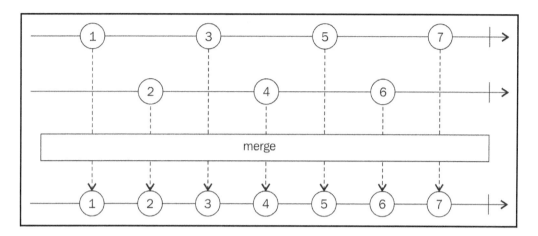

If you were developing a social media app like Twitter, you could use merge to combine all tweets from followed users into a single timeline. Let's work with the merge operator in code to understand the working in detail. We will start by commenting out the rest of the code that we wrote so far for the previous implementation and then write a bare-bones implementation or merge operator with a disposeBag, as follows:

```
import UIKit
import RxSwift
/*
executeProcedure(for: "startWith") {
    let disposeBag = DisposeBag()
    Observable.of("String 2", "String 3", "String 4")
        .startWith("String 0", "String 1")
        .startWith("String -1")
        .startWith("String -2")
        .subscribe(onNext:{
            print($0)
        })
        .disposed(by: disposeBag)
}
*/
executeProcedure(for: "merge") {
    let disposeBag = DisposeBag()
}
```

We will then create some `PublishSubjects` so that we can apply the `merge` operator on the elements that these Observables will emit:

```
executeProcedure(for: "merge") {
    let disposeBag = DisposeBag()
    let pubSubject1 = PublishSubject<String>()
    let pubSubject2 = PublishSubject<String>()
    let pubSubject3 = PublishSubject<String>()
}
```

Next, we will create new Observable sequences of those three subjects:

```
let pubSubject1 = PublishSubject<String>()
    let pubSubject2 = PublishSubject<String>()
    let pubSubject3 = PublishSubject<String>()
    Observable.of(pubSubject1, pubSubject2, pubSubject3)
```

Combine them using `merge`, as follows:

```
Observable.of(pubSubject1, pubSubject2, pubSubject3)
    .merge()
```

Then, we subscribe and print out the next elements with the following piece of code:

```
Observable.of(pubSubject1, pubSubject2, pubSubject3)
    .merge()
    .subscribe(onNext:{
        print($0)
    })
```

While implementing this, don't forget to add the subscription to the `disposeBag` that we created as the first statement of this implementation:

```
Observable.of(pubSubject1, pubSubject2, pubSubject3)
    .merge()
    .subscribe(onNext:{
        print($0)
    })
    .disposed(by: disposeBag)
```

With that done, we will now add some values to each subject:

```
Observable.of(pubSubject1, pubSubject2, pubSubject3)
    .merge()
    .subscribe(onNext:{
        print($0)
    })
    .disposed(by: disposeBag)
```

```
pubSubject1.onNext("First Element from Subject 1")
pubSubject2.onNext("First Element from Subject 2")
pubSubject3.onNext("First Element from  Subject 3")
pubSubject1.onNext("Second Element from Subject 1")
pubSubject3.onNext("Second Element from Subject 3")
pubSubject2.onNext("Second Element from Subject 2")
```

In the output console, note that these elements will be printed out in the order in which they were added to either subject:

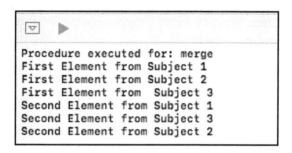

`startWith` and `merge` require that you work with Observables of the same type, that is, consider that you want to merge a `String` and an `Int`, as shown:

```
Observable.of(pubSubject1, pubSubject2, pubSubject3)
        .merge()
        .subscribe(onNext:{
            print($0)
        })
        .disposed(by: disposeBag)
    pubSubject1.onNext("First Element from Subject 1")
    pubSubject2.onNext("First Element from Subject 2")
    pubSubject3.onNext("First Element from  Subject 3")
    pubSubject1.onNext("Second Element from Subject 1")
    pubSubject3.onNext("Second Element from Subject 3")
    pubSubject2.onNext("Second Element from Subject 2")
    pubSubject3.onNext(3)
```

The compiler will throw the following error:

```
Playground execution failed: error: RxAdvancedOperators.playground:42:24: error: cannot convert value of type 'Int'
to expected argument type 'String'
    pubSubject3.onNext(3)
                       ^
```

However, what would you do if you want to combine the operators of different types? For example, a String and an Int, as we tried to do in the previous example. Curious to find the answer? Let's find out how we can do that.

Combining elements of different types

In the previous example, when we worked with the merge operator, we saw that it was easy to work with elements of the same type, but the merge operator fails when it comes to combining elements of different types. Hence, there arises a need for an operator that can combine elements of different datatypes.

Introducing zip

The zip operator lets you combine sequences of different types and apply transformations to zip them together. It will combine up to eight Observable sequences into a single sequence and will wait to emit elements from each one of the other source Observable sequences at an index until they all have emitted elements at that index. The following diagram expresses the functionality of zip briefly:

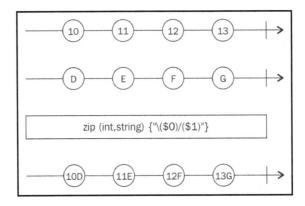

If you are developing a card game and want to wait until each player was done with the full hand before continuing, you can use zip. Why do you think we need a zip operator for a card game?

Here's the answer—as some of you might have already guessed, a card game can have numbers and strings to represent all the cards.

Now, let's see the `zip` operator in action, but before we begin writing any code for `zip`, we need to set up the playground. By setting up the playground, we mean comment out the previous implementations so far and create a bare-bones implementation for the `zip` operator with a `disposeBag`, as follows:

```
executeProcedure(for: "zip") {
    let disposeBag = DisposeBag()
}
```

Now, let's create some `PublishSubjects` of different datatypes (String and Int), as shown:

```
executeProcedure(for: "zip") {
    let disposeBag = DisposeBag()
    let intPubSubject1 = PublishSubject<Int>()
    let stringPubSubject1 = PublishSubject<String>()
    let intPubSubject2 = PublishSubject<Int>()
    let stringPubSubject2 = PublishSubject<String>()
}
```

Then, we will use the `zip` operator to combine them; `zip` is a type method on Observables that can take up to eight Observable sequences as its parameters. The closure of `zip` will receive an argument for each source Observable's element in the same order as provided, and we will embed both values in a `String`, as follows:

```
Observable.zip(intPubSubject1, stringPubSubject1,intPubSubject2,
stringPubSubject2) { intSub1, strSub1, intSub2, stringSub2 in
        "\(intSub1) : \(strSub1) AND \(intSub2) : \(stringSub2)"
    }
```

Then, we will subscribe to `nextEvents` and print out the elements, as demonstrated:

```
Observable.zip(intPubSubject1, stringPubSubject1,intPubSubject2,
stringPubSubject2) { intSub1, strSub1, intSub2, stringSub2 in
        "\(intSub1) : \(strSub1) AND \(intSub2) : \(stringSub2)"
    }
    .subscribe(onNext:{
      print($0)          })
```

Don't forget to add the subscription to the `disposeBag`:

```
Observable.zip(intPubSubject1, stringPubSubject1,intPubSubject2,
stringPubSubject2) { intSub1, strSub1, intSub2, stringSub2 in
        "\(intSub1) : \(strSub1) AND \(intSub2) : \(stringSub2)"
        }
        .subscribe(onNext:{
            print($0)
        })
    .disposed(by: disposeBag)
```

Now, let's add elements to the String subjects:

```
Observable.zip(intPubSubject1, stringPubSubject1,intPubSubject2,
stringPubSubject2) { intSub1, strSub1, intSub2, stringSub2 in
        "\(intSub1) : \(strSub1) AND \(intSub2) : \(stringSub2)"
        }
        .subscribe(onNext:{
            print($0)
        })
    .disposed(by: disposeBag)
    stringPubSubject1.onNext("is the first String element on
stringPubSubject1")
    stringPubSubject1.onNext("is the second String element on
stringPubSubject1")
    stringPubSubject2.onNext("is the first String element on
stringPubSubject2")
    stringPubSubject2.onNext("is the second String element on
stringPubSubject2")
```

Note that we still do not have any output on the output console:

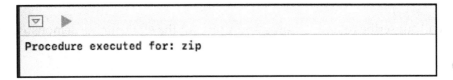

```
Procedure executed for: zip
```

This is because the `intSubject`s have not emitted anything as yet; when they do, note the change in the output console. The elements at the corresponding indexes will be combined and emitted. Let's add some elements to the `int` subjects:

```
Observable.zip(intPubSubject1, stringPubSubject1,intPubSubject2,
stringPubSubject2) { intSub1, strSub1, intSub2, stringSub2 in
        "\(intSub1) : \(strSub1) AND \(intSub2) : \(stringSub2)"
        }
        .subscribe(onNext:{
```

```
            print($0)
        })
    .disposed(by: disposeBag)
    stringPubSubject1.onNext("is the first String element on
stringPubSubject1")
    stringPubSubject1.onNext("is the second String element on
stringPubSubject1")
    stringPubSubject2.onNext("is the first String element on
stringPubSubject2")
    stringPubSubject2.onNext("is the second String element on
stringPubSubject2")
    intPubSubject1.onNext(1)
    intPubSubject1.onNext(2)
```

Even after doing that, you will see that the output console does not print anything. Did we forget to add anything? Let's try adding some elements on the other `intSubject` and then monitor the console:

```
Observable.zip(intPubSubject1, stringPubSubject1,intPubSubject2,
stringPubSubject2) { intSub1, strSub1, intSub2, stringSub2 in
        "\(intSub1) : \(strSub1) AND \(intSub2) : \(stringSub2)"
        }
        .subscribe(onNext:{
            print($0)
        })
    .disposed(by: disposeBag)
    stringPubSubject1.onNext("is the first String element on
stringPubSubject1")
    stringPubSubject1.onNext("is the second String element on
stringPubSubject1")
    stringPubSubject2.onNext("is the first String element on
stringPubSubject2")
    stringPubSubject2.onNext("is the second String element on
stringPubSubject2")
    intPubSubject1.onNext(1)
    intPubSubject1.onNext(2)
    intPubSubject2.onNext(3)
```

Note the output:

```
Procedure executed for: zip
1 : is the first String element on stringPubSubject1 AND 3 : is the first String element on stringPubSubject2
```

If the corresponding elements on all the respective subjects are present, then only the subscription prints the values; otherwise it ignores the values. Let's add one more element to the second `intSubject` and note the difference:

```
Observable.zip(intPubSubject1, stringPubSubject1,intPubSubject2,
stringPubSubject2) { intSub1, strSub1, intSub2, stringSub2 in
        "\(intSub1) : \(strSub1) AND \(intSub2) : \(stringSub2)"
        }
        .subscribe(onNext:{
            print($0)
        })
    .disposed(by: disposeBag)
    stringPubSubject1.onNext("is the first String element on
stringPubSubject1")
    stringPubSubject1.onNext("is the second String element on
stringPubSubject1")
    stringPubSubject2.onNext("is the first String element on
stringPubSubject2")
    stringPubSubject2.onNext("is the second String element on
stringPubSubject2")
    intPubSubject1.onNext(1)
    intPubSubject1.onNext(2)
    intPubSubject2.onNext(3)
    intPubSubject2.onNext(4)
```

As expected, all the elements will be printed as follows:

```
Procedure executed for: zip
1 : is the first String element on stringPubSubject1 AND 3 : is the first String element on stringPubSubject2
2 : is the second String element on stringPubSubject1 AND 4 : is the second String element on stringPubSubject2
```

It does not matter in what order the elements are emitted, they will each be paired by index. Let's see this in action:

```
Observable.zip(intPubSubject1, stringPubSubject1,intPubSubject2,
stringPubSubject2) { intSub1, strSub1, intSub2, stringSub2 in
        "\(intSub1) : \(strSub1) AND \(intSub2) : \(stringSub2)"
        }
        .subscribe(onNext:{
            print($0)
        })
    .disposed(by: disposeBag)
    stringPubSubject1.onNext("is the first String element on
stringPubSubject1")
    stringPubSubject1.onNext("is the second String element on
```

```
stringPubSubject1")
    stringPubSubject2.onNext("is the first String element on
stringPubSubject2")
    stringPubSubject2.onNext("is the cecond String element on
stringPubSubject2")
    intPubSubject1.onNext(1)
    intPubSubject1.onNext(2)
    intPubSubject2.onNext(3)
    intPubSubject2.onNext(4)
    intPubSubject1.onNext(5)
    stringPubSubject1.onNext("is the third String element on
stringPubSubject1")
    intPubSubject2.onNext(3)
    stringPubSubject2.onNext("is the third String element on
stringPubSubject2")
```

Note the output, and you will find no difference in the way the print statement is executed:

```
Procedure executed for: zip
1 : is the first String element on stringPubSubject1 AND 3 : is the first String element on stringPubSubject2
2 : is the second String element on stringPubSubject1 AND 4 : is the cecond String element on stringPubSubject2
5 : is the third String element on stringPubSubject1 AND 3 : is the third String element on stringPubSubject2
```

The overall code for the `zip` operator is this:

```
executeProcedure(for: "zip") {
    let disposeBag = DisposeBag()
    let intPubSubject1 = PublishSubject<Int>()
    let stringPubSubject1 = PublishSubject<String>()
    let intPubSubject2 = PublishSubject<Int>()
    let stringPubSubject2 = PublishSubject<String>()
    Observable.zip(intPubSubject1, stringPubSubject1,intPubSubject2,
stringPubSubject2) { intSub1, strSub1, intSub2, stringSub2 in
        "\(intSub1) : \(strSub1) AND \(intSub2) : \(stringSub2)"
        }
        .subscribe(onNext:{
            print($0)
        })
    .disposed(by: disposeBag)
    stringPubSubject1.onNext("is the first String element on
stringPubSubject1")
    stringPubSubject1.onNext("is the second String element on
stringPubSubject1")
    stringPubSubject2.onNext("is the first String element on
stringPubSubject2")
    stringPubSubject2.onNext("is the cecond String element on
```

```
stringPubSubject2")
    intPubSubject1.onNext(1)
    intPubSubject1.onNext(2)
    intPubSubject2.onNext(3)
    intPubSubject2.onNext(4)
        intPubSubject1.onNext(5)
    stringPubSubject1.onNext("is the third String element on
stringPubSubject1")
    intPubSubject2.onNext(3)
    stringPubSubject2.onNext("is the third String element on
stringPubSubject2")
}
```

We have gone over a variety of `RxOperators`. There is one more that we will work with next, which can be useful if you need to do some side work that has no direct effect on the outcome.

Performing side effects

Sometimes while working with an Observable sequence, we want to perform some action or side effect when elements are emitted, which won't change anything specifically about the elements emitted. We discussed about side effects in theory back in Chapter 2, *FRP Fundamentals, Terminology, and Basic Building Blocks*. Now, we will see the programmatic implementation.

We can use the `doOn` operator to perform side effects. Think of `doOn` as a wire tap on an Observable sequence. You can listen to the sequence but cannot modify things, and `doOn` will pass through each event. The actual method includes parameters for `onNext`, `onError`, `onCompleted` events, and the `onSubscribe` and `onDispose` handlers. Each is optional, so you can skip one or more parameters. An example scenario where you might want to use the `doOn` operator is while logging events in code.

The following diagram explains the doOn operator:

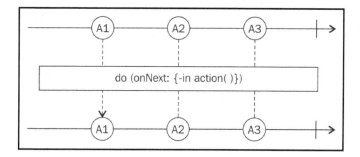

doOn in action

Let's work with doOn in code. We will use the same playground page, and start by commenting out the implementation so far. We will create a bare-bones implementation of the method for doOn and inside the implementation we will declare a disposeBag, as follows:

```
executeProcedure(for: "do(on....:)") {
    let disposeBag = DisposeBag()
}
```

Then, we will create a PublishSubject of the Int type:

```
let temperatureInFahrenheit = PublishSubject<Int>()
```

This PublishSubject will hold values that are temperatureInFahrenheit that we want to convert to Celsius.

We will chain a do(onNext:) operator on to the sequence and in it, multiply the element by itself. Although we could work with the result of this calculation within the do(onNext:) handler, it does not transform the element as a map operator would:

```
let temperatureInFahrenheit = PublishSubject<Int>()
    temperatureInFahrenheit
        .do(onNext: {
            $0 * $0
        })
```

The next event is passed through exactly as-is. We will chain in another `do(onNext:)` operator, this time to print out the beginning part of our message containing the element as a value in degrees Fahrenheit. We will select the special symbol for degrees Fahrenheit by selecting **Edit | Emoji & Symbols** from the menu and searching for degree symbol, as shown:

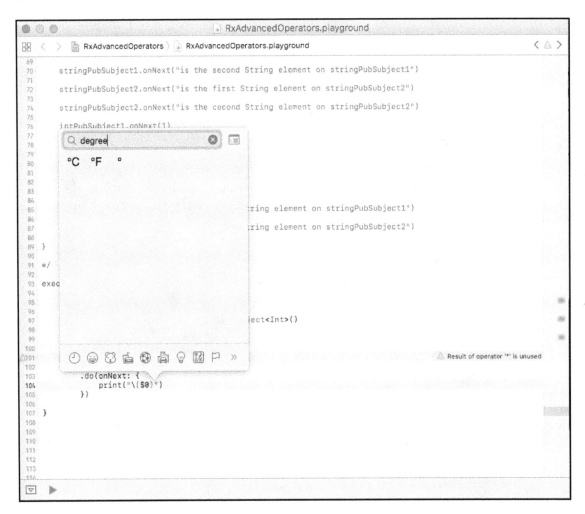

Double-click on the degree Fahrenheit symbol to access the symbol in the code:

```
let temperatureInFahrenheit = PublishSubject<Int>()
    temperatureInFahrenheit
        .do(onNext: {
            $0 * $0
        })
        .do(onNext: {
            print("\($0)°F = ", terminator: "")
        })
```

Next, we will use map to transform the element from Fahrenheit to Celsius, as shown in this code:

```
let temperatureInFahrenheit = PublishSubject<Int>()
    temperatureInFahrenheit
        .do(onNext: {
            $0 * $0
        })
        .do(onNext: {
            print("\($0)°F = ", terminator: "")
        })
        .map{
            Double($0 - 32) * 5 / 9.0
        }
```

Also, before we subscribe, we will add another call to doOn, just to show that we can include multiple handlers; onError receives an error instance, which we will print out, as shown in the code, with other events as well:

```
let temperatureInFahrenheit = PublishSubject<Int>()
    temperatureInFahrenheit
        .do(onNext: {
            $0 * $0
        })
        .do(onNext: {
            print("\($0)°F = ", terminator: "")
        })
        .map{
            Double($0 - 32) * 5 / 9.0
        }
        .do(onError: {
            print($0)
        },
            onCompleted: {
                print("Completed the sequence")
        },
```

```
        onSubscribe: {
            print("Subscribed to sequence")
    },
        onDispose: {
            print("Sequence Disposed")
    })
```

We will then subscribe to next events and print out the transform values as degrees Celsius:

```
temperatureInFahrenheit
        .do(onNext: {
            $0 * $0
    })
        .do(onNext: {
            print("\($0)°F = ", terminator: "")
    })
        .map{
            Double($0 - 32) * 5 / 9.0
        }
        .do(onError: {
            print($0)
    },
            onCompleted: {
                print("Completed the sequence")
    },
            onSubscribe: {
                print("Subscribed to sequence")
    },
            onDispose: {
                print("Sequence Disposed")
    })
        .subscribe(onNext: {
    })
```

We are using a format specifier here to print only one decimal place, and we will use the shortcut, that is, *control* + *option* + Space, to bring up the emoji picker this time:

```
temperatureInFahrenheit
        .do(onNext: {
            $0 * $0
    })
        .do(onNext: {
            print("\($0)°F = ", terminator: "")
    })
        .map{
            Double($0 - 32) * 5 / 9.0
        }
        .do(onError: {
```

```
        print($0)
    },
        onCompleted: {
            print("Completed the sequence")
    },
        onSubscribe: {
            print("Subscribed to sequence")
    },
        onDispose: {
            print("Sequence Disposed")
    })
    .subscribe(onNext: {
        print(String(format: "%.1f°C", $0))
    })
```

Of course, we will add the subscription to `disposeBag`:

```
temperatureInFahrenheit
        .do(onNext: {
            $0 * $0
        })
        .do(onNext: {
            print("\($0)°F = ", terminator: "")
        })
        .map{
            Double($0 - 32) * 5 / 9.0
        }
        .do(onError: {
            print($0)
        },
            onCompleted: {
                print("Completed the sequence")
        },
            onSubscribe: {
                print("Subscribed to sequence")
        },
            onDispose: {
                print("Sequence Disposed")
        })
        .subscribe(onNext: {
            print(String(format: "%.1f°C", $0))
        })
        .disposed(by: disposeBag)
```

Now we will add a few values to `temperatureInFahrenheit`, as follows:

```
temperatureInFahrenheit
        .do(onNext: {
            $0 * $0
        })
        .do(onNext: {
            print("\($0)°F = ", terminator: "")
        })
        .map{
            Double($0 - 32) * 5 / 9.0
        }
        .do(onError: {
            print($0)
        },
            onCompleted: {
                print("Completed the sequence")
        },
            onSubscribe: {
                print("Subscribed to sequence")
        },
            onDispose: {
                print("Sequence Disposed")
        })
        .subscribe(onNext: {
            print(String(format: "%.1f°C", $0))
        })
        .disposed(by: disposeBag)
    temperatureInFahrenheit.onNext(-40)
    temperatureInFahrenheit.onNext(0)
    temperatureInFahrenheit.onNext(37)
```

The result of the additions can be noted in the console:

```
Procedure executed for: do(on....:)
Subscribed to sequence
-40°F = -40.0°C
0°F = -17.8°C
37°F = 2.8°C
Sequence Disposed
```

Each Fahrenheit value is converted to Celsius and as per the formula; **-40°F** is equal to **-40°C**, strange aye!

The results are then followed by the dispose message. As you can see in the console, there was no error emitted during the emission of events.

We have reinforced the notion throughout the book of disposing subscriptions to a dispose bag. Let's comment out the statement where we add the subscription to dispose bag, as follows:

```
temperatureInFahrenheit
        .do(onNext: {
            $0 * $0
        })
        .do(onNext: {
            print("\($0)°F = ", terminator: "")
        })
        .map{
            Double($0 - 32) * 5 / 9.0
        }
        .do(onError: {
            print($0)
        },
            onCompleted: {
                print("Completed the sequence")
        },
            onSubscribe: {
                print("Subscribed to sequence")
        },
            onDispose: {
                print("Sequence Disposed")
        })
        .subscribe(onNext: {
            print(String(format: "%.1f°C", $0))
        })
//        .disposed(by: disposeBag)
    temperatureInFahrenheit.onNext(-40)
    temperatureInFahrenheit.onNext(0)
    temperatureInFahrenheit.onNext(37)
```

As a result, the subscription will not be disposed; you can see this in the console:

```
┌─────────────────────────────────────┐
│  ▽   ▶                               │
├─────────────────────────────────────┤
│ Procedure executed for: do(on....:)  │
│ Subscribed to sequence               │
│ -40°F = -40.0°C                      │
│ 0°F = -17.8°C                        │
│ 37°F = 2.8°C                         │
│                                      │
│                                      │
└─────────────────────────────────────┘
```

Neither the completed, nor the disposed message is printed, which means that we have leaked memory.

Instead, we will terminate the sequence by calling `onCompleted` on it:

```swift
temperatureInFahrenheit
        .do(onNext: {
            $0 * $0
        })
        .do(onNext: {
            print("\($0)°F = ", terminator: "")
        })
        .map{
            Double($0 - 32) * 5 / 9.0
        }
        .do(onError: {
            print($0)
        },
            onCompleted: {
                print("Completed the sequence")
        },
            onSubscribe: {
                print("Subscribed to sequence")
        },
            onDispose: {
                print("Sequence Disposed")
        })
        .subscribe(onNext: {
            print(String(format: "%.1f°C", $0))
        })
//        .disposed(by: disposeBag)
    temperatureInFahrenheit.onNext(-40)
    temperatureInFahrenheit.onNext(0)
    temperatureInFahrenheit.onNext(37)
```

```
temperatureInFahrenheit.onCompleted()
```

You will note that it is now terminated and properly disposed of; you can check this in the console:

```
Procedure executed for: do(on....:)
Subscribed to sequence
-40°f = -40.0°(
0°f = -17.8°(
37°f = 2.8°(
Completed the sequence
Sequence Disposed
```

So far, all the examples we have shown you have been performed on the main thread. We will go over how to manage concurrency in reactive programming using schedulers in upcoming chapters.

We have covered a number of operators so far, and the way we can work with several Observable sequences using these operators. You might be wondering how to use these concepts in a real-world application and hence we thought that it would be nice if we bound these concepts together and created a small application using the knowledge we have gained so far. In the next section, we will create a small application to address the concepts we have learned so far.

We will start with a new project in this section and build an application named Mother_Earth.

Setting the project

1. Create a single view application
2. Name the project Mother_Earth:

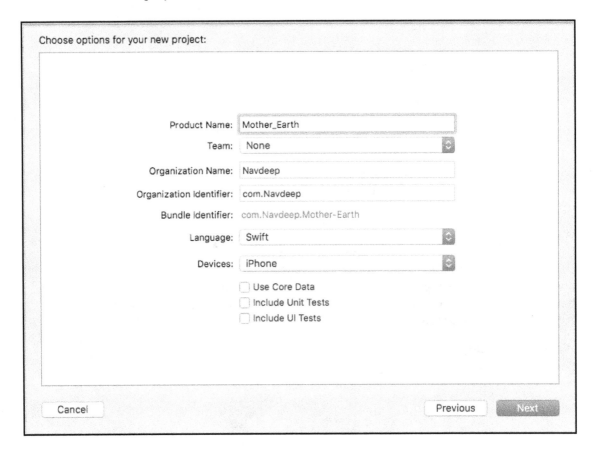

3. Open the Terminal app and go into the app project, as shown in this screenshot:

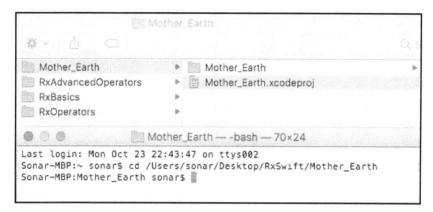

4. Initialize the `podfile` to include the `RxSwift` and `RxCocoa` dependencies:

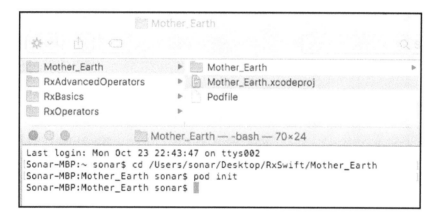

5. Open the `podfile` and paste the following code into the file:

```
use_frameworks!
target 'Mother_Earth' do
    pod 'RxSwift', '~> 3.6'
    pod 'RxCocoa', '~> 3.6'
end
```

6. Switch back to the Terminal app and enter the `pod install` command, as shown:

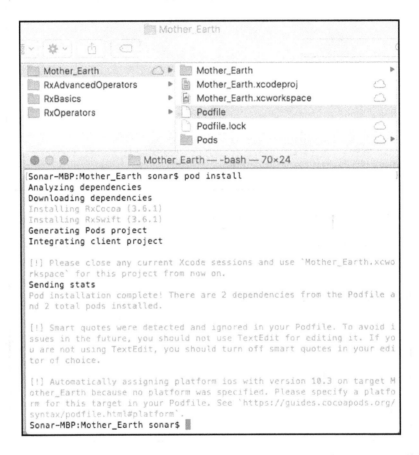

7. Open `Mother_Earth.xcworkspace`; the resulting Xcode project will look something like this:

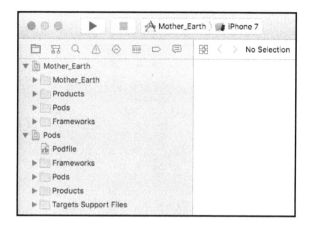

Building the app

Create the first `View` by dragging `UIViewController` onto the interface builder with the following layout:

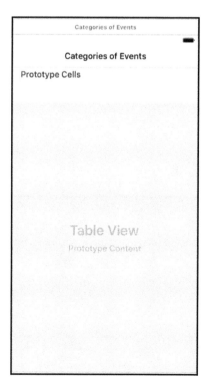

Now try to run it; you will see the following output:

Create `viewController` and name it `CategoriesVC` for the corresponding view, as follows:

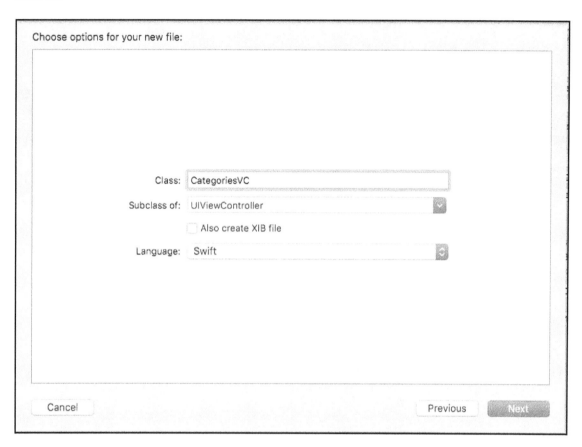

Implement the `TableViewController` methods within the `CategoriesVC` code, and embed the view controller in a navigation controller; after doing that, apply a tinted color to the navigation bar:

```swift
import UIKit
class CategoriesVC: UIViewController, UITableViewDelegate,
UITableViewDataSource {
    override func viewDidLoad() {
        super.viewDidLoad()
        // Do any additional setup after loading the view.
    }
    // MARK: UITableViewDataSource
    func tableView(_ tableView: UITableView, numberOfRowsInSection section:
Int) -> Int {
```

```
        return 0
    }
    func tableView(_ tableView: UITableView, cellForRowAt indexPath:
IndexPath) -> UITableViewCell {
        let cell = tableView.dequeueReusableCell(withIdentifier:
"categoryCell")!
        return cell
    }
}
```

Run to check whether everything works fine. Create an events view similarly using the interface builder and also create a corresponding EventsVC to manage the view.

The view should look like this:

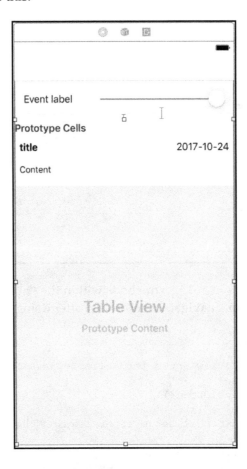

The corresponding `ViewController` will have the following code:

```swift
//
//  EventsVC.swift
//  Mother_Earth
//
//  Created by Navdeep on 24/10/17.
//  Copyright © 2017 Navdeep. All rights reserved.
//
import UIKit
class EventsVC: UIViewController {
    @IBOutlet weak var sliderView: UISlider!
    @IBOutlet weak var daysLabel: UILabel!
    @IBOutlet weak var eventsTV: UITableView!
    override func viewDidLoad() {
        super.viewDidLoad()
    }
    @IBAction func sliderMoved(_ sender: Any) {
    }
    // MARK: UITableViewDataSource
    func tableView(_ tableView: UITableView, numberOfRowsInSection section:
Int) -> Int {
        return 0
    }
    func tableView(_ tableView: UITableView, cellForRowAt indexPath:
IndexPath) -> UITableViewCell {
        let cell = tableView.dequeueReusableCell(withIdentifier:
"eventCell")!
        return cell
    }
}
```

Connect `View` to the `EventsVC` class, as shown:

We will now implement a class to control the implementation of `EventCell`. Create a new `Cocoa touch` source file and extend it from `UITableViewCell` with the name `EventCell`. This new cell class will have the following code:

```
import UIKit
class EventCell: UITableViewCell {
    @IBOutlet weak var title: UILabel!
    @IBOutlet weak var details: UILabel!
    @IBOutlet weak var date: UILabel!
}
```

Now that we have our `Views` and `ViewControllers` ready, it's time to create the `Models` that we need for our application. Check the code from the sample project of this chapter, and you will find models in the `Models` subfolder, as illustrated:

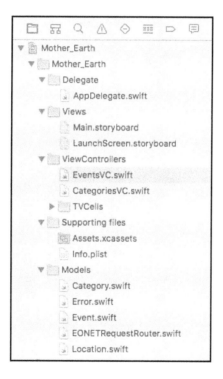

Let's start by following a generic request technique where you will handle the programmatic errors that you make by making use of Rx principles, as follows:

```
// Generic Request
    static func request(endPoint: String, query: [String: Any] = [:]) ->
Observable<[String: Any]> {
        do {
            guard let url = URL(string:
API)?.appendingPathComponent(endPoint), var components = URLComponents(url:
url, resolvingAgainstBaseURL: true) else{
                throw EONETError.invalidURL(endPoint)
            }
            components.queryItems = try query.flatMap{ (key, value) in
                guard let val = value as? CustomStringConvertible else {
                    throw EONETError.invalidParameter(key, value)
                }
                return URLQueryItem (name: key, value: val.description)
            }
            guard let finalURL = components.url else {
                throw EONETError.invalidURL(endPoint)
            }
            let request = URLRequest(url: finalURL)
            return URLSession.shared.rx.response(request: request)
                .map{ _, data -> [String: Any] in
                    guard let jsonObject = try?
JSONSerialization.jsonObject(with: data, options: []), let result =
jsonObject as? [String: Any] else {
                        throw
EONETError.invalidJSON(finalURL.absoluteString)
                    }
                    return result
            }
        }catch {
            return Observable.empty()
        }
    }
```

The strategy is simple and can be divided into the following pointers:

- Getting data from the API
- Populating the data by decoding the JSON into a dictionary
- Handling various errors that might creep in during the aforementioned two processes

Now we will make use of the preceding function to generate requests, the first one to fetch all the `Categories`:

```
// Fetch Categories
static var categories: Observable<[Category]> = {
    return EONETRequestRouter.request(endPoint: categoriesEndPoint)
        .map { data in
            let categories = data["categories"] as? [[String: Any]] ??
[]
            return categories
                .flatMap(Category.init)
                .sorted { $0.name < $1.name }
        }
        .shareReplay(1)
}()
```

In the preceding implementation, we applied the techniques that we have covered so far:

- Requesting data from the API endpoint
- Filtering out the categories objects from the JSON
- Populating the `Category` model objects and, finally, sorting them by name

Update `CategoriesVC` with the following code to bind the local data elements in the `viewController` to the ones returned from the model:

```
//
//  CategoriesVC.swift
//  Mother_Earth
//
//  Created by Navdeep on 24/10/17.
//  Copyright © 2017 Navdeep. All rights reserved.
//
import UIKit
import RxSwift
class CategoriesVC: UIViewController, UITableViewDelegate,
UITableViewDataSource {
    @IBOutlet weak var categoriesTableView: UITableView!
    let categories = Variable<[Category]>([])
    let disposeBag = DisposeBag()
    override func viewDidLoad() {
        super.viewDidLoad()
        categories
            .asObservable()
            .subscribe(onNext: { [weak self] _ in
                // Traditional way of doing things.. We will learn
Schedulers later in the book
```

```
                    DispatchQueue.main.async {
                        self?.categoriesTableView?.reloadData()
                    }
                })
                .disposed(by: disposeBag)
        }
    func startDownload(){
        let localCategories = EONETRequestRouter.categories
        localCategories.bind(to: categories)
            .disposed(by : disposeBag)
    }
    // MARK: UITableViewDataSource
    func tableView(_ tableView: UITableView, numberOfRowsInSection section:
Int) -> Int {
        return categories.value.count
    }
    func tableView(_ tableView: UITableView, cellForRowAt indexPath:
IndexPath) -> UITableViewCell {
        let cell = tableView.dequeueReusableCell(withIdentifier:
"categoryCell")!
        let category = categories.value[indexPath.row]
        cell.textLabel?.text = category.name
        cell.detailTextLabel?.text = category.description
        return cell
    }
}
```

The `categories` array in the `viewController` binds to the decoded categories returned in the JSON object, and the respective cells in the `viewController` will show the details for corresponding categories, as you can see inside the code for the `tableView(_:cellForRowAt:)` method.

The code inside `startDownload()` binds the source Observable, that is, `EONETRequestRouter.categories` to the `categories`, variable inside `CategoriesVC`, and finally we listen to those changes in `viewDidLoad()`.

Build and run, and you will see all the categories showing in the `tableView`. Next, we need to show a number of events grouped under each category in each table row. For fetching the events per category, we need to modify `EONETRequestRouter` as follows, with the addition of the following two functions:

```
fileprivate static func events(forLast days: Int, closed: Bool) ->
        Observable<[Event]> {
            return request(endPoint: eventsEndPoint, query: [
                "days": NSNumber(value: days),
                "status": (closed ? "closed" : "open")
```

```
                ])
                .map { json in
                    guard let raw = json["events"] as? [[String: Any]]
                    else {
                        throw EONETError.invalidJSON(eventsEndPoint)
                    }
                    return raw.flatMap(Event.init)
            }
    }
    static func events(forLast days: Int = 360) -> Observable<[Event]> {
        let openEvents = events(forLast: days, closed: false)
        let closedEvents = events(forLast: days, closed: true)
        return openEvents.concat(closedEvents)
    }
```

Next, we need to update categories with the respective events; for this, we need to change the code we already wrote for the startDownload() function in CategoriesVC, as follows:

```
func startDownload(){
        let localCategories = EONETRequestRouter.categories
        let downloadedEvents = EONETRequestRouter.events(forLast: 360)
        let updatedCategories = Observable
            .combineLatest(localCategories, downloadedEvents) {
                (categories, events) -> [Category] in
                return categories.map { category in
                    var cat = category
                    cat.events = events.filter {
                        $0.categories.contains(category.id)
                    }
                    return cat
                }
        }
        localCategories
            .concat(updatedCategories)
            .bind(to: categories)
            .disposed(by: disposeBag)
    }
```

The last thing is to update `tableView` to reflect the data changes under the hood, and we can do it with the help of the following lines of code in `CategoriesVC`:

```
cell.textLabel?.text = "\(category.name) (\(category.events.count))"
        cell.accessoryType = (category.events.count > 0) ?
    .disclosureIndicator
            : .none
```

Run the app, and you shall see `tableView` with a number of events grouped into categories.

Summary

This was a big chapter compared to the rest of the chapters in the book, so first of all, congratulations on completing the chapter. In this chapter, we covered concatenating and prefixing operators, then we worked with some merging and zipping operators, learned how to perform side effects, and, at the end, worked with a real-world application that utilized all the concepts that we have learned so far. Later on, we will extend the application started in this chapter to make use of schedulers in order to perform multitasking under the hood and revisit the code in order to work with the operators we have covered so far once again. In the next chapter, we will cover concepts dealing with `UIElements` in Rx.

7
React to UI Events – Start Subscribing

So far, many of you might have noted that we have used another library, `RxCocoa`, in our `pod` files, and the library was used to make view components become reactive. In this chapter, we will dig deeper to understand `RxViews` and view bindings. We will start with `RxCocoa` traits, then understand binding UI elements with data elements, and see how to bind table views and collection views in the later half of this chapter.

We will cover the following topics in this chapter:

- `RxCocoa` traits
- Binding data elements
- Table view bindings
- Collection view bindings

RxCocoa traits

`RxCocoa` traits that were previously categorized as units are structures that wrap an Observable sequence, and they exhibit the following additional characteristics that do not apply to `RxSwift` traits. They deliver events on the main thread via the main scheduler, and they are guaranteed not to fail and emit error events. These characteristics make these traits particularly useful for working with `UIElements`, for example, displaying the most recent value in a `UILabel` certain to be on the main thread and ensuring that there will be no errors.

Types of RxCocoa traits

There are three kinds of trait in `RxCocoa`, and they are as follows:

- `Driver`
- `ControlProperty`
- `ControlEvent`

We will go over each of these traits in turn now.

Driver

`Driver` intended use is to reactively bind an Observable sequence to a `UIElement`. It will also replay its latest element to its new subscriber, if there is one. We can convert an Observable sequence to a driver by calling `asDriver()` on it. As Driver cannot fail, if the Observable can fail, we will need to use one of the `asDriver()` APIs such as `asDriver(onErrorJustReturn:)` to provide a return value in the event that the underlying Observable sequence emits an error. For example, in the case of an Observable sequence of an array, we can just return an empty array.

ControlProperty

`ControlProperty` is a reactive wrapper for a property of a `UIElement`, such as `UITextField`'s `Rx.text` `ControlProperty` is a reactive wrapper around its text property. `ControlProperties` are defined in the `Rx` namespace. This helps separate and distinguish them from the standard library properties and methods. Generally, but not always, they use the same name as the standard library implementations that they wrap. Like `Driver`, a `ControlProperty` will also replay its latest element to new subscribes if there is one, and `ControlProperty` will automatically emit a completed event when its control or view is about to be deallocated.

ControlEvent

Similar to `ControlProperty`, `ControlEvent` is a reactive wrapper for a `UIElement` event. For example, `UIButton's Rx.tapControlEvent` wraps its `touchUpInside` event. It is also defined in the `Rx` namespace to differentiate it from the standard events. A `ControlEvent` will not replay its latest elements to its new subscribers though; it will only emit events as they occur to the current subscribers; for example, you would not want to replay an old tap event to a new subscriber, and a `ControlEvent` will emit a completed event when its control or view is about to be deallocated.

Binding UI elements in practice

In this section, we will work with a real-world application to show UI binding in real-world apps and how you can integrate it in your existing projects or in the apps that you make from scratch.

So far, from the previous chapters, we know how to set up `podfile` in an Xcode project and how to install the required `pod` files. In the upcoming project, we will require `RxSwift` and `RxCocoa` to start with. Since we have done the installation and project setup so many times until now, we will start with a starter project in this section. The link for the starter project is here:

`https://github.com/NavdeepSinghh/Chapter-7-Starter`

Clone or download the project from GitHub; build it so that the `Cocoapods` libraries are available, and you should be good to go.

Once the starter project is set up, you can see that we have a `ViewContoller` linked to a storyboard `View` and some other Swift files that will come in handy throughout the project.

We are starting out in a basic iOS single view project with several controls and views and a tap gesture recognizer added to the storyboard scene, and they are all wired up as `IBOutlets` in the `ViewController`. For most of these `UIControl` or `UIView` elements, there is a matching `UILabel` used to display some indication of interaction with the control or view. There is nothing special about these `UIControls` or `UIView` elements, except that we have subclassed `UITextView` and `UIButton` just to add rounded borders to them.

We have also defined a couple of properties, including a `disposeBag` instance and a `dateFormatter`, which we will use to format a `date` instance as a String later. We will use several Rx Extensions from the `RxCocoa` library, so we will need to import it into `ViewController`.

Starting from the top, we want to cause the keyboard to be dismissed whenever there is a tap on the main view. To handle this, we can use `rx.event`. This is the event operator in the `rx namespace` as of `RxCocoa 3.0`, but from here onward, we will omit using the dot `.` over and over again and just use `rxOperator`. The Rx event is an Rx wrapper that transforms gesture recognizer events into an Observable sequence. It's added as an extension to `UIGestureRecognizer`; it's a `ControlEvent` that, as we covered in the previous sections, wraps an event on a `UIElement`. Now we can subscribe to next events using `subscribe(onNext:)` and set the view's `endEditing` to true, which will cause the keyboard to be dismissed, as follows:

```
override func viewDidLoad() {
    super.viewDidLoad()
    tapRecognizer.rx.event
        .subscribe(onNext :{ [unowned self] _ in
            self.view.endEditing(true)
        })
}
```

As always, dispose of the subscription by adding it to the `disposeBag`.

We created an `unowned` capture of `self` because this is a single view app, so it is not possible for this `ViewController` to be deallocated before any code in the handler can be executed. Normally, we would create a `weak capture self`, and we added an underscore `_` to ignore the event being passed to the closure, because we don't need to do anything in the handler. This works, but we are more likely to see the use of `bind onNext operator` when working with UI; `bind(onNext:)` subscribes to next events and handles error events by throwing a `fatal error` in debug and logging it in release.

Let's work through a few examples of UI binding next and then run the app periodically to demonstrate functionality.

We will bind the text of `demoTextField` to its corresponding label, as follows:

```
demoTextField.rx.text
        .bind(to: demoTextFieldLabel.rx.text)
        .disposed(by: disposeBag)
```

rx.text is a ControlProperty that is an Rx wrapper around the text property; both
UITextField and UITextView have rx.text ControlProperties. We have used
bind(to:) to bind next events directly to the corresponding label's rx.text value. Now
whatever is typed in the text field will be displayed in the label.

We can technically skip adding the subscription to disposeBag because
ControlProperties will automatically emit a completed event on deInit(), but then we
will need to deal with the warning because the disposable returned from bind(to:) is
unused. We can just explicitly ignore it, but the best practice is to always add
subscriptions to disposeBag. This establishes uniformity and reduces the cognitive
load while reviewing the code, so we have added this subscription to the disposeBag.

For demoTextView, we will use Driver. Note that we have used the handy orEmpty
computed property on the ControlProperty text to return an empty String if the
text of textView is nil. This is just another way that Rx helps to streamline our code.

demoTextView.rx.text.orEmpty.asDriver() calling asDriver() converts the
ControlProperty, in this case, to a Driver. Remember from the previous section that Drivers cannot
fail but neither can a ControlProperty. So Driver throws a FatalError in debug, as shown:

```
public func asDriver() -> Driver<E> {
    return self.asDriver { (error) -> Driver<E> in
        #if DEBUG
            rxFatalError("Somehow driver received error from a
                source that shouldn't fail.")
        #else
            return Driver.empty()
        #endif
    }
}
```

It's just like bind(onNext:), but if an error does somehow get emitted by the source
Observable in release, driver will just return an empty sequence that simply emits the
completed event.

Back to `ViewController`; we will first use `map` to transform the text of `textView` into a `String` with a character count prefix and the character count of the text, and then we will use `drive`. We will use drive to directly bind the `character count string` on the `demoTextFieldLabel's rx.text` and add the subscription to the `disposeBag`, as shown:

```
demoTextView.rx.text.orEmpty.asDriver()
            .map{
                "Char count: \($0.characters.count)"
            }
            .drive(demoTextFieldLabel.rx.text)
            .disposed(by: disposeBag)
```

Let's run our app to check out bindings in action. Tap into the keyboard to bring up the keyboard and then tap outside the `demoTextField` to dismiss the keyboard. Now back into the `demoTextField`; as you probably know, you can either use the onscreen keyboard or connect your Mac's keyboard. We will do the latter here.

You can see that, as we type text in the `demoTextField`, that text is displayed in its corresponding label. Next, try typing something in the `demoTextView`, and you will note that the display changes to the count of the typed string value. So far, we have showed you how to bind UI using the `subscribe`, `drive`, and `bind` operators, and you can pick any one of them; it is a matter of personal preference. The most common approach is to use `drivers` for binding data to UI, such as coming from a `viewModel`, and `bind` for binding events such as taps, which are handled by a `ViewController`. We will work with an example of binding data from a `viewModel` later in the book. The most important thing while you write code is to be consistent in your choices.

Next, we will print `Tap clicked` every time the **Tap me** button is pressed. Jump back to `ViewController` so that we can start coding our way through the example. `UIButton` has an `rx.tap` extension that is a control event wrapper around `touchUpInside` events, and we will use `bind(onNext:)` to bind next events and append `"Tap clicked"` to the `label` button's text, as follows:

```
button.rx.tap
            .bind(onNext:{ [unowned self] _ in
                self.buttonLabel.text! += "Tap clicked"
            })
            .disposed(by: disposeBag)
```

We will also add some polish by setting `endEditing` to true here if the button is tapped while the keyboard is displayed, and we will call `layoutIfNeeded()` to create a nice animation when the text wraps onto a new line, so the preceding code becomes this:

```
button.rx.tap
            .bind(onNext:{ [unowned self] _ in
                self.buttonLabel.text! += "Tap clicked"
                self.view.endEditing(true)
                UIView.animate(withDuration:0.3){
                    self.view.layoutIfNeeded()
                }
            })
            .disposed(by: disposeBag)
```

Now, let's work with a `UISegmentedControl` and see how binding works in this case. `UISegmentedControl` has an `rx.value` `ControlProperty` that creates an Observable sequence of the currently selected segment. We don't want to display anything in the corresponding label, because this `SegmentedControl` starts off with nothing selected. So we will start off with the `skip` operator to skip the first emission and then we will use `bind(onNext:)` to set the text value of `SegmentedControlLabel` to the new concatenated `String`, including the selected segment, very similar to what we did to the `UIButton` example; as always, don't forget to add the subscriptions to the `disposeBag`, as follows:

```
segmentedControl.rx.value
            .skip(1)
            .bind(onNext: { [unowned self] in
                self.segmentedControlLabel.text = "Selected Segment: \
                ($0)"
            })
            .disposed(by:disposeBag)
```

We will use the same animation block to make the label display animate smoothly, as shown:

```
segmentedControl.rx.value
            .skip(1)
            .bind(onNext: { [unowned self] in
                self.segmentedControlLabel.text = "Selected Segment: \
                ($0)"
                UIView.animate(withDuration: 0.3, animations: {
                    self.view.layoutIfNeeded()
                })
            })
            .disposed(by:disposeBag)
```

Now we will bind the relative position of the `UISlider` to a `UIProgressView`. First, note that we have made the slider value range from 0 to 1 in the storyboard. `UISliders` also have an `rx.value ControlProperty`, and because we have made the slider value range from 0 to 1 in the storyboard, we don't need to transform the element in any way and just use `bind(to:)` to bind that value to `progressView`, which also expects a value from 0 to 1; short and sweet! The code will look like this:

```
slider.rx.value
        .bind(to: progressView.rx.progress)
        .disposed(by: disposeBag)
```

Let's run the app to check these bindings. We entered **Testing the text!** in `demoTextView`, and you can see the text displayed on `demoTextViewLabel`; with that, we clicked on the **Tap me** button, and you can see the text linked to the button displayed. Along with those two elements, note the length of the slider and the corresponding progress view in the following screenshot:

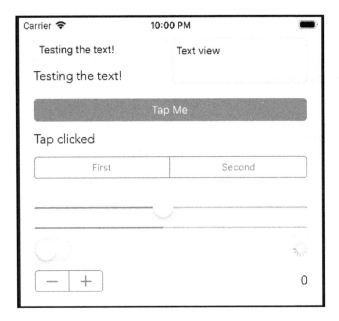

After dragging the slider, note the change in `ProgressView` here:

Play with other View elements and see the effect. So far, we have worked with
`ViewController` and for ease of understanding, made all the changes to only one method,
which is the `viewDidLoad()` lifecycle method. The consolidated code that we have written
so far is as follows:

```
override func viewDidLoad() {
    super.viewDidLoad()
    tapRecognizer.rx.event
        .subscribe(onNext :{[unowned self] _ in
            self.view.endEditing(true)
        })
        .disposed(by: disposeBag)
    demoTextField.rx.text
        .bind(to: demoTextFieldLabel.rx.text)
        .disposed(by: disposeBag)
    demoTextView.rx.text.orEmpty.asDriver()
        .map{
            "Char count: \($0.characters.count)"
        }
        .drive(demoTextFieldLabel.rx.text)
        .disposed(by: disposeBag)
    button.rx.tap
```

```
        .bind(onNext:{ [unowned self] _ in
            self.buttonLabel.text! += "Tap clicked"
            self.view.endEditing(true)
            UIView.animate(withDuration:0.3){
                self.view.layoutIfNeeded()
            }
        })
        .disposed(by: disposeBag)
    segmentedControl.rx.value
        .skip(1)
        .bind(onNext: { [unowned self] in
            self.segmentedControlLabel.text = "Selected Segment: \
    ($0)"
            UIView.animate(withDuration: 0.3, animations: {
                self.view.layoutIfNeeded()
            })
        })
        .disposed(by:disposeBag)
    slider.rx.value
        .bind(to: progressView.rx.progress)
        .disposed(by: disposeBag)
}
```

Next, we will bind `UISwitch` to the visibility and animation of a `UIActivityIndicatorView`. First, we will bind the visibility using the `rx.value` `ControlProperty` of `UISwitch`. We will use the map operator to produce the opposite BOOL so that, if the switch is "ON" or "OFF", this will produce the vice versa, and this is because we want to bind to the `ActivityIndicator`'s `rx.isHidden` observer. Don't forget to add the subscription to `disposeBag`, as follows:

```
aSwitch.rx.value
        .map { !$0 }
        .bind(to: activityIndicator.rx.isHidden)
        .disposed(by: disposeBag)
```

This acts as an `rxWrapper` around the `UIActivityIndicatorView`'s isHidden property, as shown:

This is of the `UIBindingObserver` type of the `UIElement`, in this case, a `UIActivityIndicator` and a `Bool`. `UIBindingObserver` is used in a similar manner to a `ControlProperty`, such as to enable binding transformed `next` elements to the `isHidden` property here. You will see `UIBindingObserver` types such as this referred to as bindable syncs in the documentation; all this really means is that it's a `closure` that takes the `next` element and sets it on the target property. Now we will bind the animation of the `ActivityIndicator` to the `Switch`, this time using `driver` semantics just to give another example of that approach, and we are driving the `ActivityIndicator`'s `rx.isAnimating` observer; yet again, don't forget to add the subscription to a `disposeBag`, as follows:

```
aSwitch.rx.value.asDriver()
            .drive(activityIndicator.rx.isAnimating)
            .disposed(by: disposeBag)
```

Next, we will bind a `UIStepper` to a label to display its current value as it is incremented and decremented. We are using `map` to transform the emitted `double` value to a `String` with a number down to a whole integer and then binding that value to `stepperLabel`'s `rx.text`, as follows:

```
stepper.rx.value
            .map { String(Int($0)) }
            .bind( to: stepperLabel.rx.text)
            .disposed(by: disposeBag)
```

Now run the app and play with all the changes that we have made to the view elements.

Hopefully, these examples are starting to feel pretty routine to you. It's the same pattern over and over, but you are doing a lot here with a very succinct and readable amount of `rx` code. Wrapping up the `UIBinding` examples, we will bind `UIDatePicker` to a `Label` using its `rx.date` property, and we will use map to transform the data value into a `String` using the `DateFormatter` we initially created, and then we will bind that value to the `datePickerLabel`'s `rx.text` observer. Finally, don't forget to add the subscription to the `disposeBag`, as follows:

```
datePicker.rx.date
            .map{ [unowned self] in
                "Date picked: " + self.dateFormatter.string(from: $0)
            }
            .bind(to: datePickerLabel.rx.text)
            .disposed(by: disposeBag)
```

Let's run the app and test out the remaining bindings. With the switch off, there is no `ActivityIndicator`. Switch it on and you will notice that the `ActivityIndicator` is displayed and begins animating. Use the plus (+) and minus (–) buttons on the stepper to change the value on its corresponding label, and you will note that when you select a date from the `datePicker`, the label displays the date. All this can be seen in action in the following screenshot:

So we found a whole bunch of UIControls and Views, mostly labels, in order to display evidence of interaction with them. In about 60 lines of code and some shorthand syntax, you will see the conciseness, expressiveness, and readability that RxSwift brings to your professional code. These binding features are an existing part of the reactive Swift programming paradigm, and you may want to consider starting with these concepts first when beginning to convert your apps to RxSwift. The consolidated code for the concepts we have covered so far is as follows:

```
//
//  ViewController.swift
//  RxCocoaBindings
//
//  Created by Navdeep on 5/11/17.
//  Copyright © 2017 Navdeep. All rights reserved.
//
import UIKit
import RxSwift
import RxCocoa
class ViewController: UIViewController {
    @IBOutlet weak var tapRecognizer: UITapGestureRecognizer!
    @IBOutlet weak var demoTextField: UITextField!
    @IBOutlet weak var demoTextFieldLabel: UILabel!
    @IBOutlet weak var demoTextView: TextView!
    @IBOutlet weak var textViewLabel: UILabel!
    @IBOutlet weak var button: Button!
    @IBOutlet weak var buttonLabel: UILabel!
    @IBOutlet weak var segmeåntedControl: UISegmentedControl!
    @IBOutlet weak var segmentedControlLabel: UILabel!
    @IBOutlet weak var slider: UISlider!
    @IBOutlet weak var progressView: UIProgressView!
    @IBOutlet weak var aSwitch: UISwitch!
    @IBOutlet weak var activityIndicator: UIActivityIndicatorView!
    @IBOutlet weak var stepper: UIStepper!
    @IBOutlet weak var stepperLabel: UILabel!
    @IBOutlet weak var datePicker: UIDatePicker!
    @IBOutlet weak var datePickerLabel: UILabel!
    let disposeBag = DisposeBag()
    lazy var dateFormatter: DateFormatter = {
        let formatter = DateFormatter()
        formatter.dateStyle = .medium
        formatter.timeStyle = .short
        return formatter
    }()
    override func viewDidLoad() {
        super.viewDidLoad()
        tapRecognizer.rx.event
```

```
        .subscribe(onNext :{[unowned self] _ in
            self.view.endEditing(true)
        })
        .disposed(by: disposeBag)
demoTextField.rx.text
        .bind(to: demoTextFieldLabel.rx.text)
        .disposed(by: disposeBag)
demoTextView.rx.text.orEmpty.asDriver()
        .map{
            "Char count: \($0.characters.count)"
        }
        .drive(demoTextFieldLabel.rx.text)
        .disposed(by: disposeBag)
button.rx.tap
        .bind(onNext:{ [unowned self] _ in
            self.buttonLabel.text! += "Tap clicked"
            self.view.endEditing(true)
            UIView.animate(withDuration:0.3){
                self.view.layoutIfNeeded()
            }
        })
        .disposed(by: disposeBag)
segmeântedControl.rx.value
        .skip(1)
        .bind(onNext: { [unowned self] in
            self.segmentedControlLabel.text = "Selected Segment: \
        ($0)"
            UIView.animate(withDuration: 0.3, animations: {
                self.view.layoutIfNeeded()
            })
        })
        .disposed(by:disposeBag)
slider.rx.value
        .bind(to: progressView.rx.progress)
        .disposed(by: disposeBag)
aSwitch.rx.value
        .map { !$0 }
        .bind(to: activityIndicator.rx.isHidden)
        .disposed(by: disposeBag)
aSwitch.rx.value.asDriver()
        .drive(activityIndicator.rx.isAnimating)
        .disposed(by: disposeBag)
stepper.rx.value
        .map { String(Int($0)) }
        .bind( to: stepperLabel.rx.text)
        .disposed(by: disposeBag)
datePicker.rx.dat
```

```
        .map{ [unowned self] in
            "Date picked: " + self.dateFormatter.string(from: $0)
        }
        .bind(to: datePickerLabel.rx.text)
        .disposed(by: disposeBag)
    }
}
```

Although we have gone over several examples of binding UIElements in the previous section, most likely you also want to bind these property values to events or data elements too. Hold your horses; we will cover those concepts in the next section.

Binding data to UI

We will again start out in a basic single-view project with just a TapGestureRecogniser, UITextField, and a UIButton, as shown in the following screenshot:

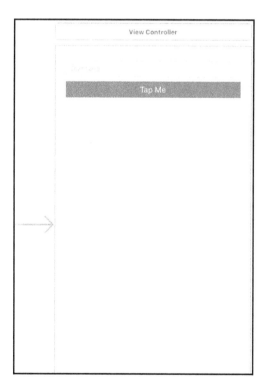

Then, make the `viewController` the initial view controller, as shown in the preceding screenshot. As you can see, the corresponding view controller has some code to handle the interactions that the user will make with the view. We will start with the following basic code and build on top of it:

```
//
//  ViewController.swift
//  RxSwiftDataBindings
//
//  Created by Navdeep on 19/11/17.
//  Copyright © 2017 Navdeep. All rights reserved.
//
import UIKit
import RxSwift
import RxCocoa
class ViewController: UIViewController {
    @IBOutlet weak var demoTapGestureRecognizer:
UITapGestureRecognizer!
    @IBOutlet weak var demoTextField: UITextField!
    @IBOutlet weak var demoButton: Button!
    let disposeBag = DisposeBag()
    override func viewDidLoad() {
        super.viewDidLoad()
    }
}
```

The elements that we see in the storyboard are wired to the view controller using `IBOutlets`. Since we are working with the `RxSwift` and `RxCocoa` libraries, we need to include them in out project, so as usual add the `podfile` to the project with the following code:

```
target 'RxSwiftDataBindings' do
use_frameworks!
pod 'RxSwift'
pod 'RxCocoa'
end
```

Now, run the `pod install` command from the Terminal, and you will get a workspace. Open the workspace project, and we are good to go!

Let's introduce the `rx.event` of `TapGestureRecognizer` to dismiss the keyboard when a tap is recognized. This is very similar to what we did with the bind UIElements project in the previous section. The code will be as follows:

```
override func viewDidLoad() {
        super.viewDidLoad()
        demoTapGestureRecognizer.rx.event
            .bind{ [unowned self] _ in
                self.view.endEditing(true)
        }
        .disposed(by: disposeBag)
    }
```

We want to bind the text from the `textField` to a `Variable`. A `Variable` is a good choice here, because we want `Observers` of that `Variable` to receive the latest or initial value upon subscription. So first, we will create a `Variable` property with an empty `String` as the initial value, as shown:

```
let demoTextFieldText = Variable("")
```

Now, we will bind the `textField`'s `rx.text.orEmpty` to the text `Variable` of `textField`:

```
demoTextField.rx.text.orEmpty
                .bind(to: demoTextFieldText)
                .disposed(by: disposeBag)
```

You might be wondering why didn't we use the `Driver` API here. `Driver` is primarily intended to drive one way from data to `UIElements`, so while you might use `Driver` to drive a label with the next element emitted from a `Variable`, you will just use `bind(to:)` to bind the text entered into a `textField` to an `Observable`. In order to see that effect of that `bind` `textFeild`'s text variable, we will create a subscription to `textFeild`'s text, as follows:

```
demoTextFieldText.asObservable()
                .subscribe{ print($0) }
                .disposed(by: disposeBag)
```

We will run the app and sure enough, entering or deleting text into the `demoTextField` results in the `textField`'s text being printed to the console, as illustrated:

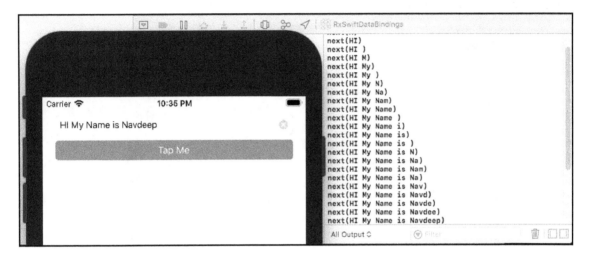

Next, we want to bind text on the **Tap Me** button to an Observable sequence, because we don't want to replay anything upon subscription. A `PublishSubject` is a good choice here. We will once again use the `rx.tap` ControlEvent of `UIButton`, and we will map it to return a String `"Button Clicked"` and bind that to the button tap's `PublishedSubject`, as shown:

```
demoButton.rx.tap
            .map { "Button Clicked" }
            .bind(to: buttonClicked)
            .disposed(by: disposeBag)
```

Now we will create a subscription to `buttonClicked`. In the handler, we will print out the element if it is a `nextEvent` or just print the event itself. The element property of an event is an optional, which will be the element if it's a `nextEvent`; otherwise, it will be `nil`:

```
buttonClicked
            .subscribe { print($0.element ?? $0) }
            .disposed(by: disposeBag)
```

Let's run the app, and you will see that, when you press the button, **Button Clicked** will be printed in the console, as depicted here:

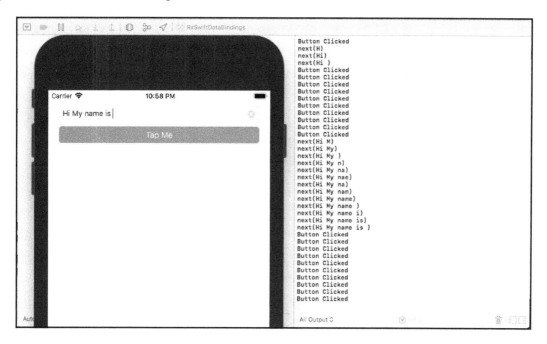

Binding to data elements is not much different from binding to `UIElements`. Coming up next, we will go over some slightly more involved bindings to `TableViews` and `CollectionViews`.

Binding UITableViews

Practically, every app needs to present and facilitate interactions with lists of data. Fortunately, `RxCocoa` and additional libraries provide several extensions to work with `Table` and `CollectionView`. We will cover `TableViews` here and `CollectionViews` in the next section. We are starting out in a basic `tableView` app written traditionally using the standard `tableView` API. Let's review it first and then refractor it to use Rx.

Open the starter project for this section, and you will see that, at the top of this section, we have an `IBOutlet` for `demoTableView` added to the `.storyboard` scene. We want to point out something here. Rather than using a `UITableViewController`, we are using a `UIViewController` and adding a `UITableView` to it; we will explain why we have done things in this manner later.

Next, we will create a simple data array of developers. These are the top 10 contributors to the `RxSwift` project at the time of writing:

```
@IBOutlet weak var demoTableView: UITableView!
    let data = [
        Developer(name: "Krunoslav Zaher", gitHubID: "kzaher"),
        Developer(name: "Yury Korolev", gitHubID: "yury"),
        Developer(name: "Serg Dort", gitHubID: "sergdort"),
        Developer(name: "Mo Ramezanpoor", gitHubID: "mohsenr"),
        Developer(name: "Carlos García", gitHubID: "carlosypunto"),
        Developer(name: "Scott Gardner", gitHubID: "scotteg"),
        Developer(name: "Nobuo Saito", gitHubID: "tarunon"),
        Developer(name: "Junior B.", gitHubID: "bontoJR"),
        Developer(name: "Jesse Farless", gitHubID: "solidcell"),
        Developer(name: "Jamie Pinkham", gitHubID: "jamiepinkham"),
        ]
```

Developer is a `struct`, and you can see that we have added the `struct` in the project navigator. The `struct` comprises a `developerNme`, `gitHubID`, and a `developerImage`, as in the following code:

```
struct Developer {
    let developerName: String
    let gitHubID: String
    var developerImage: UIImage?
    init(name: String, gitHubID: String) {
        self.developerName = name
        self.gitHubID = gitHubID
        developerImage = UIImage(named: gitHubID)
    }
}
extension Developer: CustomStringConvertible {
    var description: String {
        return "\(developerName): github.com/\(gitHubID)"
    }
}
```

Back in `ViewController`, we have set the `dataSource` and `delegate` of `demoTableView` to `self`, and then we have implemented the necessary `UITableViewDatasource` and `UITableViewDelegate` protocol methods in separate extensions, respectively. Let's run the app and see the output. You will see the list of Developers in the tableView, as follows:

Tapping on a row prints the selected developers' GitHub profiles, as shown:

Returning to the `ViewController`, we will start using `Rx` to see how we can convert an existing app to use `Rx`.

Configuring cell rows in a TableView

First, we will need to import the `Rx` libraries that we will be using, that is, `RxSwift` and `RxCocoa`, and we will do a quick build in order to make them available. We will also create a `disposeBag` property to dispose of `subscriptions`, as we did earlier.

Next, we need to convert our `data` into an `Observable Sequence`. We will use the `Observable.of` operator. *option* + click on data to see its data type, and you will see that it is an array `Observable` of the `Developer` type. The following screenshot shows this:

The code changes that we have done so far are as follows:

```
import UIKit
import RxSwift
import RxCocoa
class ViewController: UIViewController {
    @IBOutlet weak var demoTableView: UITableView!
    let data = Observable.of( [
        Developer(name: "Krunoslav Zaher", gitHubID: "kzaher"),
        Developer(name: "Yury Korolev", gitHubID: "yury"),
        Developer(name: "Serg Dort", gitHubID: "sergdort"),
        Developer(name: "Mo Ramezanpoor", gitHubID: "mohsenr"),
        ....... same array....
        ])
    let disposeBag = DisposeBag()
```

To bind data to a `tableView`, RxCocoa provides an extension method to replace the `UITableViewDataSource` protocol methods, and as you will see shortly, there are also `Rx` methods to replace the `UITableViewDelegate` protocol methods; thus, we don't need to implement those methods, and we don't need to assign self to the associated properties of the `tableView`. This is why we used a regular `UIViewController`, and it is an important point to remember. A `UITableViewController` automatically declares the adoption of the `UITableViewDataSource` and `UITableViewDelegate` protocols, and we don't want that here. Just remember to use `UIViewControllers` when trying to work with `Rx` driven `TableViews`.

We will start off by getting data as a `Driver` and note that we need to specify what is required to be done `onError()`. We will choose `onErrorJustReturn:` and return an empty `array`. Now we will use drive and, out of the several code suggestions to choose from, the one we want is `driver(with: .. curriedArgument:)`, which takes a function that will be used to bind the elements and a curry is the final value passed in order to complete the binding process. It's a rather complex function type but the implementation is straightforward, as follows:

```
data.asDriver(onErrorJustReturn: [])
        .drive(demoTableView.rx.items(cellIdentifier:"Cell"))
        { (_, developer, cell) in
            cell.textLabel?.text = developer.developerName
            cell.detailTextLabel?.text = developer.gitHubID
            cell.imageView?.image = developer.developerImage
        }
        .disposed(by:disposeBag)
```

As you can see, we have passed a binding function, that is, the `rx.items` of `tableView` which take a `cellIdentifier` string. We will use `cell`, which matches with the cell identifier we entered in the `interface builder`. It also takes a `cellType` parameter that defaults to `UITableViewCell`, so we will skip that, and it takes a configure cell closure to configure each cell. The closure is passed three values; a `rowIndex`, which we don't need in this case, an element, in this case a developer instance; and the cell itself. Don't forget to add it to the `diposeBag`. Finally, we will just cut and paste the code that sets the cell according to the data model.

As a result, now we can remove a whole lot of code required by the `UITableViewDataSource` and `UITableViewDelegate` protocol methods. So it's concise, neat, and readable!

Selecting a row in TableView

Instead of implementing `didSelectRowAtIndexPath()`, we will implement `rx.modelSelected` of `tableView`, which takes the type of `dataModel`, `Developer` in this case, and it emits a `nextEvent` containing the selected element property type that we can subscribe to and then print out the selected `developer`, as shown:

```
demoTableView.rx.modelSelected(Developer.self)
        .subscribe(onNext: {
            print("Selected Develoer:", $0)
        })
        .disposed(by: disposeBag)
```

This refractor has reduced the lines of code by at least 25%, and running the app again will produce the same result as earlier.

There are `extensions` for most of the `delegate` and `dataSource` methods in RxCocoa and matching `extensions` for `UICollectionViews`. So we encourage you to check them out. We will use a `RxCommunity` library to bind a `collectionView` in the next section.

Binding UICollectionViews

As we mentioned in the last section, we will use a community library in this section. The name of the library is `RxDataSources`. It is built on top of `RxCocoa` and `RxSwift` and provides new extensions for handling more complex tables and `collectionViews`.

We will create a `collectionView` with a set of section headers that animates changes to the `collectionView`, such as adding new sections. `RxDataSources` provides an API for doing these things reactively. We are starting out in a single-view app with the `collectionView` added to the scene; you can open the starter project for this section and build on top of it like the previous sections.

As we mentioned, we will use the `RxSwift` community library—`RxDataSources`—in this example, so we need to include the library to `CocoaPods`. Let's add the library to our `podFile` and execute `pod install` from the terminal to make that library available to our code locally. The `podFile` will look like this:

```
target 'Bind Collection Views' do
    use_frameworks!
    pod 'RxSwift'
    pod 'RxCocoa'
    pod 'RxDataSources'
end
```

Open the `xcworkspace` and switch to `ViewController`. We will import the new library using the import statement and build the project to make all the imported modules available. The first thing we recommend doing is drilling down into the library to get a basic idea of what that this library is capable of doing.

We will just work with `String` in this example, and `String` already conforms to `IdentifiableType`, so we will create a `SectionModel`, which we will name `SectionModel` and define a title for each section and a data array of the `String` type. Now we will extend `SectionModel` to adopt and conform to `AnimatableSectionModelType`, as demonstrated:

```
import UIKit
import RxSwift
import RxDataSources
struct SectionModel {
    let title: String
    var data: [String]
}
extension SectionModel : AnimatableSectionModelType{
    typealias Item = String
    typealias Identity = String
    var identity: Identity { return title }
    var items: [Item] { return data }
    init(original: SectionModel, items: [String]) {
        self = original
        data = items
    }
}
```

Now we are ready to implement `RxAnimatedCollectionView` in `ViewController`. First, we will create a `dataSource` property that is an instance of an `RxCollectionViewSectionedAnimatedDataSource`, specifying our `SectionModel` as the generic type:

```
let dataSource =
RxCollectionViewSectionedAnimatedDataSource<SectionModel>()
```

Next, we will create a data Observable sequence that is a `Variable` of the `array` of our `SectionModel`, and we will start the sequence with a single section 0 with one item in it:

```
let data = Variable([
        SectionModel(title: "Section 0", data: ["0"])
        ])
```

Now we will set a property on our `dataSource` called `configureCell`, and it's used to configure each cell. It's a closure type with four arguments, as shown in the following screenshot:

Note that it returns a `UICollectionViewCell`, so we will create a closure with these arguments, ignoring the first one, the `dataSource`, because we won't need it in our closure's body.

We will create the cell using the `dequeReusableCell()` method of `UICollectionView`, casting it as our custom `cellType` and the identifier set on the cell in the interface builder. Then, we will set the cell's `titleLabel` text and return it, as follows:

```
dataSource.configureCell = { _, collectionView, indexPath, title in
        let cell =
collectionView.dequeueReusableCell(withReuseIdentifier: "Cell", for:
indexPath) as! Cell
        cell.titleLabel.text = title
        return cell
    }
```

We also want to display a section header, so we will set and use `RxDataSources` `supplementaryViewFactory` to configure a section header for each section. It works similarly to `configureCell` and has four arguments that you can see in the following screenshot:

```
dataSource.supplementaryViewFactory                          ⓘ Expression

Declaration  var supplementaryViewFactory:
             (CollectionViewSectionedDataSource<SectionModel>,
             UICollectionView, String, IndexPath) ->
             UICollectionReusableView { get set }

Declared in  RxDataSources
```

Note that it returns a `UICollectionReusableView`. We will define each one of those arguments in the closure body and will create our `headerView` using the arguments, as shown:

```
dataSource.supplementaryViewFactory = {dataSource, collectionView, kind,
indexPAth in
        let headerView =
collectionView.dequeueReusableCell(withReuseIdentifier: "Header", for:
indexPAth) as! Header
        headerView.titleLabel.text =
dataSource.sectionModels[indexPAth.section].title
        return headerView
    }
```

Note that we need to reach into the array of `SectionModel`, which is an `array` of our `SectionModel`.

So we have set up our `dataSource`; now we just need to bind `data` to it. We will use `Driver`, because we are driving `UI` from `data`, and we will drive the `dataSource` of the `rx.item` of `CollectionView`, passing our `dataSource`:

```
data.asDriver()
        .drive(collectionView.rx.items(dataSource: dataSource))
        .disposed(by: disposeBag)
```

Let's run the app to check this out. You will see that our initial data is properly displayed:

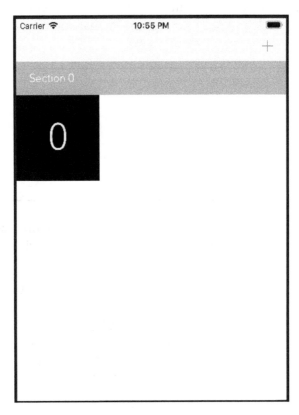

Back in Xcode, we will now add new cells when the plus barButton item is tapped. To do that, we will use the rx.tap extension of UIBarButtonItem, which works similarly to UIButtons rx.tap. We will use bind(onNext:) to do this.

We will create a random number of items for each section when it's added. To do that, we will first create a section value equal to the current count of data.value. Then, we will create an items array of String, and we will use a closure to set it. In that closure, we will create a local item's var array of String and a random number from 1 to 6, and then we will iterate through 0 to the random number, appending items with a string for each number. These will be used for the cell's titles, and we will return items as follows:

```
addBarButtonItem.rx.tap
        .bind(onNext:{ [unowned self] in
            let section = self.data.value.count
            let items: [String] = {
                var items = [String]()
```

```
                let random = Int(arc4random_uniform(6)) + 1
                (0...random).forEach {
                    items.append("\(section)-\($0)")
                }
                return items
            }()
        })
        .disposed(by: disposeBag)
```

Finally, we will set `data.value` to its current value, plus the new section and its items:

```
self.data.value += [SectionModel(
                title:"Section: \(section)",
                data: items
                )]
```

This appends the new value onto the current value and then puts that new value onto the sequence. The overall code with the addition of this line is as shown:

```
addBarButtonItem.rx.tap
        .bind(onNext:{ [unowned self] in
            let section = self.data.value.count
            let items: [String] = {
                var items = [String]()
                let random = Int(arc4random_uniform(6)) + 1
                (0...random).forEach {
                    items.append("\(section)-\($0)")
                }
                return items
            }()
            self.data.value += [SectionModel(
                title:"Section: \(section)",
                data: items
                )]
        })
        .disposed(by: disposeBag)
```

Let's run the app now to test the addition of sections. You will see something like this as soon as you tap on the plus button:

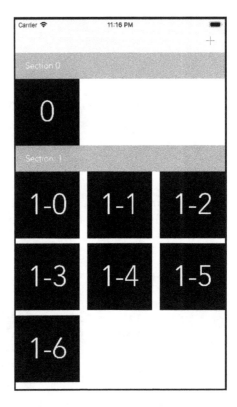

Back in Xcode, we will add one more feature to this app: the ability to move these items. For this, we will use the longPressGestureRecognizer, which is already added on collectionView. GestureRecognizers have rx.event extensions on them added by RxCocoa. We will bind nextEvents, whose elements will be instances of UILongPressGestureRecognizer. In the handler, we will switch on the state of recognizer. For .began, we will get the selected indexPath from the touch point, and we will call beginInteractiveMovementForItem() on the collectionView. For .changed, we will call updateIteractiveMovementTargetPosition() on the collectionView and for .ended, we will call endInteractiveMovement(). At the end, we will include a default to just cancel the interaction, as follows:

```
longPressGestureRecognizer.rx.event
            .bind { [unowned self] in
                switch $0.state {
                case .began:
```

```
                    guard let selectedIndexPath =
self.collectionView.indexPathForItem(at: $0.location(in:
self.collectionView)) else { break }
                    self.collectionView.beginInteractiveMovementForItem(at:
selectedIndexPath)
                case .changed:
self.collectionView.updateInteractiveMovementTargetPosition($0.location(in:
$0.view!))
                case .ended:
                    self.collectionView.endInteractiveMovement()
                default:
                    self.collectionView.cancelInteractiveMovement()
                }
            }
            .disposed(by: disposeBag)
```

Let's run the app, add some sections, and then long-press on a couple of items and move them to different sections. Pretty cool! The complete code for this ViewController is as shown:

```
import UIKit
import RxSwift
import RxDataSources
struct SectionModel {    let title: String
    var data: [String]
}
extension SectionModel : AnimatableSectionModelType{
    typealias Item = String
    typealias Identity = String
    var identity: Identity { return title }
    var items: [Item] { return data }
    init(original: SectionModel, items: [String]) {
        self = original
        data = items
    }
}
class ViewController: UIViewController {
    @IBOutlet weak var collectionView: UICollectionView!
    @IBOutlet weak var addBarButtonItem: UIBarButtonItem!
    @IBOutlet var longPressGestureRecognizer:
UILongPressGestureRecognizer!
    let disposeBag = DisposeBag()
    let dataSource =
RxCollectionViewSectionedAnimatedDataSource<SectionModel>()
    let data = Variable([
        SectionModel(title: "Section 0", data: ["0"])
        ])
```

```
        override func viewDidLoad() {
            super.viewDidLoad()
            dataSource.configureCell = { _, collectionView, indexPath, title in
                let cell =
collectionView.dequeueReusableCell(withReuseIdentifier: "Cell", for:
indexPath) as! Cell
                cell.titleLabel.text = title
                return cell
            }
            dataSource.supplementaryViewFactory = {dataSource, collectionView,
kind, indexPAth in
                let headerView =
collectionView.dequeueReusableSupplementaryView(ofKind: kind,
withReuseIdentifier: "Header", for: indexPAth) as! Header
                headerView.titleLabel.text =
dataSource.sectionModels[indexPAth.section].title
                return headerView
            }
            data.asDriver()
            .drive(collectionView.rx.items(dataSource: dataSource))
            .disposed(by: disposeBag)
            addBarButtonItem.rx.tap
                .bind(onNext:{ [unowned self] in
                    let section = self.data.value.count
                    let items: [String] = {
                        var items = [String]()
                        let random = Int(arc4random_uniform(6)) + 1
                        (0...random).forEach {
                            items.append("\(section)-\($0)")
                        }
                        return items
                    }()
                    self.data.value += [SectionModel(
                        title:"Section: \(section)",
                        data: items
                        )]
                })
            .disposed(by: disposeBag)
        }
    }
```

There's a lot more to `RxDataSources`, so we recommend reading more about it.

Summary

In this chapter, we covered some really exciting concepts related not only to `RxCocoa` and `RxSwift`, but also other community libraries. We learned about data binding to View elements and, most importantly, binding to the View elements that are used most pervasively in the Swift language, that is, `UITableViews` and `UICollectionViews`. We covered how we can bind data to these two and perform complex operations, keeping our code base tidy, readable, and concise at the same time. This chapter provided you with real-world information about how to work with `RxSwift` and `RxCocoa` code in a real-world application. We not only created a new functionality using reactive concepts but also transformed an existing application from traditional Swift to `RxSwift`. In the coming chapters, we will learn more about handling errors, work with schedulers, learn more about design patterns, and create some fantastic real-world applications.

8

RxTest and Custom Rx Extensions – Testing with Rx

Testing your code should not be cumbersome; `RxSwift` provides some really helpful libraries to streamline writing tests against your Rx code. You might even have fun while writing tests in `RxSwift`. There are two libraries in `RxSwift` that we will use while writing tests in `RxSwift`: `RxTest` and `RxBlocking`. We will cover the following topics in this chapter:

- Testing in `RxSwift`
- `RxTest`
- `RxBlocking`

Testing in RxSwift

`RxTest` and `RxBlocking` are part of the `RxSwift` repository but are made available via separate pods and hence require separate imports. `RxTest` provides useful additions for testing Rx code, including `TestScheduler`, which is a virtual time scheduler and methods for adding events at precise time intervals, whereas `RxBlocking` enables converting a regular Observable sequence to a blocking observable, which blocks the thread it's running on until the observable sequence completes or a specified timeout is reached. This makes testing asynchronous operations much easier.

RxTest

As specified earlier, RxTest is part of the same repository as RxSwift, and there is one more thing to know about RxTest before we dive into some RxTesting—RxTest exposes two types of Observable for testing purposes:

- HotObservables
- ColdObservables

HotObservables replay events at specified times using a test scheduler regardless of there being any subscribers.

ColdObservables work more like regular Observables, replaying their elements to their new subscribers upon subscription.

Testing in practice with HotObservables

We are starting off with an Xcode project with a unit test target and a single testing file. In case you are not familiar, a unit test class in iOS is a subclass of XCTestCase that provides several features, including the setUp() and tearDown() methods, that are run before every test, as shown in this code:

```
override func setUp() {
    super.setUp()
}
override func tearDown() {
}
```

We will now define scheduler and subscription properties that will be used by the tests and then, in setup, we will initialize the scheduler with an initialClock value of 0. This is the beginning of time as far as the scheduler is concerned, and once the time reaches 1000 milliseconds, we will dispose of the subscription in tearDown(), as follows:

```
var scheduler: TestScheduler!
var subscription: Disposable!
override func setUp() {
    super.setUp()
    scheduler = TestScheduler(initialClock: 0)
}
override func tearDown() {
    scheduler.scheduleAt(1000) {
        self.subscription.dispose()
    }
```

```
        super.tearDown()
    }
```

This means each test cannot take longer than one second because at that point the subscription will be disposed and doing this here avoids adding each subscription to a `disposeBag` within each test. Don't forget to add the following import statements to the file:

```
import XCTest
import RxSwift
import RxTest
import RxBlocking
```

We will begin by writing a test against the map operation. As you might be already aware, test methods must always begin with word test. We will define a local observer value of the `Int` type using the scheduler's `createObserver` operator. This observer will record received events and timestamp them. Next, we will create an Observable for this test using the scheduler's `createHotObservable()` operator. This method takes an array of recorded instances that are regular events of the specified element type. Remember that a hot observable in the context of `RxTest` plays events at absolute times, regardless of whether there are any subscribers. In this case, we will populate the array with three next events, and there is a handy next operator in `RxTest` that will create this instance for us that will take a specific time in milliseconds at which the event will be emitted along with the element value to emit in the next event. So for example, this next event will emit at 100 milliseconds with an element value of 10:

```
let observableSeq = scheduler.createHotObservable([
            next(100,10)
            ])
```

We will add a few more instances to this array to emit different values at different intervals, as follows:

```
let observableSeq = scheduler.createHotObservable([
            next(100,10),
            next(200,20),
            next(300,30)
            ])
```

Now we can move on and define the actual subject of the test. We will test that using map and multiply each element by 2 to produce the expected result. The code for the test method so far will be as follows:

```
func testMapOperator(){
        let localObserver = scheduler.createObserver(Int.self)
        let observableSeq = scheduler.createHotObservable([
            next(100,10),
            next(200,20),
            next(300,30)
            ])
        let observableForMap = observableSeq.map {$0 * 2}
    }
```

Next, we will schedule subscription into the observable at time zero using the scheduler's scheduleAt operator. We will start the scheduler and store the results. Note that RxTest makes an events property available on an observer, and we are just mapping that array of recorded to reach in and get the actual elements.

We don't normally advise that you force-unwrap anything, particularly in production code, but in the case of a test, it is acceptable because the worst that can happen is an exception and a failed test. Finally, we will use XCTAssertEqual to assert that the result is something that we expected, that is, an array of integers with values of [20, 40, 60]. So far, the overall code looks like this:

```
func testMapOperator(){
        let localObserver = scheduler.createObserver(Int.self)
        let observableSeq = scheduler.createHotObservable([
            next(100,10),
            next(200,20),
            next(300,30)
            ])
        let observableForMap = observableSeq.map {$0 * 2}
        scheduler.scheduleAt(0){
            self.subscription = observableForMap.subscribe(localObserver)
        }
        scheduler.start()
        let restultsFromMapOperation = localObserver.events.map{
            $0.value.element!
        }
            XCTAssertEqual(restultsFromMapOperation, [20,40,60])
    }
```

To run a test, you can click on the diamond icon in the gutter to run just that test or select
Product | Test from the menu to run all tests:

We will click on the diamond icon this time since we have just one test to run, and you will
note that, once the test completes processing, the diamond will become green with a check
mark indicating that the test passes, as shown:

```
     func testMapOperator(){
28       let localObserver = scheduler.createObserver(Int.self)
29       let observableSeq = scheduler.createHotObservable([
30           next(100,10),
31           next(200,20),
32           next(300,30)
33           ])
34
35       let observableForMap = observableSeq.map {$0 * 2}
36       scheduler.scheduleAt(0){
37           self.subscription = observableForMap.subscribe(localObserver)
38       }
39       scheduler.start()
```

To see what happens when it fails, we will change the array in assertion to `[10, 20, 30 ]`
and run the test again.

You will note that the test fails, and this time the diamond will become red with an X, and the assertion also prints an error, as illustrated:

```
    func testMapOperator(){
28      let localObserver = scheduler.createObserver(Int.self)
29      let observableSeq = scheduler.createHotObservable([
30          next(100,10),
31          next(200,20),
32          next(300,30)
33          ])
34
35      let observableForMap = observableSeq.map {$0 * 2}
36      scheduler.scheduleAt(0){
37          self.subscription = observableForMap.subscribe(localObserver)
38      }
39      scheduler.start()
40
41      let restultsFromMapOperation = localObserver.events.map{
42          $0.value.element!
43      }
44
45      XCTAssertEqual(restultsFromMapOperation, [10,20,30])  ◇ XCTAssertEqual failed: ("[20, 40, 60]") is not equal to ("[10, 20, 30]") -
46  }
```

You can also check the console for the reason. In our case, the console will print the following information:

XCTAssertEqual failed: ("[20, 40, 60]") is not equal to ("[10, 20, 30]")

We will undo this change and rerun the test so that it passes once again and the diamond becomes green with a check mark.

Testing in RxTest with ColdObservables

To show an example of working with a `ColdObservable` in `RxTest`, we will duplicate the previous example and change the name.

A `ColdObservable` in `RxTest` will only emit when there is a subscriber, and it will emit all its events to each subscriber on subscription. We will create two subscriptions in this example, so rather than using the subscription's `dispose()` property, we will use `disposeBag` this time. We will need two observers for this example, so we will duplicate the single one and then rename them as follows:

```
let disposeBag = DisposeBag()
let firstObserver = scheduler.createObserver(Int.self)
let secondObserver = scheduler.createObserver(Int.self)
```

Also, we will need two map `Observables` to test that each one gets all three events, so we will duplicate the original one, rename them, and change the operation so that we can distinguish them later. We will change the second one to multiply by four instead of two, as follows:

```
let firstObservableForMap = observableSeq.map {$0 * 2}
let secondObservableForMap = observableSeq.map {$0 * 4}
```

We will subscribe to the first Observable at time zero and add it to the `disposeBag` instead of assigning it to the subscription property; then we will duplicate that to subscribe to the second observable at time 150. As we used a cold observable, it should not matter when we scheduled subscription. Each subscriber should receive all the events. That's the basis of this test. We will leave the line that starts the scheduler as-is, and then we will modify the results definition to first store the first observer's events, assign the result to a variable so that we can modify it later, and then append that array with the second observer's events. Finally, we will change the assertion for the new expected results, that is, that the second map operation's results will be the original observable's values times three, appending on to the first map operator's results that are the same as earlier. Let's change the assertion to match the expected result, as follows:

```
func testMapOperatorCold(){
        let disposeBag = DisposeBag()
        let firstObserver = scheduler.createObserver(Int.self)
        let secondObserver = scheduler.createObserver(Int.self)
        let observableSeq = scheduler.createColdObservable([
            next(100,10),
            next(200,20),
            next(300,30)
            ])
        let firstObservableForMap = observableSeq.map {$0 * 2}
        let secondObservableForMap = observableSeq.map {$0 * 4}
        scheduler.scheduleAt(0){
            firstObservableForMap.subscribe(firstObserver).disposed(by:
                                                            disposeBag)
        }
        scheduler.scheduleAt(150){
            secondObservableForMap.subscribe(secondObserver).disposed(by:
                                                            disposeBag)
        }
        scheduler.start()
        var restultsFromMapOperation = firstObserver.events.map{
            $0.value.element!
        }
        _ = secondObserver.events.map{
            restultsFromMapOperation.append($0.value.element!)
```

```
        }
        XCTAssertEqual(restultsFromMapOperation, [20, 40, 60, 40, 80, 120])
    }
```

Finally, let's run the test, and you will see that the diamond next to the function name in the gutter turns green with a check mark.

Let's add a `testMapHot` test that follows the same logic as `testMapCold`, except that it uses a `HotObservable`. You can try to implement it on your own, before going on to read the implementation and match your implementation later.

Okay, let's proceed with the implementation. The solution is very simple—we just need to replace `createColdObservable` with `createHotObservable`, as follows:

```
    func testMapOperatorHot() {
        let disposeBag = DisposeBag()
        let firstObserver = scheduler.createObserver(Int.self)
        let secondObserver = scheduler.createObserver(Int.self)
        let observableSeq = scheduler.createHotObservable([
            next(100,10),
            next(200,20),
            next(300,30)
            ])
        let firstObservableForMap = observableSeq.map {$0 * 2}
        let secondObservableForMap = observableSeq.map {$0 * 4}
        scheduler.scheduleAt(0) {
            firstObservableForMap.subscribe(firstObserver).disposed(by:
                                                    disposeBag)
        }
        scheduler.scheduleAt(150) {
            secondObservableForMap.subscribe(secondObserver).disposed(by:
                                                    disposeBag)
        }
        scheduler.start()
        var restultsFromMapOperation = firstObserver.events.map{
            $0.value.element!
        }
        _ = secondObserver.events.map{
            restultsFromMapOperation.append($0.value.element!)
        }
        XCTAssertEqual(restultsFromMapOperation, [20, 40, 60, 80, 120])
    }
```

Since we used a `HotObservable`, this time the second observer will not get the first event at 100, because it didn't subscribe until after it was emitted at 150. So the expected results are [20, 40, 60, 80, 120].

Run the test once again with the expected output in the assert, and you will see the test pass.

In the next section, we will take a look at RxBlocking, which essentially turns an asynchronous operation into a synchronous one in order to test it more easily.

RxBlocking

If you are familiar with expectations in XCTest, you will know that it's another way to test asynchronous operations. Using RxBlocking just happens to be way easier. Let's start with a small implementation and see how to take advantage of this library while testing asynchronous operations.

Testing with RxBlocking

We will start a new test and create an Observable of 10, 20, and 30, as follows:

```
func testBlocking(){
        let observableToTest = Observable.of(10, 20, 30)
    }
```

Now we will define the result as equal to calling toBlocking() on the observable we created:

```
let result = observableToTest.toBlocking()
```

toBlocking() returns a blocking Observable to a straight array, as you can see here:

We will need to use the first method if we want to interrogate which is a throwing method, so we will wrap it in a do catch statement, and then we will add an `AssertEquals` statement if it is successful, as follows:

```
func testBlocking(){
        let observableToTest = Observable.of(10, 20, 30)
        do{
            let result = try observableToTest.toBlocking().first()
            XCTAssertEqual(result, 10)
        } catch {
        }
    }
```

Alternatively, an Assert fails if it's not this:

```
        do{
            let result = try observableToTest.toBlocking().first()
            XCTAssertEqual(result, 10)
        } catch {
            XCTFail(error.localizedDescription)
        }
```

That's it! Let's run the test, and you will see that the test passes. We can simplify this test with just two lines of code by forcing the try. Again, this is more acceptable on test than production code. We will comment out the do catch statement and then write the assert equals in a single line, as follows:

```
    XCTAssertEqual(try! observableToTest.toBlocking().first(), 10)
```

Rerun the test, and you will see that the test passes once again. The overall code with commented code looks like this:

```
func testBlocking(){
        let observableToTest = Observable.of(10, 20, 30)
//        do{
//            let result = try observableToTest.toBlocking().first()
//            XCTAssertEqual(result, 10)
//        } catch {
//            XCTFail(error.localizedDescription)
//        }
        XCTAssertEqual(try! observableToTest.toBlocking().first(), 10)
    }
```

How's that for succinct. Truth be told, that Observable sequence is actually synchronous already if we printed emitted elements in a subscription to it followed by a marker. The marker will be printed after the subscription's completed event.

To test an actual asynchronous operation, we will write one more test. This time, we will use a concurrent scheduler on a background thread, as follows:

```
func testAsynchronousToArry(){
        let scheduler = ConcurrentDispatchQueueScheduler(qos: .background)
    }
```

Now, we will create an Observable of the simple sequence of integers. We will use `map` to double each value, as follows:

```
let intObservbale = Observable.of(10, 20, 30)
            .map{ $0 * 2 }
```

Then, we will subscribe on the scheduler:

```
let intObservbale = Observable.of(10, 20, 30)
            .map{ $0 * 2 }
            .subscribeOn(scheduler)
```

In upcoming chapters, we will learn that it does not matter where we call `subscribeOn`. Doing so will move the entire subscription onto that `scheduler`. We will also create a subscription to print out each element as it is emitted followed by a marker; this is just to prove the asynchronous nature of this operation:

```
subscription = intObservbale.subscribe{ print($0) }
```

Now we will write a `do catch` statement that is similar to the last test calls `toBlocking` on the Observable, which should be observed on the main scheduler, as follows:

```
do{
    let result = try
intObservbale.observeOn(MainScheduler.instance).toBlocking().toArray()
    } catch {
}
```

Then, we will add the same assertions as the previous example:

```
do{
    let result = try
intObservbale.observeOn(MainScheduler.instance).toBlocking().toArray()
            XCTAssertEqual(result, [20, 40, 60])
        } catch {
            XCTFail(error.localizedDescription)
        }
```

Now we will run the test, and you will note that it passes with the green check mark in the gutter.

Note that the marker was printed before the emitted elements in the console, as shown:

```
next(20)
next(40)
next(60)
completed
Test Case '-[TestingTests.TestingTests testAsynchronousToArry]' passed (0.359 seconds).
```

This was because these operations were executed asynchronously.

Summary

RxTest, RxBlocking, and other related libraries provide amazingly streamlined testing of operations in RxSwift. In this chapter, we covered some basic examples of how to write unit tests in RxSwift using these two libraries. You might have noted the ease with which you can test the code and also how and why you can skip checking the options before making use of them in your unit tests. These tests are part of your code to ensure that the app behaves as per expectations and does not break in production. For those who prefer test-driven development, this chapter has laid down the foundation on which you can build amazing test targets. In upcoming chapters, we will cover how to write networking code in RxSwift and how to test the request and response by making use of these testing libraries.

9
Testing Your RxCode – Testing Asynchronous Code

So far, we have have covered some operators that enable you, as a developer, to write unit tests and make your code more robust, but writing test cases may provide other benefits as well. For instance, writing test cases will make your concepts more clear. It might seem a bit like working in a lab where you state your expectations inside a test and then run your code to either meet or fail the expectations; this gives you more of a sense of how things are actually working under the hood.

You can play with your code, break it as many times as you want, and then refurbish it to achieve the desired result and finally, using tests, you can ensure that your work will achieve what you expected it to achieve. In this chapter, we will extend testing to the next level and work through some other aspects of problem finding as well. We will cover the following topics in this chapter:

- Using debug for debugging
- Using total for debugging
- Testing asynchronous code

Tracking down issues – Debugging Rx code

In addition to using traditional debugging techniques, `RxSwift` also provides a couple of useful utilities to debug Observable sequences. To demonstrate this, we have created a starter project and initialized a helper class to declare the following two methods, as follows:

```
public func exampleOf(description: String, actionToPerform: () -> Void) {
    print(" ===> Example of:", description, "===>")
    actionToPerform()
}
public func delayInExecution(_ delayInterval: TimeInterval,
actionToPerform: @escaping () -> Void) {
    DispatchQueue.main.asyncAfter(deadline: .now() + delayInterval) {
        actionToPerform()
    }
}
```

The `delayInExecution()` wraps a `DispatchQueue` to execute an action asynchronously after a delay. As we are working with asynchronous code, we have also imported `PlaygroundSupport` and set `needsIndefiniteExecution` to true, as follows:

```
import PlaygroundSupport
PlaygroundPage.current.needsIndefiniteExecution = true
```

We will start by introducing a new type of Observable sequence and a new operator.

We will create a function for this example; in the function, we will create an interval sequence. Interval will create an Observable sequence that emits a new element indefinitely after the specified period has elapsed (one second in this example). So far, the implementation of the function is as follows:

```
func exampleWithPulish(){
    let intervalSeq = Observable<Int>.interval(1, scheduler:
MainScheduler.instance)
}
```

We will call publish on this sequence, which will convert the internal sequence into a connectable Observable. A connectable Observable will wait until connect is called on it before it begins emitting. Then, we will create a subscription to interval and print out emitted events, as shown:

```
let intervalSeq = Observable<Int>.interval(1, scheduler:
MainScheduler.instance)
    .publish()
```

```
intervalSeq
    .subscribe { print ($0) }
```

This example is wrapped in a function. So, we will call the function to execute the example, as shown:

```
7   func exampleWithPulish(){
8       let intervalSeq = Observable<Int>.interval(1, scheduler:
            MainScheduler.instance)
9           .publish()
10
11      intervalSeq
12          .subscribe { print($0) }
13  }
14
15  exampleWithPulish()|
```

As you can see, nothing happens. This is because it is a connectable Observable, and we haven't called connect on it yet. We will use the `delayInExecution()` helper function to call connect on the `intervalSeq` after a 2-second delay. We are explicitly ignoring the disposable return from connect because we don't want to add it to a `disposeBag` in this case, or else it will be disposed of when the program flow exits the function. Now, the `intervalSeq` Observable will start emitting next events after a couple of seconds. So far, the code is this:

```
intervalSeq
        .subscribe { print ($0) }
    delayInExecution(2) {
        _ = intervalSeq.connect()
    }
```

Also, you will note the following output in the console:

```
7   func exampleWithPulish(){
8       let intervalSeq = Observable<Int>.interval(1, scheduler:        RxSwift.(ConnectableObser...
            MainScheduler.instance)
9       .publish()
10
11      intervalSeq                                                     RxSwift.SubscriptionDispos...
12          .subscribe { print($0) }                                    (7 times)
13
14      delayInExecution(2) {
15          _ = intervalSeq.connect()                                   ()
16      }
17  }
```

```
next(0)
next(1)
next(2)
next(3)
next(4)
next(5)
next(6)
```

We will comment out the function to stop running this example, and we will add another subscription to interval, this time after a 4-second delay. Once again, ignore the returned disposable, as follows:

```
delayInExecution(2) {
        _ = intervalSeq.connect()
    }
    delayInExecution(4) {
        _ = intervalSeq
            .subscribe { print($0) }
    }
```

We have already called `connect()` on the Observable, so this new subscription will begin emitting after a 4-second delay, that is, 2 seconds after `connect()` is called, which is delayed by 2 seconds. Let's uncomment the function call and look at the result:

```
11      intervalSeq
12          .subscribe { print($0) }
13
14      delayInExecution(2) {
15          _ = intervalSeq.connect()
16      }
17
18      delayInExecution(4) {
19          _ = intervalSeq
20              .subscribe { print($0) }
21      }
22  }
23
24  exampleWithPulish()
25
```

```
next(0)
next(1)
next(1)
next(2)
next(2)
next(3)
next(3)
next(4)
next(4)
next(5)
next(5)
next(6)
next(6)
```

We can see both subscriptions printing emissions from the same Observable sequence. This simple example demonstrates that, once you get into multiple subscriptions on a single Observable, determining what's going on can be a bit more challenging. We can see two next events with the same elements after the first emission, which makes sense because the first is delayed before `connect()` is called. However, the second starts its countdown right away, so it begins emitting two seconds after the first. If we need to determine which of these printed events is associated to which subscription, we can use unique strings for each print statement. However, there is a better way.

Debugging with debug

We will comment out the function call again to stop running this example. The debug operator will print out details about every event. We will just add it to the initial subscription, as follows:

```
func exampleWithPulish(){
    let intervalSeq = Observable<Int>.interval(1, scheduler:
MainScheduler.instance)
    .publish()
    intervalSeq
        .debug()
        .subscribe { print($0) }
    delayInExecution(2) {
        _ = intervalSeq.connect()
    }
    delayInExecution(4) {
        _ = intervalSeq
            .subscribe { print($0) }
    }
}
exampleWithPulish()
```

Next, we will uncomment the function call and let the playground run this example. As you can see in the console logs, you will see much more information this time, as illustrated:

```
11      intervalSeq                                          RxSwift.(SinkDisposer in _B.
12         .debug()
13         .subscribe { print($0) }                          (7 times)
14
15      delayInExecution(2) {
16         _ = intervalSeq.connect()                          ()
17      }
18
19      delayInExecution(4) {
20         _ = intervalSeq                                    ()
21            .subscribe { print($0) }                        (6 times)
22      }
23  }
24
25  exampleWithPulish()
```

```
2018-01-16 23:18:23.221: RxSwift_Chapter9.playground:12 (exampleWithPulish()) -> subscribed
2018-01-16 23:18:26.416: RxSwift_Chapter9.playground:12 (exampleWithPulish()) -> Event next(0)
next(0)
2018-01-16 23:18:27.416: RxSwift_Chapter9.playground:12 (exampleWithPulish()) -> Event next(1)
next(1)
next(1)
2018-01-16 23:18:28.416: RxSwift_Chapter9.playground:12 (exampleWithPulish()) -> Event next(2)
next(2)
next(2)
2018-01-16 23:18:29.416: RxSwift_Chapter9.playground:12 (exampleWithPulish()) -> Event next(3)
next(3)
next(3)
2018-01-16 23:18:30.416: RxSwift_Chapter9.playground:12 (exampleWithPulish()) -> Event next(4)
next(4)
next(4)
2018-01-16 23:18:31.416: RxSwift_Chapter9.playground:12 (exampleWithPulish()) -> Event next(5)
next(5)
next(5)
2018-01-16 23:18:32.416: RxSwift_Chapter9.playground:12 (exampleWithPulish()) -> Event next(6)
next(6)
next(6)
```

Note that it prints the subscription and then each event that it receives. Debug can optionally take a message to print out, so we will indicate that this is the first subscription, as follows:

```
intervalSeq
        .debug("First")
        .subscribe { print($0) }
```

If you check the console now, you will note that it is a bit easier to follow. Let's do the same for the second subscription:

```
delayInExecution(4) {
        _ = intervalSeq
```

```
        .debug("Second")
        .subscribe { print($0) }
}
```

Note the console logs, as shown:

```
11      intervalSeq                                    RxSwift.(SinkDisposer in _B.
12          .debug("First")
13          .subscribe { print($0) }                   (4 times)
14
15      delayInExecution(2) {
16          _ = intervalSeq.connect()                  ()
17      }
18
19      delayInExecution(4) {
20          _ = intervalSeq                            ()
21              .debug("Second")
22              .subscribe { print($0) }               (3 times)
23      }
24  }
25
26  exampleWithPulish()
27
```

```
2018-01-16 23:26:07.882: First -> subscribed
2018-01-16 23:26:10.890: First -> Event next(0)
next(0)
2018-01-16 23:26:11.888: Second -> subscribed
2018-01-16 23:26:11.889: First -> Event next(1)
next(1)
2018-01-16 23:26:11.889: Second -> Event next(1)
next(1)
2018-01-16 23:26:12.889: First -> Event next(2)
next(2)
2018-01-16 23:26:12.890: Second -> Event next(2)
next(2)
2018-01-16 23:26:13.889: First -> Event next(3)
next(3)
2018-01-16 23:26:13.890: Second -> Event next(3)
next(3)
```

You will note that it is really easy to follow which event is from which subscription. Actually, we don't even need to print out events in the handlers, so we will just make both the handlers empty, as follows:

```
intervalSeq
        .debug("First")
        .subscribe { _ in }
    delayInExecution(2) {
        _ = intervalSeq.connect()
    }
    delayInExecution(4) {
        _ = intervalSeq
            .debug("Second")
            .subscribe { _ in }
    }
```

Then, you will note that the console logs are much better than the previous case as well. So, let's say that we call dispose on the second subscription, not realizing what effect that will have:

```
delayInExecution(4) {
        intervalSeq
            .debug("Second")
            .subscribe { _ in }
            .dispose()
    }
```

Note the console logs, as in the following screenshot:

```
11          intervalSeq
12              .debug("First")
13              .subscribe { _ in }
14
15          delayInExecution(2) {
16              _ = intervalSeq.connect()
17          }
18
19          delayInExecution(4) {
20              intervalSeq
21                  .debug("Second")
22                  .subscribe { _ in }
23                  .dispose()
24          }
25      }
26
27  exampleWithPulish()
```

```
2018-01-16 23:32:31.592: First -> subscribed
2018-01-16 23:32:34.778: First -> Event next(0)
2018-01-16 23:32:35.715: Second -> subscribed
2018-01-16 23:32:35.715: Second -> isDisposed
2018-01-16 23:32:35.778: First -> Event next(1)
2018-01-16 23:32:36.778: First -> Event next(2)
2018-01-16 23:32:37.778: First -> Event next(3)
2018-01-16 23:32:38.778: First -> Event next(4)
2018-01-16 23:32:39.778: First -> Event next(5)
2018-01-16 23:32:40.778: First -> Event next(6)
2018-01-16 23:32:41.778: First -> Event next(7)
2018-01-16 23:32:42.778: First -> Event next(8)
```

You can see that our second subscription is disposed of right away.

There is another useful utility to keep track of things in iOS. Let's cover that in the next section.

Debugging with total

RxSwift includes another utility operator that counts all Observable allocations, called total. This is not enabled by default. To enable it, the trace resources flag needs to be added to the RxSwift target. The most reliable way to do this with CocoaPods is to set this flag to the debug configuration in the pod file's post install hook. Check the pod file of the starter project for this section, and you will note the install hook, as follows:

```
post_install do |installer|
    installer.pods_project.targets.each do |target|
        target.build_configurations.each do |config|
            config.build_settings['CONFIGURATION_BUILD_DIR'] = '$
                                   PODS_CONFIGURATION_BUILD_DIR'
            if config.name == 'Debug'
                config.build_settings['OTHER_SWIFT_FLAGS'] ||= ['-D',
                                      'TRACE_RESOURCES']
            end
        end
    end
end
```

Returning to the playground, we will begin by printing out the total property as shown:

```
print(RxSwift.Resources.total)
```

Note that total is a type method on resources and in this case, the total is zero. Now we will create a dispose bag instance and print the total again using the previous print statement, and you will see in the console logs that the total is 2 this time. You might ask: **Why is it 2 this time?**

The answer to that question is in the implementation details. We can just accept this by creating a disposeBag that increments the total by 2, but let's delve more deeper to answer the question. *command* and click on DisposeBag() to go to its definition. You will see that DisposeBag inherits from DisposeBase. *command* and click on DisposeBase and you will see that it increments the total in its init. However, back in the DisposeBag definition, you will note that DisposeBag has a private var_lock that is an instance of SpinLock(). Let's *command* and click into SpinLock() and see that it is an alias for RecursiveLock. Also, *command* and clicking into RecursiveLock shows that even RecursiveLock increments the total.

Back to the playground; `Resources.total` only tracks Rx allocations. For example, consider that we create an instance of `NSObject` before the dispose bag, as follows:

```
exampleOf(description: "total") {
    print(RxSwift.Resources.total)
    let object = NSObject()
    let disposeBag = DisposeBag()
    print(RxSwift.Resources.total)
}
```

The total is still 2, but now we will create an Observable sequence of string and print the total again, as shown:

```
print(RxSwift.Resources.total)
    let stringSequence = Observable.just("I am a string")
    print(RxSwift.Resources.total)
```

Then, you will see that the total is now 3, as shown in the following screenshot:

```
4    exampleOf(description: "total") {
5        print(RxSwift.Resources.total)
6
7        let object = NSObject()
8        var disposeBag = DisposeBag()
9        print(RxSwift.Resources.total)
10
11       let stringSequence = Observable.just("I am a string")
12       print(RxSwift.Resources.total)
```

```
===> Example of: total ===>
0
2
3
```

Then, we will subscribe to the Observable and print total in the handler, as follows:

```
stringSequence
        .subscribe(onNext: { _ in
            print(RxSwift.Resources.total)
        })
        .disposed(by: disposeBag)
```

Also, you will note that the total will now be 4, as illustrated:

```
10
11          let stringSequence = Observable.just("I am a string")
12          print(RxSwift.Resources.total)
13
14          stringSequence
15              .subscribe(onNext: { _ in
16                  print(RxSwift.Resources.total)
17              })
18              .disposed(by: disposeBag)

===> Example of: total ===>
0
2
3
4
```

Let's print total again after the subscription too and note in the console logs that the total is still 4, because the subscription is still allocated. So we will set the `disposeBag` to a new instance of `DisposeBag()` before the print statement that will call for disposal of all its contents. We will also need to make `disposeBag` a variable so that it can be changed, as follows:

```
let object = NSObject()
    var disposeBag = DisposeBag()
    print(RxSwift.Resources.total)
    let stringSequence = Observable.just("I am a string")
    print(RxSwift.Resources.total)
    stringSequence
        .subscribe(onNext: { _ in
            print(RxSwift.Resources.total)
        })
        .disposed(by: disposeBag)
    disposeBag = DisposeBag()
    print(RxSwift.Resources.total)
```

You will then note that the total has now decremented by 1 for the subscription that was disposed.

We will print the total once more after the example block, as follows:

```
exampleOf(description: "total") {
    print(RxSwift.Resources.total)
    let object = NSObject()
    var disposeBag = DisposeBag()
    print(RxSwift.Resources.total)
    let stringSequence = Observable.just("I am a string")
    print(RxSwift.Resources.total)
    stringSequence
        .subscribe(onNext: { _ in
            print(RxSwift.Resources.total)
        })
        .disposed(by: disposeBag)
    disposeBag = DisposeBag()
>   print(RxSwift.Resources.total)
}
print(RxSwift.Resources.total)
```

Now, you will see that it has returned to zero, as shown:

```
11        let stringSequence = Observable.just("I am a string")
12        print(RxSwift.Resources.total)
13
14        stringSequence
15            .subscribe(onNext: { _ in
16                print(RxSwift.Resources.total)
17            })
18            .disposed(by: disposeBag)
19
20        disposeBag = DisposeBag()
21        print(RxSwift.Resources.total)
22   }
23   print(RxSwift.Resources.total)
24

===> Example of: total ===>
0
2
3
4
3
0
```

Using total, and the debug operator that we covered in the last section, will help you resolve any issues you encounter in your `RxSwift` world.

Testing asynchronous code

Let's make use of a real-world example to start with—suppose you are driving down from location A to location B and along the way you want to track only the traffic lights and nothing else that is on the road; that is, you want to ignore any tolls or check posts, and so on, and focus only on the traffic lights. In other words, you want to filter out traffic lights from all the other things that you might encounter during your journey.

So how will we filter them out? The first concept that might come to your mind will be streams, since that's the concept that underpins Rx, and the second will be subscriptions. So, if you subscribe to those streams, you will be able to filter out those events. If you don't subscribe to those streams and those events happen, then they are gone. Gone forever!

So, in our case, the visualization will look like this:

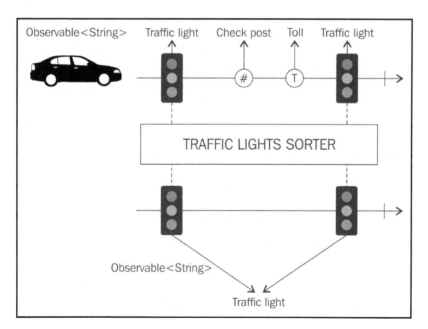

The traffic light sorter will filter out anything that is not a traffic light, and here's the first bit of the code:

```
import RxSwift
struct TrafficLightsSorter {
        let trafficLightStream: Observable<String>
        init(trafficStream: Observable<String>) {
        // Do something to filter out non traffic lights
        }
}
```

The struct is initialized with `trafficStream`, that is, the stream of events comes on the road and a `trafficLightStream` property, that is, the stream of filtered traffic lights.

Next, we will see how to approach writing tests for such a scenario. We will start our test as follows:

```
func testCanSortTrafficLightsFromTrafficStream(){
        let disposeBag = DisposeBag()
        let scheduler = TestScheduler(initialClock: 0)
        let testObserver = scheduler.createObserver(String)
}
```

Test scheduler helps us send events one at a time, so we can expect a stream of events lined one after the other. This is very important when it comes to testing Rx code because Rx sends events through at a particular time; thus in this example, we have `testScheduler` sending through subjects. In our second part, we have our testful observer. The testful observer notes down everything that goes through the observer that you are looking at, so it notes events and the times at which the events happened. Hence, we can use this to compare our expectations to the final results. So when we are testing, we put in a set of test inputs and then we compare that to the outputs we get. Let's take a look at the following piece of code and try to understand what it's trying to achieve:

```
func testCanSortTrafficLightsFromTrafficPosts(){
        private let disposeBag = DisposeBag()
        let scheduler = TestScheduler(initialClock: 0)
        let testObserver = scheduler.createObserver(String)
        //Given
        let testInput = ["lights", "post", "lights", "lights", "post"]
        let observableInput = testInput.toObservable(scheduler)
        let trafficLightsSorter = TrafficLightsSorter(trafficStream:
                                                        testInput)
        //When
        //Then
}
```

You can see that our `testScheduler` is starting at `initialClock` zero, which is the concept of test time. In `RxTest`, the time at which things happen is fake; it just happens as defined at regular intervals. This is great, since it means that our tests don't have to do real time. Hence, if you are testing that your stream will receive data over 20 minutes, you don't have to wait for 20 minutes while testing the code. In the example, we declared our `testInput`, which is an array, and then we turned that array into a stream of observable events. That stream of events is then passed on to scheduler, which will in turn spit out those events one by one over the period of the test. We then create our `trafficLightsSorter`, which is our subject under test, and in that input we pass in the `testInput`.

Next, we subscribe our `testObserver`, which is the spy to the `trafficStream` of `trafficLightsSorter`, which in turn is the result of the operation that we are doing as follows:

```
func testCanSortTrafficLightsFromTrafficPosts(){
        private let disposeBag = DisposeBag()
        let scheduler = TestScheduler(initialClock: 0)
        let testObserver = scheduler.createObserver(String)
        //Given
        let testInput = ["lights", "post", "lights", "lights", "post"]
        let observableInput = testInput.toObservable(scheduler)
        let trafficLightsSorter = TrafficLightsSorter(trafficStream:
                                                        testInput)

        //When
        trafficLightsSorter.trafficLightsStream
                .subscribe(testObserver)
                .addDisposableTo(disposeBag)
        scheduler.start()
        //Then
    }
```

As a final step, we start our scheduler as follows:

```
func testCanSortTrafficLightsFromTrafficPosts(){
        private let disposeBag = DisposeBag()
        let scheduler = TestScheduler(initialClock: 0)
        let testObserver = scheduler.createObserver(String)
        //Given
        let testInput = ["lights", "post", "lights", "lights", "post"]
        let observableInput = testInput.toObservable(scheduler)
        let trafficLightsSorter = TrafficLightsSorter(trafficStream:
                                                        testInput)

        //When
        trafficLightsSorter.trafficLightsStream
```

```
        .subscribe(testObserver)
        .addDisposableTo(disposeBag)
scheduler.start()
//Then
let expectedEvents = [
                        next(1, "lights"),
                        next(3, "lights"),
                        next(4, "lights"),
                        completed(8)
                      ]
XCTAssertEqual(expectedEvents, testObserver.events)
}
```

Finally, we declare the expectation and that's it! We compare our expectation to the result of the operation.

Summary

Often while writing complex programs, developers end up in situations that don't seem to work according to the logic they conceived while writing that piece of code at first. This is when debugging comes into the picture, trying to break the complex logic into smaller functionalities and then understand individual pieces.

In this chapter, we learned about debugging operators and then covered testing asynchronous code. Since you will be writing a lot of networking code for your real-world applications, this chapter laid down the foundation for making your networking code more robust.

10
Schedule Your Tasks, Don't Queue!

As we already covered in the previous chapters, an Observable and the operators that we use on it will execute and notify the observer on the same thread on which the `subscribe` operator is used. So far, we have done a lot of work on the main thread. Schedulers are an abstraction that lets us specify distinct queues on which to perform the work. It is always a good idea to move intensive work off the main thread to keep the app responsive for users. Schedulers make it easy to do this.

Scheduler can be serial or concurrent. We use serial schedulers if we want to ensure that the work is carried out on that queue in the order in which it was added to the queue. Otherwise, we can just use a concurrent queue. In this chapter, we will learn about the following topics:

- Queues and schedulers
- Scheduler Singletons
- `ConcurrentDispatchQueueScheduler`
- `SerialDispatchQueueScheduler`
- `OperationQueueScheduler`

Queues and schedulers

There are built-in scheduler types that work with **Grand Central Dispatch (GCD)** queues and NSOperationQueues, including SerialDispatchQueueScheduler, which can dispatch work on a specified serial dispatch queue; ConcurrentDispatchQueueScheduler, which will dispatch on a concurrent dispatch queue; and OperationQueueScheduler, which will perform the work on a specified NSOperationQueues.

We can also specify our own custom schedulers by conforming to the immediateScheduler protocol.

Scheduler Singletons

There are a couple of Singleton schedulers that we can use for some common needs such as the following:

- CurrentThreadScheduler
- MainScheduler

CurrentThreadScheduler represents the current thread and is the default scheduler. The MainScheduler, on the other hand, represents the main thread and is typically used for all UI-related work.

Specifying a scheduler

To specify a scheduler on which a subscription is created, handler-executed, and disposed of, we use the subscribeOn operator. This is not normally used; instead, we just use ObserverOn, which specifies the scheduler events: next, error, and completed. The important thing to remember is that subscribeOn will direct which scheduler a subscription operates, whereas ObserveOn will only direct which scheduler to use after or below where ObserveOn is used in a chain. Let's look at this in a marble diagram first and then jump into a code example in the coming section.

We are starting on in the main thread, which is represented by the timeline here:

We will call ObserverOn and specify scheduler1, as shown:

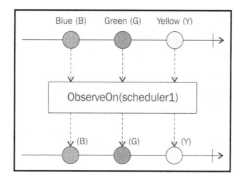

Imagine that we will do some intensive work here, so we are specifying the background queue to receive the events on for a map operation, as follows:

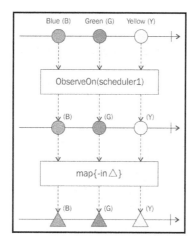

Finally, we will call `subscribeOn` and specify `scheduler2`. We specified where we want subscriptions to be created, where the handlers are executed, and where they will be disposed of. This is not normally necessary; we are just demonstrating how it works:

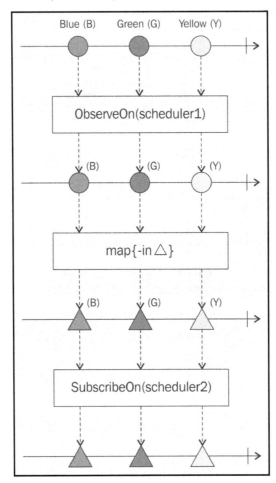

Using the `subscribeOn` operator here will direct subscriptions for the entire chain. That means we will no longer be on the main thread initially:

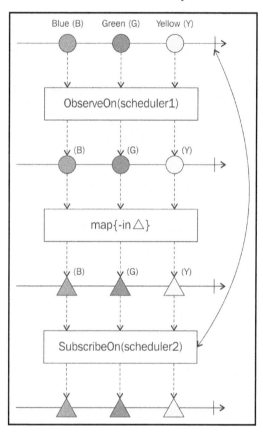

It will be on the queue, as shown in the preceding diagram by `scheduler2`. We are still observing on `scheduler1`; nothing has changed there, and finally we will use `ObserveOn` again to receive the transformed elements from the map operation back on the main thread, as illustrated:

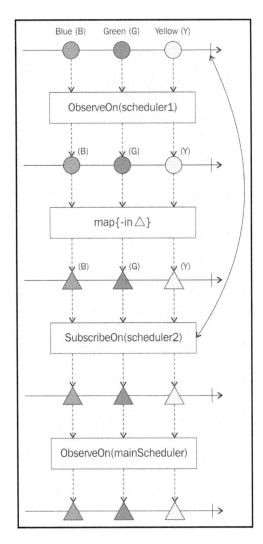

Schedulers in practice

Let's now work with a code example to see schedulers in action. We will start out in a playground in which we will import `PlaygroundSupport` and set `needsIndefiniteExecution` to true, because we will write concurrent code. We have also added two images to the `resources` folder for the playground page.

We have displayed the assistant editor, which you can enable by navigating to **View** | **Assistant Editor** | **Show Assistant Editor**, as shown in the following screenshot:

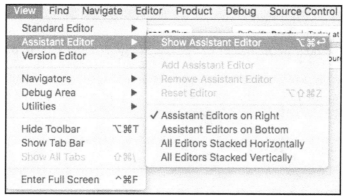

If you look at the setup project, you will note that we have some setup code in the playground:

```
import PlaygroundSupport
PlaygroundPage.current.needsIndefiniteExecution = true
import RxSwift
let imageView = UIImageView(
    frame: CGRect(
        x: 0,
        y: 0,
        width: 128,
        height: 128
    )
)
PlaygroundPage.current.liveView = imageView
```

This code creates an `imageView` and then sets it to be the live view for the playground page. We have also created image data for the Swift and Rx images that we added to the `resources` folder as follows:

```
let swift = UIImage(named: "Swift")!
let swiftImageData = UIImagePNGRepresentation(swift)!
let rx = UIImage(named: "Rx")!
let rxImageData = UIImagePNGRepresentation(rx)!
let disposeBag = DisposeBag()
```

Imagine that this image data was retrieved via a `URLSessionRequest`, and you can see that we have added a `disposeBag` as well.

We will demonstrate how to push the work of creating `UIImages` from data onto a background thread.

 Just a side note: If this data were coming from a `URLSession` request, it would already be on a background queue.

ConcurrentDispatchQueueScheduler

In this example, we are starting out on the main thread. First, we will create an `imageData` `PublishSubject` of type data. We will be adding the Swift and Rx image data values onto this sequence later on. Next, we will create a `concurrentScheduler` by making use of the `ConcurrentDispatchQueueScheduler` convenience initializer, which takes a **Quality of Service (QoS)** enum and sets that to the background, as follows:

```
let imageData = PublishSubject<Data>()
let concurrentScheduler = ConcurrentDispatchQueueScheduler(qos:
.background)
```

Now we will use `ObserveOn` to indicate that we want events received from the sequence on the `concurrentScheduler` we created, and we will use map to transform that data into a `UIImage` instance, as follows:

```
imageData
    .observeOn(concurrentScheduler)
    .map { UIImage(data: $0) }
```

By doing this work on a background queue, we are ensuring peak performance on the main thread. However, once we have a UIImage, we need to go back to the main thread in order to display it, so we will use ObserveOn again, this time passing in the MainScheduler Singleton instance. Then, we will subscribe(onNext) to set the image on the imageView, and finally we will add the subscription to the disposeBag, as shown:

```
imageData
    .observeOn(concurrentScheduler)
    .map { UIImage(data: $0) }
    .observeOn(MainScheduler.instance)
    .subscribe(onNext: {
        imageView.image = $0
    })
    .disposed(by: disposeBag)
```

Although we are observing on the main thread here, we do want to mention that disposeBag is thread-safe. If we were creating a subscription on a different thread, it would be okay to add that subscription to this disposeBag. Now we will add the Swift imageData to the imageData sequence:

```
imageData.onNext(swiftImageData)
```

Now, observe that the imageView displays the Swift image as shown here:

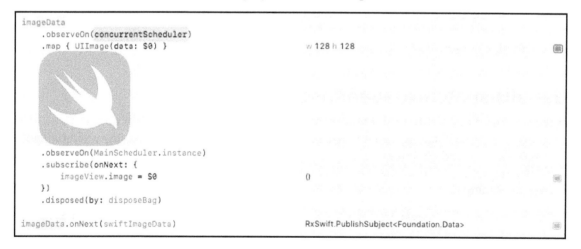

Now, we will add the `rxImageData` onto the image data subject, as follows:

```
imageData.onNext(rxImageData)
```

Also, see the Rx image displayed, as follows:

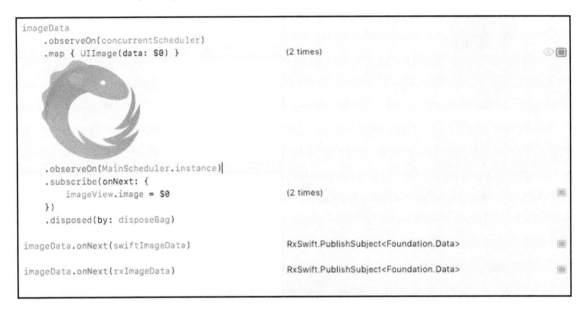

That was an example of using a global concurrent dispatch queue.

SerialDispatchQueueScheduler

It would not be much different if you wanted to create your own dispatch queue. To demonstrate, we will create a custom dispatch queue using the `DispatchQueue` initializer that takes a label and attributes that can be used to specify the queue type. We will make it a concurrent queue, but this time we will create a serial dispatch queue scheduler with that queue, as shown:

```
let conQueue = DispatchQueue(label: "com.Navdeep.conQueue", attributes:
.concurrent)
let serScheduler = SerialDispatchQueueScheduler(queue: conQueue,
internalSerialQueueName: "com.Navdeep.serQueue")
```

We would use a serial queue if we planned to do additional work on the same queue, and wanted to ensure that the work is carried out in the order in which it was added to the queue. The reason why we used a concurrent queue with a serial initializer is that we want to point out that, even if you pass a concurrent queue to the serial dispatch queue scheduler initializer, it will still create a serial queue. Let's see what is stated in the documentation:

```
17 It is extremely important that this scheduler is serial, because
18 certain operator perform optimizations that rely on that
      property.
```

It is extremely important that this scheduler be serial so that, no matter what type of queue is passed in, an internal serial queue will be created, as you can see in the screenshot showing an excerpt from the documentation:

```
22 will be assumed, and internal serial proxy dispatch queue will be
      created.
```

So now we will use this `serialScheduler` instead of the earlier concurrentScheduler with the `observeOn` operator, as follows:

```
imageData
    .observeOn(serScheduler)
    .map { UIImage(data: $0) }
>    .observeOn(MainScheduler.instance)
    .subscribe(onNext: {
        imageView.image = $0
    })
    .disposed(by: disposeBag)
```

OperationQueueScheduler

To work with the operation queue API instead of GCD, first we need to create an `OperationQueue` instance and then create an `OperationQueueScheduler` with that operation queue, as follows:

```
let opQueue = OperationQueue()
let opQueueScheduler = OperationQueueScheduler(operationQueue: opQueue)
```

Finally, we can use the opQueueScheduler instead of the serial queue scheduler with the ObserveOn operator, as demonstrated:

```
imageData
    .observeOn(opQueueScheduler)
    .map { UIImage(data: $0) }
    .observeOn(MainScheduler.instance)
    .subscribe(onNext: {
        imageView.image = $0
    })
    .disposed(by: disposeBag)
```

The overall code for this demonstration can be summarized as follows:

```
import PlaygroundSupport
PlaygroundPage.current.needsIndefiniteExecution = true
import RxSwift
let imageView = UIImageView(
    frame: CGRect(
        x: 0,
        y: 0,
        width: 128,
        height: 128
    )
)
PlaygroundPage.current.liveView = imageView
let swift = UIImage(named: "Swift")!
let swiftImageData = UIImagePNGRepresentation(swift)!
let rx = UIImage(named: "Rx")!
let rxImageData = UIImagePNGRepresentation(rx)!
let disposeBag = DisposeBag()
let imageData = PublishSubject<Data>()
let concurrentScheduler = ConcurrentDispatchQueueScheduler(qos:
.background)
let conQueue = DispatchQueue(label: "com.Navdeep.conQueue", attributes:
.concurrent)
let serScheduler = SerialDispatchQueueScheduler(queue: conQueue,
internalSerialQueueName: "com.Navdeep.serQueue")
let opQueue = OperationQueue()
let opQueueScheduler = OperationQueueScheduler(operationQueue: opQueue)
imageData
    .observeOn(opQueueScheduler)
    .map { UIImage(data: $0) }
    .observeOn(MainScheduler.instance)
    .subscribe(onNext: {
        imageView.image = $0
    })
```

```
        .disposed(by: disposeBag)
    imageData.onNext(swiftImageData)
    imageData.onNext(rxImageData)
```

Summary

Now that we have gone over how to create and work with Observable sequences using `RxSwift` operators and how to use schedulers to direct where the work is performed, we can look at how to work with Rx APIs that are specific to `Cocoa` platforms, such as iOS. In this chapter, we covered most concurrent, serial, and operational schedulers; by now, you will have realized that, under the hood, schedulers use queues to perform operations, either GCD queues or operational queues.

11
Subscribe to Errors and Save Your App

Many Observables can emit error events, and there are operators available to preemptively catch and handle those errors or retry the operation. Also, there are `drivers` that guarantee not to terminate with an error event that can determine what to return in the event an error does occur ahead of time.

We did this earlier by simply returning an empty array. We will show some examples of using `Driver`, which is defined in `RxCocoa`.

In this chapter, we will learn the following:

- Catching and handling errors
- Error handling operators
- Catch, retry, related terms, and concepts

Error handling

We will start this section with the starter project for this chapter and dive straight into code as you already are well aware of how to set up the `RxSwift` workspace and how to create one from scratch if need be. For the time being, open the starter project, and you will see that we have already created a `SupportCode` file in which we have declared an enum called `CustomError`, as follows:

```
public enum CustomError: Error {
    case test
}
```

Just to verify that we are on the same page, check the following screenshot and ensure that you have a similar project structure:

We will start with the `catchErrorJustReturn` operator on the playground page.

The catchErrorJustReturn operator

The `catchErrorJustReturn` operator recovers from an error event by returning an observable sequence that emits a single element and then terminates. We will create a `PublishSubject` that will emit an error, as follows:

```
example(for: "catchErrorJustReturn") {
    let disposeBag = DisposeBag()
    let pubSubject = PublishSubject<String>()
    subject.catchErrorJustReturn("")
}
```

Now we will subscribe and print out the emitted events. We will use the `catchErrorJustReturn` operator on it to return a smiley, as follows:

```
let disposeBag = DisposeBag()
    let pubSubject = PublishSubject<String>()
    pubSubject.catchErrorJustReturn("Demon Error")
        .subscribe{ print($0) }
        .disposed(by: disposeBag)
```

We will add a value to this subject, as shown:

```
pubSubject.catchErrorJustReturn("Demon Error")
        .subscribe{ print($0) }
        .disposed(by: disposeBag)
    pubSubject.onNext("First element")
```

Note in the console, that it emits the next event containing that element, as shown:

Then we will add an error, passing in our `CustomError` test case that we created in the `SupportCode` file as follows:

```
pubSubject.catchErrorJustReturn("Demon Error")
        .subscribe{ print($0) }
        .disposed(by: disposeBag)
    pubSubject.onNext("First element")
    pubSubject.onError(CustomError.test)
```

You will note that the `catchErrorJustReturn` operator causes the smiley face to be emitted and then it completes, as shown:

```
7       let disposeBag = DisposeBag()
8       let pubSubject = PublishSubject<String>()
9
10      pubSubject.catchErrorJustReturn("Demon Error")
11          .subscribe{ print($0) }
12          .disposed(by: disposeBag)
13
14      pubSubject.onNext("First element")
15      pubSubject.onError(CustomError.test)
16  }
17
```

```
... Example for: catchErrorJustReturn .....
next(First element)
next(Demon Error)
completed
```

Next up is the `catchError` operator.

The catchError operator

Like `catchErrorJustReturn`, it will catch and switch to another observable. The difference is that the recovery observable does not need to immediately emit and terminate. It can continue emitting. Let's start by creating the `PublishSubject`, and we will also create a recovery sequence as follows:

```
example(for: "catchError") {
    let disposeBag = DisposeBag()
    let pubSubject = PublishSubject<String>()
    let recoverySeq = PublishSubject<String>()
}
```

We will use the `catchError` operator on the subject to print out the error and then return the recovery sequence, as shown:

```
let disposeBag = DisposeBag()
    let pubSubject = PublishSubject<String>()
    let recoverySeq = PublishSubject<String>()
    pubSubject.catchError({
        print("Error=", $0)
        return recoverySeq
    })
```

Now we will subscribe and print events, as illustrated:

```
pubSubject.catchError{
        print("Error=", $0)
        return recoverySeq
        }
        .subscribe { print($0) }
        .disposed(by: disposeBag)
```

First, we will add a value to this subject, and then we will add an error, as we did in the previous example:

```
pubSubject.catchError{
        print("Error=", $0)
        return recoverySeq
        }
        .subscribe { print($0) }
        .disposed(by: disposeBag)
    pubSubject.onNext("First element")
    pubSubject.onError(CustomError.test)
```

Note that the completed event has not emitted in the console logs:

```
18   example(for: "catchError") {
19        let disposeBag = DisposeBag()
20        let pubSubject = PublishSubject<String>()
21
22        let recoverySeq = PublishSubject<String>()
23
24        pubSubject.catchError{
25            print("Error=", $0)
26            return recoverySeq
27            }
28            .subscribe { print($0) }
29            .disposed(by: disposeBag)
30
31        pubSubject.onNext("First element")
32        pubSubject.onError(CustomError.test)
33        pubSubject.onNext("Second element")
34        |
35   }
```

```
... Example for: catchErrorJustReturn .....
next(First element)
next(Demon Error)
completed

... Example for: catchError .....
next(First element)
Error= test
```

Let's add another value to the subject, as follows:

```
pubSubject.onNext("First element")
    pubSubject.onError(CustomError.test)
    pubSubject.onNext("Second element")
```

Now, you will note that the value is not emitted, as depicted here:

```
31        pubSubject.onNext("First element")
32        pubSubject.onError(CustomError.test)
33        pubSubject.onNext("Second element")
34
35  }
36
```

```
... Example for: catchErrorJustReturn .....
next(First element)
next(Demon Error)
completed

... Example for: catchError .....
next(First element)
Error= test
```

This is because the subject terminated with an error event, but the subscription switched to the recover sequence. So let's add a value to the recovery, as follows:

```
pubSubject.onNext("First element")
    pubSubject.onError(CustomError.test)
    pubSubject.onNext("Second element")
    recoverySeq.onNext("Third element")
```

You will note that this event is emitted by the recovery sequence, as shown:

```
31        pubSubject.onNext("First element")
32        pubSubject.onError(CustomError.test)
33        pubSubject.onNext("Second element")
34
35        recoverySeq.onNext("Third element")
36    }
37    |
```

```
... Example for: catchErrorJustReturn .....
next(First element)
next(Demon Error)
completed

... Example for: catchError .....
next(First element)
Error= test
next(Third element)
```

Next, we will discuss the retry operator.

The retry operator

The `retry` operator does not really handle the error. It just ignores it, and it will resubscribe to an Observable that emits an error. Let's start with the implementation. We will define a `shouldEmitError` that equals true, which we will use as a quick way to prevent our sequence subscription from retrying indefinitely in this example. Now we will create an Observable sequence of the `Int` type, as follows:

```
example(for: "retry") {
    let disposeBag = DisposeBag()
    var shouldEmitError = true
    let observableSeq = Observable<Int>.create{ observer in
    }
}
```

We will add two next events to the `observer`, which will be emitted to the subscribers. This is another way to create an Observable sequence using create and manually building it up with next error and/or completed events:

```
let observableSeq = Observable<Int>.create{ observer in
        observer.onNext(10)
        observer.onNext(20)
    }
```

`create` takes a closure parameter that takes an `observer` and returns a `disposable` and `create returns` an Observable. We don't have to do anything to disposable returned by the closure, such as adding it to the `disposeBag`. The observable sequence is handled normally; in other words, normal rules apply. So we will use disposables create operator to return disposable that does nothing on disposal. It's good to have some sense of the inner workings, but don't get too hung up on it if it is too elusive, especially when you first start working with it. So we have added a couple of next events and now we will conditionally add an error event. We will check to see whether `shouldEmitError` is true, which it is initially, and if so, we will create and add an error event and then set `shouldEmitError` to `false`. We will use a `retry` operator in a moment. When this error event is encountered, subscribers will be resubscribed and the sequence will start emitting from the beginning, but the error event will not be emitted again, because `shouldEmitError` will be `false`. So far, our code looks like this:

```
let observableSeq = Observable<Int>.create { observer in
        observer.onNext(10)
        observer.onNext(20)
        if shouldEmitError{
            observer.onError(CustomError.test)
            shouldEmitError = false
        }
        return Disposables.create()
    }
```

We will add a next and completed event that will be emitted upon resubscription, as follows:

```
if shouldEmitError{
        observer.onError(CustomError.test)
        shouldEmitError = false
    }
    observer.onNext(30)
    observer.onCompleted()
    return Disposables.create()
}
```

Now that we have created the Observable sequence, we will subscribe to it and print out emitted events, as follows:

```
example(for: "retry") {
    let disposeBag = DisposeBag()
    var shouldEmitError = true
    let observableSeq = Observable<Int>.create { observer in
        observer.onNext(10)
        observer.onNext(20)
        if shouldEmitError{
            observer.onError(CustomError.test)
            shouldEmitError = false
        }
        observer.onNext(30)
        observer.onCompleted()
        return Disposables.create()
    }
    observableSeq.subscribe{ print($0) }
    .disposed(by: disposeBag)
}
```

In the console log, note that the Observable sequence emits the error and terminates, as illustrated:

```
39   example(for: "retry") {
40       let disposeBag = DisposeBag()
41       var shouldEmitError = true
42
43       let observableSeq = Observable<Int>.create { observer in
44           observer.onNext(10)
45           observer.onNext(20)
46
47           if shouldEmitError{
48               observer.onError(CustomError.test)
49               shouldEmitError = false
50           }
51
52           observer.onNext(30)
53           observer.onCompleted()
54
55           return Disposables.create()
56       }
57
58       observableSeq.subscribe{ print($0) }
59       .disposed(by: disposeBag)|
60   }
```

```
next(Third element)

... Example for: retry .....
next(10)
next(20)
error(test)
```

We will insert the `retry` operator before the subscription, as shown:

```
example(for: "retry") {
    let disposeBag = DisposeBag()
    var shouldEmitError = true
    let observableSeq = Observable<Int>.create { observer in
        observer.onNext(10)
        observer.onNext(20)
        if shouldEmitError{
            observer.onError(CustomError.test)
            shouldEmitError = false
        }
        observer.onNext(30)
        observer.onCompleted()
```

```
        return Disposables.create()
    }
    observableSeq.retry()
    .subscribe{ print($0) }
    .disposed(by: disposeBag)
}
```

Also, the subscriber will be resubscribed, the error event will not be emitted the second time, so the third next event will be emitted and then the sequence will terminate with the completed event, as in the following screenshot:

```
39  example(for: "retry") {
40      let disposeBag = DisposeBag()
41      var shouldEmitError = true
42
43      let observableSeq = Observable<Int>.create { observer in
44          observer.onNext(10)
45          observer.onNext(20)
46
47          if shouldEmitError{
48              observer.onError(CustomError.test)
49              shouldEmitError = false
50          }
51
52          observer.onNext(30)
53          observer.onCompleted()
54
55          return Disposables.create()
56      }
57
58      observableSeq.retry()
59      .subscribe{ print($0) }
60      .disposed(by: disposeBag)
61  }
```

```
... Example for: retry .....
next(10)
next(20)
next(10)
next(20)
next(30)
completed
```

The retry operator will retry repeatedly infinitely until it successfully terminates with a completed event. If you want to limit the number of retries, you can use the overload of `retry` that takes a `maxAttemptsCount` integer parameter. This is a little unintuitive though, since the operator name is `retry` but the integer you pass is the total number of times the subscription will be attempted. In other words, if you want to subscribe and then retry once if the subscription emits error, pass in the value of 2 to `retry`. As we mentioned, `Drivers` guarantee not to fail, that is, terminate with an error event. This does not mean that it somehow magically prevents errors from happening. It just means that `Drivers` will require you to preemptively determine what to do in case an error does occur. Similar to regular Observable sequences, `Drivers` can just return sequences that emit a single element and terminate. We are talking about `onErrorJustReturn`, which we have already used a few times, but now we will specifically look at its implementation and usage.

onErrorJustReturn

We will create a `PublishSubject` and while trying to invoke `asDriver`, we will get three options in code completion; select `onErrorJustReturn` and add `1000` as the value, as follows:

```
example(for: "Driver onErrorJustReturn"){
    let disposeBag = DisposeBag()
    let pubSubject = PublishSubject<Int>()
    pubSubject.asDriver(onErrorJustReturn: 1000)
}
```

Then, we will use `drive(onNext)` to print out each element as it is emitted, as follows:

```
let disposeBag = DisposeBag()
    let pubSubject = PublishSubject<Int>()
    pubSubject.asDriver(onErrorJustReturn: 1000)
        .drive(onNext: {
            print ( $0 )
        })
        .disposed(by: disposeBag)
```

Now, we will add a couple of values to the subject sequence, as follows:

```
pubSubject.asDriver(onErrorJustReturn: 1000)
        .drive(onNext: {
            print ( $0 )
        })
        .disposed(by: disposeBag)
    pubSubject.onNext(10)
    pubSubject.onNext(20)
```

Also, in the console logs, note that they are emitted as shown:

```
63    example(for: "Driver onErrorJustReturn"){
64
65        let disposeBag = DisposeBag()
66        let pubSubject = PublishSubject<Int>()
67
68        pubSubject.asDriver(onErrorJustReturn: 1000)
69            .drive(onNext: {
70                print ( $0 )
71            })
72            .disposed(by: disposeBag)
73
74        pubSubject.onNext(10)
75        pubSubject.onNext(20)
76    }
```

```
next(30)
completed

... Example for: Driver onErrorJustReturn .....
10
20
```

Then, we will add an error as follows:

```
pubSubject.onNext(10)
pubSubject.onNext(20)
pubSubject.onError(CustomError.test)
```

In the console logs, note that `1000` is emitted, as shown:

```
63  example(for: "Driver onErrorJustReturn"){
64
65      let disposeBag = DisposeBag()
66      let pubSubject = PublishSubject<Int>()
67
68      pubSubject.asDriver(onErrorJustReturn: 1000)
69          .drive(onNext: {
70              print ( $0 )
71          })
72          .disposed(by: disposeBag)
73
74      pubSubject.onNext(10)
75      pubSubject.onNext(20)
76      |
77      pubSubject.onError(CustomError.test)
78  }
```

```
completed

... Example for: Driver onErrorJustReturn .....
10
20
1000
```

This sequence is now terminated, so adding another value to it does nothing. Next, we will discuss `onErrorDriveWith`.

onErrorDriveWith

Let's just copy and paste the last example and change the description as follows:

```
example(for: "Driver onErrorDriveWith"){
    let disposeBag = DisposeBag()
    let pubSubject = PublishSubject<Int>()
    pubSubject.asDriver(onErrorJustReturn: 1000)
        .drive(onNext: {
            print ( $0 )
        })
        .disposed(by: disposeBag)
    pubSubject.onNext(10)
    pubSubject.onNext(20)
    pubSubject.onError(CustomError.test)
}
```

We will also create a recovery subject and change the `asDriver` call to use `onErrorDriver` using the recover subject, which also has to specify what needs to be done on error. So we will also just return `1000`, as follows:

```
example(for: "Driver onErrorDriveWith"){
    let disposeBag = DisposeBag()
    let pubSubject = PublishSubject<Int>()
    let recoverySubject = PublishSubject<Int>()
    pubSubject.asDriver(onErrorDriveWith:
recoverySubject.asDriver(onErrorJustReturn: 1000))
        .drive(onNext: {
            print ( $0 )
        })
        .disposed(by: disposeBag)
    pubSubject.onNext(10)
    pubSubject.onNext(20)
    pubSubject.onError(CustomError.test)
}
```

This time, you will note that the first two next events are emitted in the console but not the third, as shown:

```
80  example(for: "Driver onErrorDriveWith"){
81
82      let disposeBag = DisposeBag()
83      let pubSubject = PublishSubject<Int>()
84
85      let recoverySubject = PublishSubject<Int>()
86
87      pubSubject.asDriver(onErrorDriveWith: recoverySubject.asDriver(onErrorJustReturn:
            1000))
88          .drive(onNext: {
89              print ( $0 )
90          })
91          .disposed(by: disposeBag)
92
93      pubSubject.onNext(10)
94      pubSubject.onNext(20)
95
96      pubSubject.onError(CustomError.test)
97  }
```

```
20
1000

... Example for: Driver onErrorDriveWith .....
10
20
```

This is because that subject terminated with an error. Now recovery is driving, so add 100 to recovery, as follows:

```
pubSubject.onNext(10)
  pubSubject.onNext(20)
  pubSubject.onError(CustomError.test)
  recoverySubject.onNext(100)
```

This will cause it to be emitted as shown:

```
80   example(for: "Driver onErrorDriveWith"){
81
82       let disposeBag = DisposeBag()
83       let pubSubject = PublishSubject<Int>()
84
85       let recoverySubject = PublishSubject<Int>()
86
87       pubSubject.asDriver(onErrorDriveWith: recoverySubject.asDriver(onErrorJustReturn:
            1000))
88           .drive(onNext: {
89               print ( $0 )
90           })
91           .disposed(by: disposeBag)
92
93       pubSubject.onNext(10)
94       pubSubject.onNext(20)
95
96       pubSubject.onError(CustomError.test)
97
98       recoverySubject.onNext(100)
99   }
```

```
1000

... Example for: Driver onErrorDriveWith .....
10
20
100
```

onErrorRecover

At times, we might want to perform an additional action before recovering from an error like this; for this, we have `onErrorRecover`. It schedules a recovery sequence to run on the next loop. In order to show this on playground, we need to write this on a global scope, that is, not enclose it in the example (`for`) method call, and we will also need to import playground support and set `needsIndefiniteExecution` to `true`. This will give schedule recovery time to execute. We will write something like this:

```
print("... Example for: Driver onErrorRecover.....")
import PlaygroundSupport
PlaygroundPage.current.needsIndefiniteExecution = true
```

We will now duplicate the code from within the first example again, and this time, we will use `onErrorRecover`, which can be written as trailing closure on `asDriver`. We will print the error, and then we will return the single element sequence for simplicity sake, but this could have been a `Driver`, like we used in the previous example, that would keep on driving. The code will look as follows:

```
print("... Example for: Driver onErrorRecover.....")
import PlaygroundSupport
PlaygroundPage.current.needsIndefiniteExecution = true
let disposeBag = DisposeBag()
let pubSubject = PublishSubject<Int>()
pubSubject.asDriver{
    print( "Error:", $0 )
    return Driver.just(1000)
    }
    .drive(onNext: {
        print ( $0 )
    })
    .disposed(by: disposeBag)
pubSubject.onNext(10)
pubSubject.onNext(20)
pubSubject.onError(CustomError.test)
```

In the console, you will note that the first two elements are printed, then the error, and then the recover `Driver`, as shown:

```
104   print("... Example for: Driver onErrorRecover.....")
105   import PlaygroundSupport
106   PlaygroundPage.current.needsIndefiniteExecution = true
107
108   let disposeBag = DisposeBag()
109   let pubSubject = PublishSubject<Int>()
110
111   pubSubject.asDriver{
112       print( "Error:", $0 )
113       return Driver.just(1000)
114       }
115       .drive(onNext: {
116           print ( $0 )
117       })
118       .disposed(by: disposeBag)
119
120   pubSubject.onNext(10)
121   pubSubject.onNext(20)
122
123   pubSubject.onError(CustomError.test)
```

```
100
... Example for: Driver onErrorRecover.....
10
20
Error: test
1000
```

Summary

Handling errors preemptively, as we saw in this chapter, will make your code robust and when you are using `Driver`, you usually need to specify how you want to handle errors like this. It is always a good practice to anticipate and act on the occurrence of errors while developing any software. In this chapter, we worked with different operators that allow us to strategize the methodology that we can adopt, depending on the situations and the logic inside the code. In this chapter, we covered how to handle scenarios when our code might encounter an unexpected event. In the next chapter, we will extend this approach of addressing common scenarios using the design patterns.

12
Functional and Reactive App-Architecture

Design patterns are conceptual tools for solving complex software problems. We will be discussing the ones that appear in Cocoa, but they exist in all programming languages and some span multiple languages. For example, MVC is applicable to any application driving a user interface regardless of the language it is written in. Design patterns appear at different levels of the application structure, from the organization of the code modules to data structure creation to communication. Some are like two-stage object creation you are already using, while others, like key value observing, or KVO, are more esoteric and are not found in every project.

These patterns are simple and elegant solutions that have evolved over time and may have become generally accepted as the best way to address certain design challenges. In this chapter, we will cover different design patterns that we use for building our applications; these are as follows:

- Singletons
- KVO (Key value observing)
- KVC (Key value coding)
- Notifications
- Delegation

These design patterns not only solve common software problems but are also referred to quite frequently in Apple documentation as well, so knowing them is helpful while you try to read through the documentation.

Design patterns

We will go through a quick inventory of common design patterns that are used most extensively while working with iOS apps. The first design pattern we will look at is the two stage Object creation; it divides the process into separate memory allocation and initialization steps. This might appear cumbersome, but as we will see later, it allows greater flexibility in how we customize initialization methods. This facilitates code reuse both within classes and between classes in the inheritance hierarchy; then we will look at Singletons.

The Singleton pattern encapsulates a shared resource within a single unique class instance. This instance arbitrates access to the resource and storage-related state information. A class method provides the reference to this instance, so there is no need to pass the reference around; any object that has access to the Singleton's class header can use the Singleton. The following diagram briefly describes Singletons in action:

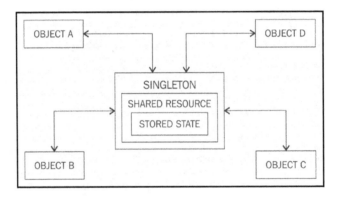

Next, we will look at key value coding or KVC and key value observing, aka KVO. KVC is a universal dictionary interface that uses keys and key paths for setting and accessing object properties. This interface opens the door to a number of powerful techniques, including KVO.

KVO allows the key coding interface to be used by one object to examine the property of a second object. The observing object is changed every time the property is modified. This allows the observer to respond to specific state conditions within other objects with minimal coupling. The observer only needs to know the simple key path. The diagram below briefly describes KVC in action:

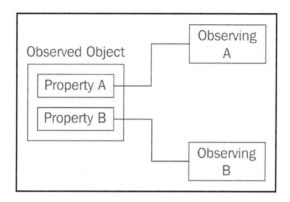

NSNotifications work by having interested objects register for specific message types. When any instance posts a notification of that type, all the registered objects are notified. The system works something like a radio station broadcasting on a certain frequency; any radio tuned to that frequency can listen in. Like a radio station, the posting object has no idea how many, or if any, objects are listening and listeners don't know the source of any notification. The notification system allows for objects to pass signals between them with almost no coupling. Objects posting or listening have no information about other objects participating in the system. Notifications are an extreme example of decoupled communication. The following diagram briefly describes notifications in action:

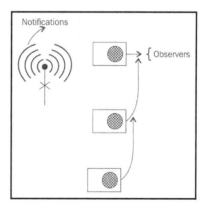

Model view controller (**MVC**) is the most abstract pattern that we will be examining. It structures the relationship between objects that provide data and those that present information in a user interface. In MVC, classes are either the member of the model that manages application data or the view that manages the interface of the controller that acts as the mediator between the model and the view. This separation into three separate subsystems clarifies the roles and responsibilities of each and allows classes to be more specialized.

The given diagram briefly describes MVC in action:

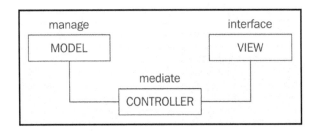

In the coming sections, we will discuss each one of these design patterns in detail, starting with the Singleton design pattern.

Singleton design pattern

We will now look at the Singleton pattern. This design pattern defines the structure of a class that can have only one instance. A Singleton encapsulates a unique resource and makes it readily available throughout the application. The resource might be hardware, a network service, a persistent store, or anything else that can be modeled as a unique object or service. One example from Cocoa touch is a physical device running an iOS application; for an executing app, there is only one iPhone or iPad with a single battery and a screen. UIDevice is a Singleton class here, since it provides one channel to interact with the underlying features. In case the unique resource has a writable configuration this sort of discrepancy, it can lead to problems such as race condition and deadlock. Since they are unique, Singletons act as a control, ensuring orderly access to the shared resource. Singletons may often be modeled as a server within the application that accepts requests to send, store, or retrieve data and configure the resource state.

Implementation

Implementation of the Singleton pattern often typically creates a single object using the factory method, and this instance/object is called a shared instance in most cases. Since the access to the instance is passed on through a class method, the need to create an object is eliminated. Let's look at the Singleton implementation in the code in the following section.

For this exercise, we will use the command line tool Xcode template to create a project and name it Singleton. Our Singleton class will be called `SingletonObject`, which we will create as a normal `Cocoa` class, and it will be a subclass of `NSObject`. The project setup will look like this so far:

Let's add a class method called `sharedInstance` as discussed earlier, since this is how the class will make the Singleton available. Its return value will be of the `SingleObject` type, as follows:

```
func sharedInstance() -> SingletonObject {
    }
```

You will note the compiler error at this time since the function does not return the value as promised in the function signature, but we will change it soon. The function will store the instance in a static local reference called `localSharedInstance`. Static locals are much like global objects; they retain their value for the lifetime of the application, yet they are limited in scope. These qualities make them ideal to be a Singleton since they are permanent and yet ensure that our Singleton is only available through `sharedInstance`. This is one of the ways in which our Singleton implementation ensures that the Singleton stays singular. The basic structure of shared instance consists of a conditional block that tests whether a Singleton instance has been allocated, but to your surprise, that's the older way of doing things or may be the way to go in other languages, but in Swift, the implementation has changed to merely one line, and we don't require a method. The implementation looks like this:

```
class SingletonObject: NSObject {
    static let sharedInstance = SingletonObject()
}
```

Simple, isn't it? In the next section, we will discuss some pros and cons of using the Singleton design pattern.

Singleton design pattern – Pros and cons

Singletons are not the answer to every problem. Like any tool, they can be short in supply or can be overused. Some developers are critical of Singletons for various reasons. We will examine this critique and discuss ways to address them briefly. The criticisms, for the most part, fall into two categories:

- Singletons hinder unit testing: A Singleton might cause issues for writing testable code if the object and the methods associated to it are so tightly coupled that it becomes impossible to test without writing a fully-functional class dedicated to the Singleton.
- Singletons create hidden dependencies: As the Singleton is readily available throughout the code base, it can be overused. Moreover, since its reference is not completely transparent while passing to different methods, it becomes difficult to track.

To avoid these complications, when considering the Singleton pattern, you should make certain that the class is a Singleton and also, while thinking of designing the Singleton design pattern, keep testing in mind and use dependency injection whenever possible, that is,try to pass Singleton as a parameter to the initializer whenever possible.

Key value coding (KVC)

KVC is a generic way of accessing an object's properties and variables using a dictionary style interface. It might seem like a slightly cumbersome way of accessing instance data, but KVC actually provides a flexible, adaptable, and useful means of talking to objects. The method for accessing a variable or property using KVC is value(`forKey:`). In the following example, we are trying to access the value of the `data` property and store it in a variable of type data, as follows:

```
var data = value(forKey: "data")
```

Setting a value is done using `setValue(value:forKey:)`. The mechanism of KVC is adaptive in storing and retrieving of values and operates using an order of precedence similar to arithmetic operators. When accessing instance data, the following sequence of priority implies; for example, if we call `value(forKey:)` using a hypothetical key, some var KVC will first try to retrieve a value using standard property accessor method; failing that, it will look for methods _var and _get some var, then it will try instance variables, and finally, if no source for a var is found, KVC will call `value(forUndefinedKey:`. Let's see KVC in action.

KVC – Implementation

We can use the same project that we used for the previous section and create a new class called `KVCObject.swift`; this class is a subclass of `NSObject`. For now, leave the class as empty and move over to the `main.swift` file.

We will now create a new instance of `kvcObject` and then write a print statement that tries to print the request of KVO for a value associated with the `stringToFind` key, as shown:

```
var kvcObject = KVCObject()
print("KVC value = \(kvcObject.value(forKey: "stringToFind"))")
```

After building and running the project, you will note that the program crashes with a console log error message, as illustrated:

```
   import Foundation
10 var kvcObject = KVCObject()
11 print("KVC value = \(kvcObject.value(forKey: "stringToFind"))")                    2 = | Thread 1: signal SIGABRT

▽  ▶  ▷  △  ⊥  ⊥  ⬭  ⅋  ⋗  ⊡  ⊡  | ■ Singleton ⟩ ⬤ Thread 1 ⟩ ☲ 12 main

2017-12-30 20:02:18.226144+1100 Singleton[4139:8384178] [DYMTLInitPlatform] platform initialization successful
2017-12-30 20:02:18.280224+1100 Singleton[4139:8384110] *** Terminating app due to uncaught exception 'NSUnknownKeyException', reason:
'[<Singleton.KVCObject 0x101257650> valueForUndefinedKey:]: this class is not key value coding-compliant for the key stringToFind.'
*** First throw call stack:
(
    0   CoreFoundation                      0x00007fff8cf6057b __exceptionPreprocess + 171
    1   libobjc.A.dylib                     0x00007fffa21c11da objc_exception_throw + 48
    2   CoreFoundation                      0x00007fff8cf604c9 -[NSException raise] + 9
    3   Foundation                          0x00007fff8ea5bdce -[NSObject(NSKeyValueCoding) valueForUndefinedKey:] + 226
    4   Foundation                          0x00007fff8e92da7c -[NSObject(NSKeyValueCoding) valueForKey:] + 283
    5   Singleton                           0x0000000100002c40 main + 480
    6   libdyld.dylib                       0x00007fffa2aa2235 start + 1
    7   ???                                 0x0000000000000001 0x0 + 1
)
libc++abi.dylib: terminating with uncaught exception of type NSException
(lldb)
```

That happened because we did not provide any source for the key that it's asking for.

Now let's switch back to `KVCObject`, and let's implement the
`valueForUndefinedKey()` method; this method will be a net for catching requests for
keys that we have no value for, and the implementation of our method will be as follows:

```
override func value(forUndefinedKey key: String) -> Any? {
        print("we do not have any key for \(key)")
        return nil
    }
```

As a result of the implementation, you will note that the console logs reflect the function
that was invoked:

```
11   class KVCObject: NSObject {
12
13       override func value(forUndefinedKey key: String) -> Any? {
             print("we do not have any key for \(key)")
15           return nil
16       }
17   }
```

```
2018-01-01 16:29:48.438635+1100 Singleton[4872:8654402] [DYMTLInitPlatform] platform initialization
successful
we do not have any key for stringToFind
KVC value = nil
Program ended with exit code: 0
```

This function will catch the execution if someone requests a key that we don't have. As you
might have noted, this method also provides us with an opportunity to return a default
value for that key, so we have returned `nil` as a string in our case.

Now, let's make things a little more interesting—switch back to the `main.swift` file and
add another print statement for another key, as follows:

```
print("KVC vallue of Second Key = \(String(describing:
kvcObject.value(forKey: "numberToFind")!))")
```

Building and running again will result in the following console log, and as you might have
guessed, our function will again be invoked to provide a default value, as you can see here:

```
2018-01-01 16:51:48.765388+1100 Singleton[4948:8661962] [DYMTLInitPlatform] platform initialization
successful
we do not have any key for stringToFind
KVC value = nil
we do not have any key for numberToFind
KVC vallue of Second Key = nil
Program ended with exit code: 0
```

Let's add an instance variable called `stringToFind` to `KVCObject`, and now we will need an initializer as well to give it an initial value, as follows:

```
@objc dynamic var stringToFind: String
public override init() {
        self.stringToFind = "First value"
        super.init()
    }
```

This will replace the value for the `stringToFind` key with `"First value"`, as shown:

```
13    @objc dynamic var stringToFind: String
14
15    public override init() {
16        self.stringToFind = "First value"
17    }
18    override func value(forUndefinedKey key: String) -> Any? {
19        print("we do not have any key for \(key)")
20        return "nil"
21    }
22
```

```
2018-01-02 22:42:03.343969+1100 Singleton[5490:8690606] [DYMTLInitPlatform] platform initialization
successful
KVC value = First value
we do not have any key for numberToFind
KVC value of Second Key = nil
Program ended with exit code: 0
```

Notifications

Notifications are a mechanism for broadcasting a simple message throughout an application. A notification can be posted from anywhere, and any object instance can register for a notification that a message has been posted. Notifications work similar to radio signal station broadcasting on a specific frequency, and objects registered for a notification are like radios tuned to that frequency. As the analogy suggests, coupling between notification posters and listeners is minimal.

Adding observers and posting notifications are both done through a Singleton instance of `NSNotificationCenter` available through the `NSNotification` class method `defaultCenter`. A poster has no idea about the listener or number of listeners if a notification is raised, because the listeners register with `NotificationCenter` directly using the `addObserver` method. An object can stop receiving notifications at any time by sending a `removeObserver` message to `NotificationCenter`.

`NSNotificationCenter` allows small amounts of data to be piggybacked along with the notifications. There is a form of the post method that allows us to append dictionary defined by the user to the notification posted by the poster. This information is available to the observer through the `userInfo` property of the `NSNotification` parameter passed with the notifying callback:

```
- (void) postNotificationName: (NSNotificationName) aName
object: (id) anObjectuserInfo: (NSDictionary *) aUserInfo;
```

As we mentioned, notification registration is done with an `addObserver` method call. There are two forms; one specifies a selector callback, as follows:

```
- (void) addObserver: (id) observer selector: (SEL) aSelector
name: (NSNotificationName) aName object: (id) anObject;
```

The other provides a block:

```
- (id<NSObject>) addObserverForName: (NSNotificationName) name  object: (id) obj
queue: (NSOperationQueue *) queue  usingBlock: (void (^) (NSNotification
*note)) block;
```

The first form takes the following arguments:

- Observing object
- A selector method that will execute on that object
- Name of the notification
- A sender object

An Observing object and selector must be provided, but the name of the notification and sender object may be `nil`. If the notification name is `nil`, the selector will be called when any notification is posted; if the sender object is `nil`, the selector will be called regardless of which object posts the notification. Setting both to `nil` indicates an interest in observing all notifications.

The second form takes the following argument:

- Name of the notification
- Object which is posting the notification
- Operation queue
- A block to execute

Other than a selector, the block to execute in response to the notification is provided. The queue allows you to specify an NSOperation queue to which the block will be added for execution. All parameters except the block may be nil, which would specify that the block should be run on the posting thread in response to any object posting any notification.

Notifications – Implementation

Let's create a single view application and name it NotificationsExample. Switch over to the appdelegate and add code to listen in on all the notifications that are being passed around within our iOS application. To do so, we will first create a reference to NotificationCenter's default center by making a call to the class method NotificationCenter.default. Then, we will send a message to the notification center to add the Observer, as follows:

```
func application(_ application: UIApplication,
didFinishLaunchingWithOptions launchOptions:
[UIApplicationLaunchOptionsKey: Any]?) -> Bool {
    // Override point for customization after application launch.
    let notificationCenter = NotificationCenter.default
    notificationCenter.addObserver(forName: nil, object: nil,
    queue: nil) {notification in
        print("Notification captured \(notification.name)")
    }
    return true
}
```

The block that we have implemented in the preceding code basically defines that it will be executed anytime any notification is posted. Execute the code, and you will note that the console will log all the notifications, as shown:

```
9   import UIKit
10
11  @UIApplicationMain
12  class AppDelegate: UIResponder, UIApplicationDelegate {
13
14      var window: UIWindow?
15      func application(_ application: UIApplication, didFinishLaunchingWithOptions
            launchOptions: [UIApplicationLaunchOptionsKey: Any]?) -> Bool {
16          // Override point for customization after application launch.
17          let notificationCenter = NotificationCenter.default
18          notificationCenter.addObserver(forName: nil, object: nil, queue: nil) {notification
                in
19              print("Notification captured \(notification.name)")
20          }
21          return true
22      }
23  }
```

```
☑  ▶  ⅠⅠ  △  ↓  ↥  ⟦⟧  ⅝  ⊞ NotificationExample
Notification captured Name(_rawValue: _UIApplicationStatusBarHiddenStateChangedNotification)
Notification captured Name(_rawValue: UIWindowDidBecomeVisibleNotification)
Notification captured Name(_rawValue: UIWindowDidBecomeKeyNotification)
Notification captured Name(_rawValue: UIApplicationDidFinishLaunchingNotification)
Notification captured Name(_rawValue: UIViewAnimationDidCommitNotification)
Notification captured Name(_rawValue: UIViewAnimationDidStopNotification)
Notification captured Name(_rawValue: _UIWindowContentWillRotateNotification)
Notification captured Name(_rawValue: _UIWindowContentWillRotateNotification)
Notification captured Name(_rawValue: UIDeviceOrientationDidChangeNotification)
Notification captured Name(_rawValue: _UIApplicationDidRemoveDeactivationReasonNotification)
Notification captured Name(_rawValue: UIDeviceOrientationDidChangeNotification)
Notification captured Name(_rawValue: UIDeviceOrientationDidChangeNotification)
Notification captured Name(_rawValue: _UIApplicationDidRemoveDeactivationReasonNotification)
Notification captured Name(_rawValue: UIApplicationDidBecomeActiveNotification)
Notification captured Name(_rawValue:
UIStatusBarItemViewShouldEndDisablingRasterizationNotification)
Notification captured Name(_rawValue: UIStatusBarTimeItemViewDidMoveNotification)
Notification captured Name(_rawValue: UIStatusBarTimeItemViewDidMoveNotification)
```

Next up, we will discuss the design pattern that is most abundantly used in iOS programming, and this design pattern is MVC.

Model view controller – MVC

The **model view controller** (**MVC**) is more abstract than the others that we have discussed so far. This design pattern divides the structural components into three parts; these parts are as follows:

- The model: Houses application logic
- The view: User interface
- The controller: The glue or binding entity between the view and the model

The model

The model is the core of the application. The business logic of the application, or, in simpler terms, the capabilities of the application on a whole can be termed as the model component of an application. The logic within the model layer might deal with storing and managing data to maintain the state of the application. All the network communications that your application makes, the parsing and complex calculations that it performs on the received data, all comes under the model layer.

The view

The view is the interface to the application. State of the application is represented by the view. In order to enhance decoupling in the application architecture, views should not have any logical component in their implementation other than the ones required to take inputs or display data on a screen.

The controller

The controller manages communication between the view and the model. It also encapsulates the functionality that is specific just to governing the interaction between various logical components, as a result of which model and view subsystems remain decoupled. The controller can be termed as the binding element between the model and views.

The software virtue that MVC exhibits is modularity, which helps developers to manage the complexity of developing an application. It allows the model, view, and controller modules to focus on a limited range of functionality. In short, it allows them to specialize.

As a general rule, the modular design is preferred over a holistic one.

MVC is unique among the patterns that we have looked at so far in its general applicability. It was originally introduced in *SmallTalk* in the '70s, and it is language- and platform-agnostic. The model view controller design pattern may be applied to the development of any application that supports a graphical user interface or GUI. We will illustrate MVC with an example from the physical world.

Let's take the example of an old-school landline telephone. The key functionality of this device is a subsystem that physically connects to the line leading to the home or business and transmits and receives signals to and from that wire. Since this is the core of what a phone does, we will call this the model. The interface for very early phones was a horn-shaped microphone mounted on the front of the device and a speaker that the user had to hold next to their ear. Later, the interface evolved so that the speaker and microphone were integrated into a handset and dialling a number evolved from speaking to an operator to dial router and later to a keypad. Though there is no screen, the speaker and the microphone are an interface. So they are analogous to the view. The controller in this example will be the other parts required to complete the device, for instance, the casings, the connections between interface elements, and the core phone components. In the '70s, the core phone functionality, that is, the model was integrated to a new device. This one coupled the line communication hardware to an interface that modulated binary signals into one suited for telephone systems, that is, one in the human auditory range. This new device was the dial up modem. The analogy is telling, in that, it is the core phone or model functionality that endured largely and remained unchanged for long. Likewise, in the software world, interface subsystems tend to be changed the most, driven by user feedback and evolving interface styles and standards. In the upcoming sections, we will work with simple MVC examples to dig into the concept a little more.

MVC implementation

The first place a Cocoa developer encounters MVC is in the structure of an application when a new project is created in Xcode. Let's create a single view application once again; ensure that you include core data that is checked while creating the project and name it as MVCTemplate. Other than `appdelegate`, note that all other components are already members of the model, view, or controller. `MVCTemplate.xcdatamodeld` is the data model created by the core data. The `storyboard` is the `View`, and the `ViewController` modules are part of the controller subsystem. Arguably, `appdelegate` also fits within the controller.

You can't really do any logic within the XML, as shown in the following screenshot for you to explore on your own:

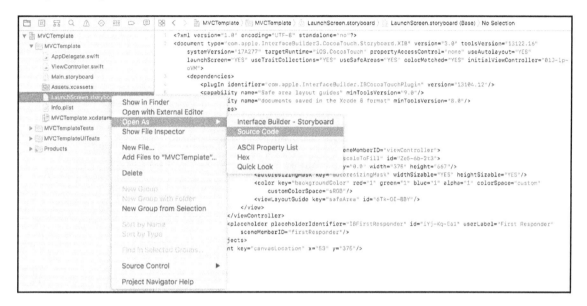

While the nib and storyboard objects are instantiated at runtime, Xcode assumes no need for logic beyond low-level event handling that is rather left to controller subsystem to handle. The skeleton for the controller is laid out in the `UIViewController` subclass modules. Looking through the methods provided by the `UIViewController` class creates a clear picture of the expected functionality relative to the view.

The relationships shown are not always present and certainly not required, but they are the most common ones between the three subsystems. The majority of the interactions are between the model and the controller or between the controller and the view.

Since the controller is described as glue or insulation between the other two components, this makes sense, as depicted here:

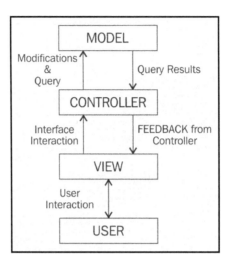

One relationship that might seem surprising is the data displayed from the model directly to the view. In some cases, it is useful to provide the model state directly to the view so that it can be displayed verbatim. Note that this relationship is directional. User interaction should not directly affect the model state without some processing by the controller, as illustrated:

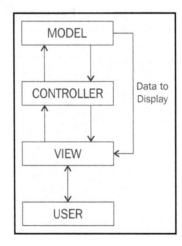

MVC is used extensively in iOS projects, and in the coming chapters, we will discuss some of the shortcomings associated with this design pattern and how to address those shortcomings using some other design patterns such as the **model view view model (MVVC)** design pattern, which is the favorite design pattern when it comes to RX programming.

Summary

In this chapter, we dived into the fundamentals of software development in general and explored some of the most widely used design patterns in iOS development. We explored MVC in more detail than others, since it is used in almost all iOS projects and forms the foundation of a majority of applications. In the previous chapters, we used these design patterns multiple times but many a times, we just use things without knowing the underlying concept. This chapter gave you an insight to identify exciting design patterns in the existing code base and to allow you to think in the capacity where you can understand the problem at hand and choose between the design patterns that we discussed in this chapter and beyond. Design patterns is a vast subject in itself, and this chapter provided you with a mere introduction to the concept. We highly encourage you to take some time out, explore design patterns on your own as well, and pick the ones that suit your needs the best. Think of them as tools in your arsenal that you might need anytime to do the job at hand more efficiently.

Finish a Real-World Application

13

In the book, we have covered many different concepts related to Rx, and now is the time to put most of them into practice. Since most applications require API interactions in some way or the other, this chapter will work on an app that will make use of networking code to fetch and display some meaningful information on the `tableView`. The main objectives of this chapter are as listed:

- Networking in `RxSwift`
- Creating a real-world application
- `ViewModel`
- `RxAlamOfire`

Networking in RxSwift

We can't do much in an app these days without interacting with a remote server. `RxSwift` offers useful extensions for working with the `URLSession` API, and there are some excellent community networking libraries available for `RxSwift`, including `RxAlamOfFire` and Moya. Both utilize `AlamOfire` under the hood actually, and they make writing networking code as enjoyable as it should be. We will go through a pretty standard example for this chapter so that it is easy for you to relate to.

We will create a type ahead search app of GitHub repositories for GitHub user ID.

Project setup

We will start out in a single view app with a `tableView`. Open up the starter project for this chapter, and you will see that we have created a `searchController` and configured it using `configureSearchController()` to include the `searchBar` of the `searchController` as the `tableHeaderView` of `tableView`, as follows:

```
func configureSearchController() {
        searchController.obscuresBackgroundDuringPresentation = false
        searchBar.showsCancelButton = true
        searchBar.text = "scotteg"
        searchBar.placeholder = "Enter GitHub ID, e.g., \"scotteg\""
        tableView.tableHeaderView = searchController.searchBar
        definesPresentationContext = true
    }
```

Also, we have already bound the data sequence of a `viewModel` to the `tableView`, as shown:

```
viewModel.data
            .drive(tableView.rx.items(cellIdentifier: "Cell")) { _,
repository, cell in
            cell.textLabel?.text = repository.name
            cell.detailTextLabel?.text = repository.url
        }
            .addDisposableTo(disposeBag)
```

This is the first time we are actually using a `viewModel` in this book. We have used the same `rx.items(cellIdentifier)`, which we discussed while working with `tableViews` in the previous chapters. We have created a `struct` repository with `repoName` and `repoURL` string properties, as follows:

```
struct Repository {
    let repoName: String
    let repoURL: String
}
```

Also, we have defined a `viewModel` class with a `searchText` variable of string as shown:

```
class ViewModel {
    let searchText = Variable("")
    lazy var data: Driver<[Repository]> = {
        return Observable.of([Repository]()).asDriver(onErrorJustReturn:
[])
    }()
}
```

The purpose of a `viewModel` is to abstract from the code that prepares the data for use by the `viewController`, such as binding to the UI. The data property just has a placeholder return so that this project will compile. We will replace it shortly. This data sequence is implemented as a `Driver` of array of repository—`Driver<[Repository]>`—and as we see in the `viewController`, it'll drive the `tableView`. Remember that `Driver` will not emit an error, and it will automatically deliver events on the main thread.

Project implementation

We will start by implementing a `repositoriesBy()` helper method that will take a Github ID parameter and return an Observable of array of Repository. In a production app, we would put this functionality in an `APIManager`, but we are intentionally doing this in one file to make it easier to follow. First, we will guard that the GitHub ID parameter is not empty, and then we will successfully create a URL to use our fetch request, as follows:

```
static func repositoriesBy(_ githubID: String) -> Observable<[Repository]>
{
        guard !githubID.isEmpty,
            let url = URL(string:
"https://api.github.com/users/\(githubID)/repos") else {
            return Observable.just([])
        }
    }
```

If the creation of the URL fails, we will return just an empty array of Observables. You can find GitHub's documentation for the API at `https://developer.github.com/v3/repos/#list-user-repositories`.

In order to test out the response from the aforementioned URL, you can try it on a browser. For example, my GitHub ID is `NavdeepSinghh`, and in order to create a URL to fetch my repositories, I use the following URL:

`https://api.github.com/users/NavdeepSinghh/repos`

Then, if you open this link in the browser, you will see a list of all the repositories under my GitHub ID and some more details, as illustrated:

Here, we can see that we get back an array of dictionaries and the two data points that we are interested in:

- "name": "book-notes"
- "html_url": "`https://github.com/NavdeepSinghh/book-notes`"

Switch back to Xcode, and let's work on the implementation to pull this data and make full use of it within our application.

Fetching and parsing data

Next, we will get hold of the shared singleton of `URLSession` and use the `rx.json` extension on `URLSession`, passing the URL we created, as shown:

```
guard !githubID.isEmpty,
        let url = URL(string:
"https://api.github.com/users/\(githubID)/repos") else {
        return Observable.just([])
    }
    return URLSession.shared.rx.json(url: url)
```

`rx.json` returns an Observable sequence of the response JSON. As errors can occur regularly in networking, we will use retry with a max attempt count of 3 so that it retries twice and then, if a third error occurs, we will use `catchErrorJustReturn` to return an empty array, as follows:

```
    return URLSession.shared.rx.json(url: url)
    .retry(3)
    .catchErrorJustReturn([])
```

We don't need to do this here because the error is handled in the implementation of data because it's a `Driver` and `Driver` cannot emit an error. Here, we just wanted to point out that, if we were not using `Driver`, we need to see this catch. We will just comment it out to leave it as a reference.

We want to point out that `URLSession` already returns, so we don't need to specify a background queue to do the parsing on. If we did want to specify a specific background queue, we would use an `observeOn` operator here, just like we did in the schedulers chapter earlier in the book.

Next, we will use map to transform the Observable sequence but, rather than writing the mapping code within the map operator, we will abstract it to a parseJson() method that takes a json and returns an array of repositories. We will start by using a guard to cast the json as an items array of dictionaries of String keys and Any values; if that fails, we will just return an empty array, as follows:

```
static func parse(json: Any) -> [Repository] {
        guard let items = json as? [[String: Any]]  else {
            return []
        }
    }
```

Then, we will create an empty array of repositories to hold each repository instance we create from the json. We will iterate over the items array using the forEach method and in there use a guard to extract the local name and URL String values from the dictionary, as illustrated:

```
guard let items = json as? [[String: Any]]  else {
        return []
    }
    var repositories = [Repository]()
    items.forEach{
        guard let repoName = $0["name"] as? String,
            let repoURL = $0["html_url"] as? String else {
                return
        }
    }
```

Then, we will create a new repository instance and append it to the repositories array and finally, we will return the repositories array, as follows:

```
var repositories = [Repository]()
        items.forEach{
            guard let repoName = $0["name"] as? String,
                let repoURL = $0["html_url"] as? String else {
                    return
            }
            repositories.append(Repository(repoName: repoName, repoURL:
repoURL))
        }
        return repositories
```

Now, back in the `repositoriesBy()` method, we will pass this method to the map operator. Remember that when we pass the function type directly as a parameter, we just write the name and not the parameter list. This works with functions with a single parameter list and the parameter is inferred to be each value exposed by, in this case, map. We are not subscribing here; we are just passing through an input to an output, as follows:

```
static func repositoriesBy(_ githubID: String) -> Observable<[Repository]>
{
        guard !githubID.isEmpty,
            let url = URL(string:
"https://api.github.com/users/\(githubID)/repos") else {
            return Observable.just([])
         }
        return URLSession.shared.rx.json(url: url)
        .retry(3)
        //.catchErrorJustReturn([])
        .map(parse)
    }
```

That takes care of fetching and creating the repositories.

Now we will make data use the `repositoriesBy()` method.

Binding fetched data to View elements

First, we will delete the placeholder return. We want to transform the `searchText` into an array of repositories. We should point out that the unauthenticated GitHub API we are using has a rate limit of 10 requests per minute. We will use the `throttle` operator here to only take the latest element received through the specified time. This will prevent triggering multiple network requests in rapid succession. We will also use the `distinctUntilChanged` operator, which will allow only unique contiguous elements to pass through. As the change to text in `searchText` triggers the operation in this app, this is not necessary here, but we have Search button so that the user can click on the button to explicitly initiate a search. This will help in executing multiple searches in a row on the same string if the user keeps tapping on the search button over and over, as follows:

```
lazy var data: Driver<[Repository]> = {
        return self.searchText.asObservable()
        .throttle(0.3, scheduler: MainScheduler.instance)
        .distinctUntilChanged()
    }()
```

Now we will use `flatMapLatest`. From the previous chapters, you might remember that `flatMapLatest` switches to the latest Observable sequence and applies a transform to each element. We will pass the static `ViewModel.repositoriesBy()` method directly to `flatMapLatest`, which will return an Observable array of repositories each time search results are returned and finally, we will use `asDriver(onErrorJustReturn)` to convert this to a `Driver`, just returning an empty array on error, as depicted:

```
lazy var data: Driver<[Repository]> = {
        return self.searchText.asObservable()
        .throttle(0.3, scheduler: MainScheduler.instance)
        .distinctUntilChanged()
        .flatMapLatest(ViewModel.repositoriesBy)
            .asDriver(onErrorJustReturn: [])
    }()
```

Now, let's move over to `ViewController`; here, we will bind the `rx.text` of `searchBar` to the `searchText` sequence of `ViewModel` using `orEmpty` to handle the text value being nil, as shown:

```
viewModel.data
            .drive(tableView.rx.items(cellIdentifier: "Cell")) { _,
repository, cell in
                cell.textLabel?.text = repository.name
                cell.detailTextLabel?.text = repository.url
            }
            .addDisposableTo(disposeBag)
        searchBar.rx.text.orEmpty
        .bind(to: viewModel.searchText)
        .disposed(by: disposeBag)
```

As text is entered into `searchField`, it will put onto the `searchText` sequence of `ViewModel`, triggering the network call we set up. This will also handle when the cancel button is tapped on.

We will also use the data sequence of `viewModel` to drive the title of `navigationItem` using its `rx.title` extension, using `map` to count the number of elements in the data array and embed that value in a string, as follows:

```
searchBar.rx.text.orEmpty
            .bind(to: viewModel.searchText)
            .disposed(by: disposeBag)
    viewModel.data.asDriver()
            .map { "\($0.count) Repositories" }
            .drive(navigationItem.rx.title)
            .disposed(by: disposeBag)
```

That's it!

Build and run

Let's run the app and try to enter some search text in the Search bar. I will enter my GitHub ID.

You will see the following results:

You will see some repositories either created or contributed to. Delete the text and type in a new GitHub ID to see that person's repositories as well. You might have noted that the overall process of invoking the API, parsing, and then displaying took a lot less time and comparatively less code. RxSwift does much of the heavy lifting and makes code quick to write and easy to follow.

Some other cool libraries

Now, let's take a look at a couple of really great libraries in the RxSwift community.

The first is RxAlamofire, which wraps the elegant Alamofire library. If you are used to using Alamofire, you will feel right at home here. Here's what an rx.json call would look like using RxAlamofire:

```
_ = session.rx
        .json(.get, stringURL)
        .observeOn(MainScheduler.instance)
        .subscribe { print($0) }
```

You can find all the information for that cool library at https://github.com/RxSwiftCommunity/RxAlamofire.

The second is Moya. Moya seems to be the crowd favorite, looking at the stars this repository has got on GitHub; you can find it at https://github.com/Moya/Moya.

Moya is an abstraction layer that significantly streamlines networking code. In Moya, you use providers like these to make all requests:

```
provider = MoyaProvider<GitHub>()
provider.rx.request(.userProfile("ashfurrow")).subscribe { event in
    switch event {
    case let .success(response):
        image = UIImage(data: response.data)
    case let .error(error):
        print(error)
    }
}
```

Moya also makes use of Enums to represent your endpoints, such as the `userProfile` endpoint here:

```
provider = MoyaProvider<GitHub>()
provider.reactive.request(.userProfile("ashfurrow")).start { event in
    switch event {
    case let .value(response):
        image = UIImage(data: response.data)
    case let .failed(error):
        print(error)
    default:
        break
    }
}
```

You can read about all these and many more features that the library provides on the links provided in this section.

Summary

The bottom line is that for Networking in `RxSwift`, you have several choices. Our suggestion is that you learn how to use the core `RxCocoa` networking extensions first and then check out Moya; or, if you are already a heavy `Alamofire` user, `RxAlamofire` is the way to go.

In this chapter, we created a real-world simulation of a small-scale application that is usable to a certain extent. We learned how to bundle most of the concepts that we covered throughout the book in this application. This chapter provided you with the gist of how to invoke APIs, how to parse data that was returned from the API, and then, using a `ViewModel`, how to plug the data into the `View`. The design pattern that we used was MVVM, which is the most favorable design pattern when it comes to writing `RxSwift` code.

In this book, we have introduced you to reactive programming with reactive extensions for Swift in iOS. There is a lot more to explore in the Rx world and a vibrant community. We encourage you to read through the documentation on the `RxSwift` repository home page; you can use the following link to go through the documentation. `RxSwift` documentation for further reading is available at `https://github.com/ReactiveX/RxSwift/tree/master/Documentation`.

There are plenty of sample projects that you can download from the repo and review one at a time.

Also, check out the `RxSwift` community libraries at `https://github.com/RxSwiftCommunity`; these resources will help broaden your knowledge of `RxSwift` and Rx in general as well. Thank you for joining us. We hope you found this book helpful and interesting. All the best!

Other Books You May Enjoy

If you enjoyed this book, you may be interested in these other books by Packt:

Mastering Swift 4 - Fourth Edition
Jon Hoffman

ISBN: 978-1-78847-780-2

- Delve into the core components of Swift 4.0, including operators, collections, control flows, and functions
- Create and use classes, structures, and enumerations
- Understand protocol-oriented design and see how it can help you write better code
- Develop a practical understanding of subscripts and extensions
- Add concurrency to your applications using Grand Central Dispatch and Operation Queues
- Implement generics and closures to write very flexible and reusable code
- Make use of Swift's error handling and availability features to write safer code

Swift 4 Protocol-Oriented Programming - Third Edition
Jon Hoffman

ISBN: 978-1-78847-003-2

- Understand the differences between object-oriented programming and protocol-oriented programming
- Explore the different types that Swift offers and what pitfalls to avoid
- Delve into generics and generic programming
- Learn how to implement Copy-On-Write within your custom types
- Implement several design patterns in a protocol-oriented way
- Design applications by prioritizing the protocol first and the implementation types second

Leave a review - let other readers know what you think

Please share your thoughts on this book with others by leaving a review on the site that you bought it from. If you purchased the book from Amazon, please leave us an honest review on this book's Amazon page. This is vital so that other potential readers can see and use your unbiased opinion to make purchasing decisions, we can understand what our customers think about our products, and our authors can see your feedback on the title that they have worked with Packt to create. It will only take a few minutes of your time, but is valuable to other potential customers, our authors, and Packt. Thank you!

Index

P

prefixing 136, 138

Q

Quality of Service (QoS) 244
queues 238

R

retry operator
  using 257, 261
Rx code, debugging
  about 220, 222
  asynchronous code, testing 233, 236
  debug, using 224, 228
  total, using 229, 233
RxAlamofire
  reference 296
RxBlocking
  about 215
  used, for testing 215, 217
RxCocoa traits
  about 173
  ControlEvent 175
  ControlProperty 174
  Driver 174
  types 174
RxSwift foundation
  about 43
  marble diagrams 46
  Observables 44
  Reactive extensions 43
  schedulers 49
  subject 45
RxSwift
  CocoaPods, using 59
  environment, preparing 58
  environment, setting 58
  installing 59
  installing, with Carthage 60
  Login page 61
  networking 287
  reference 58
  RxTest 208
  testing 207

using 57
RxTest 208

S

schedulers
  about 243
  ConcurrentDispatchQueueScheduler 244
  OperationQueueScheduler 247
  SerialDispatchQueueScheduler 246
side effects
  app, building 161, 167, 170
  doOn operator, using 149, 154, 157
  performing 148
  project, setting up 158
single trait 100
singleton design pattern
  about 272
  cons 274
  implementation 272
  pros 274
Singleton scheduler
  about 238
  specifying 238, 242
  using 243
special cases
  about 28
  default parameter values 29
  new string 28
  single-tuple and multiple-argument function types,
    difference 28
  tuple destructuring, adding 28
Strings
  changes/improvements 16
  grapheme clusters, changes interpretation 18
  protocol 17
  string.characters, avoiding 16
subjects, Observables
  BehaviorSubject 92
  PublishSubject, using 87, 91
  ReplaySubject 94
  variable 97
Swift 4
  access modifiers 19
  Carthage/CocoaPods projects, using 30
  changes/improvements, in Strings 16

www.ingramcontent.com/pod-product-compliance
Lightning Source LLC
Chambersburg PA
CBHW080624060326
40690CB00021B/4813